AMERICA
IN EUROPE

Europe welcoming merchants from the New World.
Illustration from Abbé Raynal's
Histoire de la Colonisation et du Commerce
des Européens dans les Deux Mondes
(1780).

Photograph: Bibliothèque Nationale de Paris

AMERICA IN EUROPE

A History of the New World in Reverse

Germán Arciniegas

Translated from the Spanish by
Gabriela Arciniegas and R. Victoria Arana

HARCOURT BRACE JOVANOVICH, PUBLISHERS

SAN DIEGO   NEW YORK   LONDON

Copyright © 1975 by Germán Arciniegas
English translation copyright © 1986 by Harcourt Brace Jovanovich, Inc.

Library of Congress Cataloging in Publication Data

Arciniegas, Germán, 1900–
America in Europe.

Translation of: América en Europa.
Bibliography: p.
1. America—Discovery and exploration.
2. Europe—Intellectual life.
3. Europe—Civilization—American influences.
I. Title.
E121.A713   1986   970.01   85-21924
ISBN 0-15-105555-6

Designed by Michael Farmer
Printed in the United States of America
First edition
A B C D E

HBJ

To Gabriela

Contents

Contents

Contents

Contents

CHAPTER 12

DINNER IS SERVED

AMERICA
IN EUROPE

Preface

Many are the books written about the influence of European thought on America, yet there are none to speak of on the opposite phenomenon: the impact of America on European thought and history—which is why this book may seem to have been thought out in reverse. Ideas have moved in one direction or the other, beginning on the day the first colonies were established, but to insist on the contributions of Europe to the New World is superfluous by now. Taking the opposite course, one notes with surprise the decisive role America has played in each new epoch of European thought. In the first place, as a negative fact—one that reaches far back into the distant centuries. Suffice it to say that before the existence of a new continent was revealed, science was unable to come to any positive conclusion regarding the structure of the cosmos. In order for Copernicus to present his system definitively, America had to appear. Until then, the idea of a solar system was a mere adventure of the mind. Everything from the time of the revelation of America on back seems to us today as fictional as a novel, as mythical as a painting. With America, the modern world begins. Scientific progress begins, philosophy thrives. By means of America, Europe acquires a new dimension and emerges from its shadows.

The void this book aspires to fill—spanning as it does the whole process of history, a process revealing itself in the phenomenon of evolution (of ideas, of literature, and of the arts)—has not been similarly addressed before. But this book does not pretend to do the spadework that has already been done in many concrete fields of inquiry by specialized researchers, nor does it pretend to be exhaustive. What the author proposes here is to follow the march of European thought almost panoramically, focusing on salient episodes. Obviously, one cannot do more than present a showcase of specimens; and, in doing no more than that, one would in any case never arrive at the end of the investigation nor at the projection of all its potential consequences. More than anything, this volume is intended as a stimulus: to invite the curious to complete the outline, confident that if they assume the vantage point taken in this work, they will find further remarkable and gratifying proofs for the concepts it is here only possible to sketch.

I think I have not exaggerated the role that things American have played in the progress of ideas. I am not so naive as to think that the origin of each new concept the world has ever had must be traced to America. Many American novelties have long ere now agitated European thought. What is remarkable is that the American experience has so often proved the determining factor in the literal realization of so many ideas. The case of Columbus serves as a symbolic example. Toscanelli had already said in Florence that one could reach the Orient by marching continuously westward; in fact, with those words he was only reiterating a notion that had long been humanly imagined as possible. But it was the voyage of Columbus and the physical manifestation of America that transformed mere fiction, so to speak, into undeniable reality. Perhaps the description of American society made by Amerigo Vespucci, considered so original by Sir Thomas More, acquired its Platonic, poetical ingredient because Vespucci had been reared in a family enlightened by the humanism of Marsilio Ficino. More telling yet, in the verbal portrait of Incan society penned by the Inca Garcilaso, we can discern strokes characteristic of the same Florentine brush. Nevertheless, whatever else we may perceive in such texts, it is the terra firma of America, we must conclude, that offers the Old World the immediate possibility of abandoning fantasy and entering reality.

Similarly, only when the foundations for the world's newest democracy are laid in Philadelphia, only when the modern republic is thus created, do those spectral ideas elaborated in the prose of European speculators finally take shape in the flesh. What astonishes is the transfiguration that occurs within the American milieu. Theories touching America convert themselves into living substances. Something that had earlier been exported to the New World as an imaginative invention produces, upon its return to Europe, the greatest revolutionary ferment.

If America has been the crucible where the greatest of man's illusions have been fused, if from America have emerged the cornerstones of the political philosophy that has transformed the world, if with these elements the very foundations of European thought have been changed, these statements do not imply a dearth of contributions made by European man. The white man removed to the New World changes the framework of his life; he is a European, perhaps improved, who acquires a new consciousness of his freedoms, a new spirit of independence—in short, the whole frame of mind that I make bold to call "American." Herein lies such a universality of experience—and of causes, too—that it may excuse the arrogant pretensions of specialness with which spokesmen of the two American continents express themselves when they give voice to one or another sort of macronationalism.

The observations that gave rise to this book rest on an objective regard for the American phenomenon as a whole. Although the writer is a Latin American, he cannot escape reflecting upon the fact that the whole hemisphere is so often conceptualized (and by himself as well) as of a piece. The importance of the ideas of such thinkers as Copernicus, Descartes, Thomas More, or the authors of the French Revolution arises from their formulation of such a notion as "continental America," whether the points of reference be, in specific instances, the Antilles or Brazil or Philadelphia.

Since this book tries above all to promote another choice—a new perspective—it does not pretend to exhaust the study of a history about which one might project infinitely (it would be childish to make such a claim). I strive merely to gather together a coherent set of examples extending barely to a certain critical moment in the nineteenth century. What comes afterward is in plain view of any observer: figuring out the subsequent scenarios should prove to be a very simple task. The world is, in fact, no longer seen as a consequence of what Europe thinks and publishes. Each time there is dialogue or controversy, new voices intervene; and, on this new global stage, America has come to be the decisive actor in the solution of world wars or in the debates or struggles that commit to peace. The respect for the very remote past has extended to American archaeology, which is now seen as part of the universal panorama. And American novels, poetry, music, and art have come to exert a growing influence—well beyond their places of local origin. To discuss the thousands of ramifications of all of this would require a book having many more pages and a much greater number of details than this one boasts. For the moment, let us say that America exists, that it does indeed generate ideas and events, and breathtakingly continues to illustrate the *historical* reality of a planet that, in revolving as it goes, permits every last segment of its great sphere to be bathed in sunlight.

1

•

The Foreshadowed
Continent

The New Europe and Her American Era

_____

After the advent of Christianity, no other event has brought about such a radical change in European thinking as the actual discovery of America. Up to the apocalyptic day on which the new continent revealed itself to the Occident, it was possible to consider Earth the creation of the gods. But, even so, as the achievement of the gods, Earth was lame, unfinished; a marvelous machine, yes . . . but lacking an essential part. It was a half-planet (of which fact some scholars were aware), a planet that reason could not explain, a world bordering on mythology and fable. When it dawned on Vespucci that another continent existed—a continent apart from the three already known—and when he proposed that it be named "the New World" (having been most understandably surprised), his words were an understatement. What would be new thenceforward was not merely the enormous expanse of land he announced—the balancing, the missing hemisphere—but the whole world. Europe would soon be new, the Occident would be new, and new also would be the compass of man's imagination.

With knowledge of the sphere incomplete, all westward routes ended at the Pillars of Hercules. And, her highway to further knowledge obstructed, Science, too, like the sailors of Europe, found herself blocked. The Age of Reason could never have existed before Columbus. As a man of science, the natural philosopher of antiquity moved within the narrowest of parameters. Look: his reason wanders in twilight, and he is forced to rely on instinct, to trust often to dumb luck. He is little more than irrational. But with the voyage of 1492, Occidental man is fledged, matures, enters fully upon modern realities. The geographical change the expedition produced is destined, as we shall see, to alter the old theories of the universe, theories so long accepted by the powerful and the wise. America thus liberates European thinking, redeems it. This is the first feat of magic resulting from her appearance on an unmeasurably dilated Western horizon. America makes Copernicus, Galileo, and Descartes possible. Without her experimental ground, virgin territory until then, without the physical foundation for fertile inductive thought she still represents, today's familiar theories could never have been proven, and without them science would have continued a sleeping beauty. The most learned men could not have formulated new scientific principles without empirical proofs. A portion of America's destiny, as she undertook her new role in the modern age, was to permit the appearance of such outstanding thinkers, the glory of the Renaissance and the forerunners of our own age. How much did Europe draw on our own newly revealed planet? in what measure? on what dates?—these are questions we must still explore. But an undeniable truth we can admit at once: just as soon as it was possible to sail around the world, all the rest of what we now know was on its way.

The "Discovery" could have taken place a century before 1492, or a century after. A Columbus, bold enough to step across the wide, menacing Atlantic, could have appeared at any given moment, once the time was ripe. I mean "ripe" in the sense that before any real commercial interest existed, all voyages over that ocean—like those of the Vikings, for instance—were written on water and lost in the infinite silence of the shackled ages. If the

"Columbus" so fancied had been not the actual one of 1492 but another person setting out at another time, the meridian for modern ideas need simply be drawn forward or backward accordingly, but probably not more than a hundred years; and we would either be a century ahead or a century behind ourselves. Bertrand Russell, in tracing the pattern of scientific evolution, does not hesitate to say with the proud individualism of his Saxon phlegm that there are unique persons—venturers, adventurers, wanderers blessed by Fortune—who blaze the trails. "If . . . we take away some hundred men from the history of European thought, we would still be groping through the labyrinths of the Middle Ages."

What made Columbus possible? Why was it that, as soon as he opened the Atlantic, that ocean became the most profitable trade route for European vessels? Recall what a quantity of gold, silver, pearls, slaves, tobacco, brazilwood—the riches of the time—was immediately being transported in Spanish ships, in legitimate traffic . . . or smuggled by the French and Dutch, or pirated by such forerunners of the British Empire as were Drake, Hawkins, Raleigh! . . . or carried by the Portuguese who founded their Lusitanian America in Brazil, thereby doubling the size of their empire. All of this business, as well as the events that followed the initial bustle, can be seen as the masterpiece of the mercantile middle class, the Renaissance's enterprising class of burghers. In 1500, the world was already oriented toward the merchant. Merchants enabled each nation to make a profit from seagoing explorations and put the discoveries to work for an already mature and powerful bourgeoisie, the motor behind the Great Expeditions. America's presence accelerated the historic process. Europe began thinking faster. A new tempo was introduced, and a different notion of schedules and calendars—all as speedy as the inertia inherited from countless centuries of torpor would permit. A world economy—more or less as we know it today—began its takeoff. . . . And in Europe was born what could rightfully be called "the American Era."

At that time also Reason and Magic once again came face to face, as they had done so often before. Their confrontation has been a constant element in European history. Philosophers, cosmographers, poets, dialoguers, peripatetics, novelists of antiquity—all struggled with science and with fiction in their attempts to fill the centuries-old void that wrapped itself around the gods' favorite world. Moving upon theoretic planes, they formulated contradictory explanations, shaped arbitrary images. Science there was, but it was a science mounted on empty air. Twenty centuries before Columbus, the Chaldeans, the Egyptians, and the Greeks had attempted to discover scientific answers to their questions; in the end, the efforts to ascertain truth yielded to Magic. We must agree with Bertrand Russell that the Greeks saw the world more as poets have always done than as scientists do. That was so, according to Russell, because the Greeks believed manual activity unfit for gentlemen; thus, any sort of study requiring hands-on experimentation seemed to them somewhat vulgar. We can connect their class-conscious prejudice, perhaps, to a related fact: where the Greeks actually made the most notable scientific progress was in astronomy—the study of visible but intangible bodies.

As soon as America appears, there is a change in the earth's dimensions, in the possibilities for experiment. The sphere about which some had already had hunches now materialized, was twice as big. But even more impressive than the physical evidence was the immediate geometric progression in the development of the mind's horizons. The intellectual sphere did not simply double, but increased a hundredfold. A fascinating history was to follow. Today, we are seeing its events from the long perspective of five hundred years. Europe and her thinkers came into their own in their new world—the new European world that now existed because of America. They had the entire planet within vista. Magellan had sailed around it! Nevertheless, those who doubted were far more plentiful than those who accepted the news. Blessed be the cavilers! Science is forever being arrested beyond all reason by the disciples of Saint Thomas. No learned man would believe until he put his finger into the wound. So, Magic would not die. Not even during the Age of Reason. Magic is more stubborn and better sustained, in general, than doubt, than skepticism. Those who advocated science had to see everything for themselves—Cook, LaCondamine, Humboldt. Those who were for Magic ruled secretly, as they rule today, over occult sciences. They fashioned their own deities.

In Diderot's Encyclopedia

In 1751, the *Encyclopedia* is first published—*Summa* of the Enlightened Century's wisdom and knowledge, monument to Reason, first principle of the French Revolution, compendium of all the learning of enlightened Europe. In it, the word "America" is allotted just fifty lines—one fourth of a page—while "Alsace" is given eighteen times that space. America was barely worth one eighteenth what Alsace was worth. As the work on the second edition progressed, all the things having to do with America began to reveal themselves so palpably in words pertaining to geography, history, plants, animals, cities, that when the *Supplement* was planned, years later, it was obvious the original information would have to be revised—and expanded, so that finally the word "America" cuts a fine new figure in an article nineteen pages long that begins like this:

For the philosophers, world history perhaps offers no event as singular as the discovery of the new continent, which, together with the seas that surround it, comprises a whole hemisphere of our planet, of which the ancients knew but 180 degrees of longitude, or perhaps only 130 by strict deduction, for such is Ptolemy's error when he places the mouths of the Ganges at the 148th degree and the modern astronomers place them at around 108; in other words, Ptolemy errs in an excess of 40 degrees, having apparently no idea about anything farther than Indochina, the eastern limit of the world as it was known at that time.

Let us not be surprised by such hesitations and contradictions in the *Encyclopedia*. In the sixteenth century, man discovers that, given the existence of an American continent and a Pacific Ocean as well, the small world imagined by the Greeks and still thinkable in Columbus's day becomes an immense globe, the forthcoming object of the most audacious explorations. Even so, a hundred years pass before the English—driven to it by religious emergencies—establish the first colonies in North America. The Encyclopediasts of the first moment, those of 1751, when they dispatched with the subject matter in fifty lines, seemed to have no clear notion of what had in fact been going on all around them.

The science of the Greeks may have been star-struck, but it was still science and the early theories of the Egyptians and Chaldeans were perhaps even more reliable than those of the Greeks. Whatever the case, Greek speculative philosophy, arising from such penetrating studies as those of Aristarchus of Samos, Seleucus of Babylon, and Pythagoras, is notable for its closer approximation to reality than the Summae Theologicae of the Middle Ages. After all, the Greeks invented and manipulated their gods so that those deities remained at the service of their inventors' creative intelligence, whereas in the Middle Ages speculations were metaphysical, asleep from birth, lulled by the contemplative symphony of Revelation and Grace. The blackout that struck the West after the fall of the Roman Empire hurled the achievements of ancient natural philosophers into cultural limbo.

Aristarchus of Samos formulated (one thousand eight hundred years before Copernicus) the hypothesis that the earth was a planet moving within a complex system, rotating on its axis and revolving around the sun. The time that elapsed between Aristarchus and Copernicus represents eighteen centuries of silence and fear. We are scarcely able to conceive such waste. The accumulated scientific wealth of the Chaldeans, the Egyptians, and the Greeks is frozen between parentheses that close only when Columbus declares that the route across the Sargasso Sea is open and when Amerigo Vespucci announces the splendors of a continent that was, up to that point, thought to be lost to human sight, submerged beneath the waters.

Some people still consider it strange that Vespucci's message should be thought by anyone to have produced a greater impact upon Western intellectual history than Columbus's message could have done; and these same people question as well the fact that the New World should have been named "America" instead of "Colombia." An explanation is not hard to come by. Columbus only proved that the Greeks' small world was, as many believed it to be, a sphere. With only one variant: their terrifying sea of reefs and slime was clean and navigable. Toscanelli the Florentine was proven right. In the same spirit, the Genoese found it possible to conclude: "I have reached Japan." But Vespucci's message was altogether different: he talked about *another continent*. His discourse expanded the globe to twice its size. *His* was news indeed, and it truly revolutionized all earlier preconceptions.[1] A group of friars, or canons, at the Abbey of Saint-Dié were much wiser and more intuitive than our present-day cavilers: they are the ones who realized the magnitude of the announcement and coined the word "America," the name immediately adopted. Even more alert was the Venetian editor who gave Vespucci's letter the title *Mundus Novus*. These of his contemporaries realized the significance of Vespucci's news, unlike those others I have alluded to, who for the last four hundred years have been blindly heaping trash over Vespucci's name.[2]

From Greek Science Fiction to Medieval Tale

The poetic charm of Atlantis and the horror of its frightful end—as Plato presented that marvelous legend in his precursor to modern science fiction—made a strong impression on the minds of Greek mariners and on the minds, too, of all those who later sailed in the wakes of the early Greek ships. The story made an impression that lasted for centuries. The realism of Plato's images is imposing. In the dialogues of Timaeus and Critias, Atlantis appears as a fabulous continent, formidable, prepossessing at first, then sinking—one of the greatest catastrophes ever described in any literature or journalism. Within the span of a day and a night, the sea swallowed Atlantis: the vast island became a vast ocean bristling with reefs, impassable. This fictional account, and the miry lower depths of which the Platonic narrative speaks, effectively blocked off the Atlantic. The terror lasted twenty centuries.

The most striking thing about Plato's book is not the invention of Atlantis but the divination of another continent, of another world, of another ocean. Continent, world, and ocean invented in part by the scientific calculations of ancient sages, in part by legend. Plato says that he consulted ancient writings where he found reference to a powerful oversea country whose armies set out to conquer Asia and Europe and to defy the divine Greece. The armies, in his own words, came from "another world" (America, let us say) on the Atlantic Ocean. From that "America"—as large as Asia and Libya together—"one could pass in those days to other islands, and, from there, have access to the continent, spreading before them and bordering on the true sea. For everything on this side of the strait is similar to a port whose entrance is narrow while that which is on the other side forms a real sea, and the land which surrounds it can rightfully claim the name of continent." To the surprise of Plato's ghost, twenty centuries later Amerigo Vespucci declared the Platonic legend a reality in fact.

Everything in Plato smacks of the extraordinary. No other word can describe the passage, itself novelistic, in which Plato tells about the clash between his "America" and a Europe represented at that moment by Greece. It is something like the conflict devoutly wished for by so many of our contemporaries, a conflict that would render the Old World victorious over an empire located on the other side of the Atlantic. Every time one reads these pages, one finds sharper and sharper edges: "On that Isle of Atlantis, the kings had created a great and admirable nation, extending dominion over the whole island, over the neighboring islands and over some parts of the continent as well. On this side of the strait, our side, we were Libya as far as Egypt, and Europe as far as the Tyrrhenian Sea. One day, powerful Atlantis assembled all her forces and sought, with one blow, to subjugate our country—Europe—and all the nations on this side of the water. Solon then, with his mighty

Athenian power, made his courage and strength shine in the eyes of the world." And that was how Europe, under Solon, met the American challenge in the first intercontinental war, contained its armies, and—in the span of a single battle—won the liberty of the Old World. Shortly thereafter, Atlantis sank. Curtain.

The Magic Medieval Tale

Echoing the expressions of Diderot's *Encyclopedia,* we can say that there has occurred no more singular spectacle in the world of ideas than the Western blackout following the collapse of the Roman Empire. It was a catastrophe like that of Atlantis—Plato could have written it. The barbarians came, threw a tombstone over Europe, and the vanquished remained groping, not yet exposed to a science that could aid them in an exploration of the world about them, hopelessly abandoned to a destiny controlled by magic—this also a Platonic heritage, if one insists on the fabulous aspects of Atlantis.

Today, when we visit ruins and museums, doing our own bit of archaeology on what remains or is dug out of the ancient cities— temples, aqueducts, bridges, theaters, arenas, images of gods and emperors, mausoleums of patricians and matrons—we see the near perfection attained in those days in architecture, in figurative and abstract art. And then there was a total breakdown. The generations that followed were orphaned, blind, enslaved. They returned to the caves. And when again in the eleventh and twelfth centuries, more temples were raised, statues sculpted, images of the Divine Majesty painted, it was with the naïveté of folk art. The basilicas of the year 1000 are rude, elementary monuments compared with the Parthenon, as are the temples of Paestum and Syracuse, the ruins of Balbek, the imposing shell of the Colosseum or of the Roman Pantheon. One thousand years—five hundred, in the best of cases—were the survivors of the invasions obliged to wait before beginning over again. Those who arrived at the end of those quiet centuries—naked, ignorant—either invented or searched out the history of the lost civilizations, so as to resurrect them and give them new life. They rescued the Roman arch and vault, found lost books, dug their hands into archaeological garbage heaps. They were the Columbuses who traveled pastwards and discovered antiquity. History has that positive aspect about it: it encourages, stimulates, stirs ambitions. Memory pushes humanity forward.

After fifteen hundred years, Ptolemy is discovered—saved by the Arabs—and his discoverers experience the thrill of finding themselves suddenly gazing upon a forgotten science. Plato, resurrected in Medici Florence, creates a new school of disciples even more fervent than those who listened to him speak in his own day. The Renaissance attains its prime. Still, the struggle continues between awakening Reason and unyielding Magic. The idea of a spherical earth posited by Eudoxus of Cnidus in Plato's time is questioned in Salamanca nine hundred years later. Poor Columbus. His common sense tells him the world is round, but on the eve of his first voyage he finds he must forever abandon contact with a science that Spain repudiates and withdraw into the Scriptures and the books of the Holy Fathers, hoping there to find divine or divinatory "arguments" that will open the way westward for a society that still lives beneath the sign of the Dark Ages. When science does not prove useful, may the old tales help him on his way!

We have seen how a story can influence the great adventures of history. With a story, Plato halted ships for twenty centuries, and with the same narrative kept alive "the ideal." Greece was rational, scientific, humanistic, as far as it could be; the rest it achieved through its imagination. Dialogues, treatises, rhapsodies, comedies, tragedies were composed, constituting in the end a body of literature very much like that of modern times because of the problems that perplex it, the curious, uninhibited spirit that animates it, the humanization of the divine, the mythological divinization of the human. Greece takes a magnifying glass to the Olympian gods so that they become everyday folk who can enter a mortal's home or meddle with a young maiden's country outing. At the same time, it projects kings and heroes into the clouds that encircle the heights of Mount Olympus. When one enters the zone of the Middle Ages, that fabulous heritage is transformed into the magical, diabolical, Christian tale. More than tale, it is a magic lantern. From the murky gloom of the cathedral, the view through the stained glass offers a tantalizing image of theology, demonology, the labyrinths of metaphysics. The old fantasy metamorphoses into lives of saints, of enchanted knights, into miracle tales of crusaders and pilgrims.

To this day, it is difficult for fiction to produce images as vivid as the combats between angels and devils of medieval times. The monsters and paradises of the Middle Ages convert Greek mythology into a baroque altarpiece. Stepping away from the sunlit blue of the Mediterranean and into the Black Forest of Central Europe, what else might we expect in the way of results? The popularity of romances and of poetry was assured by the captive receptivity of a credulous humanity whose eyes were ever fixed on the terrors of the Last Judgment. At the entrance to every cathedral, the dead (in sculpted realism) ascend, raising their tombstones, and, to the sound of apocalyptic trumpetings, assemble for the supreme trial. Dominating the whole scene, from within his almond-shaped ring of fire, sits the Heavenly Majesty, who looks only upon the Just, headed in a stream for Paradise. Below, in wild skirmish, the devil clutches one of the sides of a scale on which souls are being weighed as Golden Saint Michael pluckily defends them. From a steep crag fall the certified reprobates, into the claws of hellish demons and monsters. Over the tapestries of such fiction, humanity walked cautiously, restrained by a holy fear of the Lord. Fear was the master of their destinies. The storyteller worked on these fantasies. His characters were saints or demons; their feats, chimerical.

From the Greeks, medieval authors took traditional tales like that of the Amazons or of the kingdom of California. Then came the adventures of chivalry, which introduced themselves into the same old legends. All of it influenced the adventurers who set out to discover and then to conquer America—even the unlettered ones; for those who had not read the books had heard the tales.

The magical story was far more influential as a stimulus than philosophy or history could ever have been, not for the common man alone but for the learned as well. In the mind of a soldier, the tale of Amadis of Gaul is more convincing than a Platonic dialogue. The soldier might as easily have been a pure and simple illiterate adventurer as an Hernán Cortés, who was educated at Salamanca. The vast majority of the conquistadors, high-born or low-, had no schooling; the lack of it did not prevent them from becoming, as in the case of Belalcázar, "the greatest of the great." But the knowledge they all shared was in the tales. The Greek practice of listening—whether one happened to be scholarly or ignorant—to the rhapsodies of blind Homer comes to mind. Science had less power over Columbus than did the ramblings of the author Pierre d'Ailly.

The magical elements of medieval fiction culminate in a rebirth of Plato's dreams. Thus did the new American tale begin.

A Series of Discoveries

The topic of the discoveries is older by far than Columbus. It is born with the Crusades. The Orient—before that a prodigality assigned to oblivion—takes shape unexpectedly, and Jerusalem becomes a bridgehead on the route to Japan. The knights who set out to free the Holy Sepulcher likely returned from their adventure with a thorn from the crown of Christ—but they came, too, with pearls, rugs, cinnamon . . . or news about such luxuries. Asia began to weave her fascination. Mercantile ambitions grew: the golden threads of Christian legend interlace with silken ones from unknown Persia and India and Japan. One must not speak of "the discovery of America," but of a series of discoveries following in succession, climaxing in the restoration of the lost continent of Atlantis. This last eclipses all the discoveries that preceded it, and its unforeseen outgrowths (to this day) offer the European a new role in world history.

If we begin with the Crusades and rank the many discoveries, the two major ones would have to be Asia and America. In religious thought, in the arts, in commerce, the Oriental current is a historic constant penetrating the West in a thousand ways. But from 1492 on, America, and everything to do with America, alters the whole process. Why was there such a difference between the reasons that led to the discovery of Asia and those that led to the discovery of America? Why did the human flow of European emigrants spill over America alone? Why is Africa yet another world—the third or fourth—held tardily in reserve for a still-later exploration? Why? why? why?—such an uncountable number of questions! They only multiply as soon as our curiosity pronounces them.

The discovery of Asia is a serious concern of ours because the idea endures that America has to be like Asia. Columbus sails in search of that Asia, and Europe is drawn instead to these other "Indies"—with their own monsters and their own treasures.

Asia's Columbus was another Italian: Marco Polo. There were differences: Columbus was Genoese, Marco Polo Venetian. There were similarities: Genoese or Venetians, it would be hard to say which were the more consummate merchants; both had participated avidly in the Crusades and subsequently in the establishment of colonies to systematize trade.

The glittering Byzantine Empire, the golden Orient, were, for Venetians and Genoese, the magnets that attracted the compass of their impulses. Logically, Asia represents the first station in the progress of commerce. It is Venice's turn, and she looks toward the East. In order to understand Columbus, we have to start with Marco Polo. The discovery of Asia came two and a half centuries before the other one. The distance between the dates of the two discoveries shows how slowly things progressed in those days. Between Marco Polo and Columbus we would have to consider King Henry the Navigator. With Henry, Portugal casts a line onto Africa. But Henry still faces eastward, his back square to America.

When Marco Polo was born, Asia represented a mystery, even though everyone was aware of her existence. Trade followed the scent of pepper, cinnamon, nutmeg, ivory, and pearls. But Asia, like Europe, was enclosed within her own sphere of action. They were two worlds separated by a curtain no one was interested in raising. There was commercial exchange, and there were even some Christian schismatics who had followed Nestor and created a left-wing church behind that curtain. Theirs was a Christian outpost in China: a potential bridge. But each continent respected the age-old frontier.

The boundary between the two spheres was so sharply drawn that any attempt to make a geographical exploration was virtually paralyzed. Asia was for the Asians, for whose civilization Western admiration was based more on intuition than on anything resembling reliable information. Its discovery begins with Marco Polo's precursors. Friar Julian of Hungary in the twelfth century reported a possible invasion of Europe by the Tartars, who were gathering military concentrations on the border. The news reached the ears of Pope Innocent IV. King Frederick at the time was waging a war whose immediate consequence would have been to undermine the Church's temporal power. Innocent called an extraordinary council, excommunicated Frederick, proposed a European union to defend the continent from the invaders, and sent Prester John of Perugia as ambassador to the Tartar monarch. Prester John made a tour of the countries on the other side of the curtain and, in 1247, wrote a book: *Historia Mongolorum.* It is the direct forerunner of Marco Polo's *The Million.* According to Leonardo Olschki—the erudite biographer of Marco Polo—*Historia Mongolorum* is the travel book that inaugurates that genre in Europe.

Prester John's book describes the monsters that were to populate the fantastic, medieval geographies from then on. He tells about *cinocephali* (men with dogs' heads) and monopodes "relegated, as are other such monsters, to the regions of the Arctic, beyond all personal and human experience." Prester John learns the lore from conversations at the court of Emperor Kuyuk. Monsters aside, the book abounds in precise, realistic information.

The pope never conceived of the discovery of Asia in terms of conquest, nor were the other monarchs moved by any such ambitious notion. As for the Church, whatever action was deemed necessary emerged always as an answer to the pressing questions—how to strengthen the Christians' line of defense and how to preclude invasions. Merchants, on the other hand, saw in Asia the possibility of some kind of trade, and so it was that the Polo family—and its most famous member, Marco—became interested. Marco Polo spent twenty-five years inside Asia, without ever reaching Japan. The emperor of China bestowed honors on him when Marco served as ambassador and later as governor. The Great Khan saw him neither as a spy nor as an enemy. Upon his return from this unprecedented experience, Marco, imprisoned, confided his adventures to a cell mate. That narrative eventually became *The Million,* the most fascinating report on the world hidden behind the curtain. The Venetian died 168 years before Columbus's first ocean voyage.

The travel literature that began with Prester John and Marco Polo could not have been more stimulating. China and India, according to Marco Polo, with their great cities, paper money, printing presses, and so on, impress the visitor as superior civilizations. Having an exceptional facility for acquiring exotic languages, amiable and affable by nature, at ease in the courtier's role, Marco Polo traveled to Shansi, Szechuan, Tibet, Karakorum, Cochinchina, Sumatra, Ceylon. He saw a multitude of animals, plants, minerals—and, also, of princes, peasants, merchants. In *The Million,* we hear the first news of oil—in Bazu; it is remarkable as fuel and useful medically. He refers to gold—to be found in some Japanese mines which he did not manage to visit. That Japanese gold was the "El Dorado" that Columbus set out to find.

To the East for Trade, to America for Conquest

The trail that Marco Polo blazed was followed for nearly two centuries by the most diverse of explorers. One explorer who was almost Polo's contemporary was Friar Giovanni da Montecorvino, an Italian who visited Persia, India, and China and finally established a Christian church in Beijing. A Franciscan, also Italian, Odoric of Perdenone, went as far as China. It is said he baptized thirty thousand heathen. The Moroccan Ibn Battuta started out from Egypt and visited Iraq and India and Beijing. Behind these evangelists and sightseers followed the merchants. The Italians had agents, consuls, warehouses, fleets to cater to the unceasing demand for cinnamon, pepper, cloves, nutmeg, pearls, amber, and sugar. The voyage that began in the interest of reconquering the Holy Sepulcher ended quite differently—in dressing the courts and the gentry in silks and brocades. All of this transpired without ever removing the mystery from those fabulous empires that for centuries were kept at a respectful distance—the sort of distance one keeps from a Bengal tiger.

The city that became Florence developed its commercial interests gradually, eyes fixed on the Orient; its enterprises were concentrated in the hands of a single guild—that of the physicians and spice dealers. Long before the Crusades, as long ago as "antiquity," pepper was considered to have medicinal properties and to provide the ultimate refinement in food.

> Not only did it give prestige to the tables of the wealthy and of the distinguished; but, as St. Pier Damiani recalls, the austere Camandolite monks, according to the 1080 constitution, were permitted to acquire two pounds a year to season their food at the monastery. Pepper was held in such high esteem that Florentines did not hesitate to send parcels as gifts to king and ambassador, along with other spices. Pepper was given in return for merchandise, as a tribute, as payment for rent. Part of the debt contracted by Genoa with the Florentine traders in 1154 was paid off in pepper, brazilwood, cotton, indigo, incense, and alum. The Florentine Ghino di Ugolini Frescobaldi promised to give a pound of pepper every year on All Saints' Day in payment for the rental of certain lands. From the beginning of the fourteenth century, that is to say, from the time of the most ancient ordinance of the physicians' and spice dealers' guild, we find that it was an accepted custom to offer consuls and other officials of the Florentine craft guilds pepper, cinnamon, saffron, and other precious spices in payment for their receipts, a custom also in

practice in other cities where spices were offered to emperors, princes, popes, monasteries, and lay persons, and even to victorious soldiers as booty after battle.[3]

As we can see, even before the Crusades, spices that came from the East had a special place in local consumption; and it should not astonish us to learn that those who enrolled in the Holy Wars found—along with the enterprise that assured them an afterlife in Heaven—a natural complement in being near those fabled places whence came the delightful seasonings that made life so much better on earth. In fact, the Crusades furthered commerce. When Marco Polo tells how pepper is cultivated throughout India and cinnamon on the Ganges; that the best camphor in the world comes from Sumatra (it fetched the same price as gold); that nutmeg is Java's wealth—he was in effect pointing out the precise routes that medieval trade later found itself treading.

The search in America for the Oriental commodity known as brazilwood in fact caused half of South America to be named Brazil. The links reveal themselves in such seemingly trivial facts.

Florence was ahead of the other republics in the development of a bourgeoisie. Above all, she became an intellectual center, represented the "flowering" of the centuries. But she was an inland Florence; she possessed no fleets but transported her merchandise on ships belonging to Pisans, Genoese, Venetians, Neapolitans, Sicilians, Provençals. In Constantinople, the Genoese had their colony in the center of the city—with warehouses, banks, stores, everything that buyers, sellers, or transporters might need. But the big difference between Europe's relations with the Orient and her relations with America is remarkable: there was no effort whatsoever to conquer the Orient.

Commerce between the Occident and the countries that produced spices, perfumes and fragrances was not made directly by the western Christians. The latter, except on rare occasions, limited themselves to a few days' journey along the Mediterranean coasts or the Black Sea or the Caspian. People from other nations traveled the trade routes to their nether ends: the Persians at the time of the Byzantine Empire; the Arabs after their expansion over the three continents then known; the Mongols, especially after their conversion to Christianity; even some of the Tartar tribes. The ports of Tripoli, Beyrouth, Tyre and Acre were starting points for roads to Jerusalem and Damascus. Jerusalem was a compulsory stop for all pilgrims returning from Mecca, and the products arriving from the Orient across the Red Sea and the port of Dieddah were sold in that city.[3]

Exchanges in the marketplace among Christians, Mohammedans, or whatever, who met without reservations in certain cities to transact business, who met without the least thought of conquest, went on for nearly five centuries. But what happens on the other hand when America is actually discovered? As soon as navigation through the Atlantic is opened, Europe pours itself into the New World. In forty years America is explored, from Labrador to the Strait of Magellan; those who arrive, ignorant about the native civilizations, affirm the right to subjugate, to burn temples and idols, to impose the religion of Christ. Vessels with Castilian flags are followed by those of Portugal, England, France, Holland, Denmark. Among the expeditionaries one finds Italians, Greeks, Germans, Poles. . . . They penetrate the great rivers, sail into the interior, north and south: the Amazon, the Mississippi, the Orinoco, the Plata, the Magdalena. They climb the Andes, follow the contours of the Pacific; they cross deserts and jungles; they catalogue hundreds, myriads, of islands; they defy the solitude of the pampas, of the icy moors, of the rain forests. Spurred on by a lust for adventure, they are not lone explorers but a massive crowd of ensorcelled Europeans, dashing after the elusive lure of El Dorado. In the end, even the women follow. The Spaniards were probably the most audacious, when up to that moment they had seemed the least likely to be globe-trotters! The word "discovery" was soon forgotten. The new word was "conquest." In the New World, the Aztecs or Incas could well have been as solidly established as the Chinese in their fabled capital cities. That of course did not matter. The indigenous peoples were crushed, enslaved. A desire to appropriate the land, the water, the air, awakened dormant, unrecognized ambitions. Balboa marched into the Pacific Ocean till the water was up to his knees and took possession of it in the name of the king of Spain. A frenzy of Europeanization, Christianization, culturalization ensued—transformations effected according to the barbaric methods of each self-styled group of conquerors; and the various regions began to be brought, one by one, under the banners of Spain, Portugal (this, with the pope's specific blessing), England, and France. The enterprise was so spectacular that there was no longer any talk of discoveries but only of *the* discovery. The discovery of America made the trade with Asia fade into the mists like a fairy tale about the Chinese or the Arabs or the Indians. Actually, the essence of what "discovery" means (to know, to reveal, to understand the other) was lost and redefined utterly by the conqueror.

The result is scarcely apparent for all its clarity, dazzle, resplendency. Today, more descendants of Europeans populate America than remain in Europe. More children of Spaniards live in America than live in Spain; of Portuguese than in Portugal; of Italians than in Italy; of Englishmen than in England; of Irishmen than in Ireland. Perhaps the same could be said regarding Israelis, Poles, Greeks, Germans, Norwegians, Swedes, Danes, Dutch, Arabs, Finns. Three languages at least have found their greatest expansion in the American hemisphere: Spanish, Portuguese, English. The modern capitals of the Spanish and Portuguese languages have moved to America; and, from the time of *Webster's Dictionary* and of the *Encyclopaedia Britannica,* the English language has grown with greater speed and richness in America than in England.

The essential result of these developments has been more than a physical transference of multitudes to territories upon a new continent. These travelers brought with them the cultural products, the languages, the religions of Europe, the laws and ideas. It was not frivolously that from the beginning these newcomers dotted their maps with such coinages as New Spain, New England, New France, Nova Scotia, New Sweden, New Amsterdam, New Granada, New Galicia, New Andalucia, New York, New Orleans. Golden Castile! And with cities that multiply themselves on the atlas: Cambridge, Granada, Trujillo, Mérida, Córdoba, Valencia, Harlem, Santiago, Seville, Rome, Ithaca, Athens, Segovia, Salamanca . . .

The most remarkable aspect of this evolution is the alteration of the old tempo for change. What was not done in Asia in five centuries was accomplished in America in fifty years. A world quiescent, self-contained, suddenly springs to life. Spain needed seven centuries to reconquer the lands that the Arabs had occupied on the peninsula, but between 1492 and 1542 she devoured lands that were many times larger than those of Europe. Europe was slow to accept certain ideas (those, for instance, of Copernicus, Galileo, Descartes)—ideas generated on her own territory. The acceleration I refer to occurred on the other side of the Atlantic. And the events, the popular events, were even more decisive than the ideas. A change of horizon. The masses moved, and it was nearly possible to speak of a New Europe within Europe's old borders. Even if in general it was left unsaid, the transformation that America produced in the Occident was thoroughgoing. We could ask ourselves, Exactly where was this New World that emerged in the sixteenth century? Was it west of the Atlantic? Or was it in a Europe that awakened to a different life and a different destiny when just the day before it had been nothing more remarkable than the same old world?

2

·

Imago Mundi

The Ghosts of an Unknown World

When Columbus steers his three caravels westward, he is not heading for the utterly unknown. He is moving toward a magical reality. He sets out to locate a land already occupied: those populous regions, conquered already by fable. Medieval man, to whose society the admiral belongs, is more likely to believe in the fancifully elaborated than in the real and tangible. The giants and pygmies of fictional jungles exist for the learned and the ignorant alike with the same certainty as the folk they jostle in the marketplace or greet in the town square, see in church or pass on the highway to and from the countryside. The islands and the mainland of the other hemisphere have got to be the home of Cyclopses, of a whole race of big-eared people, of dog-faced tribes, of Amazons. And it goes without saying that gold and precious gems will be found there in quantity—as in no other place on earth. Fifteenth-century Europe thinks in terms of fables. Storybook. It was not in the least bit different five centuries earlier and continues the same within the Italy now touched by the lights of humanism. Everyone: philosophers, theologians, poets, geographers, astrologers and astronomers, mystics, masters, witches, the preaching friar, the knight and the arms bearer, the maid and her mistress, the woman at the inn, the prince and the princess—not one of them has failed to look at his or her image in the crystal ball. Those who teach doctrine and preach it move around with magic lanterns projecting full-color images of Hell and of Paradise. Stained-glass windows. Journalism, reporting, "true stories," memorized romances and tales of chivalry—all from the same bolt. Not a pope nor a king, not a banker nor a merchant grown wealthy will begin construction of a palace, go on a trip, undertake anything, or take any sort of action whatsoever without first consulting a personal astrologer. Out of books and, still more often, out of poems—at a time when the air tingles with the stuff of poetry and everything is charmed or beautified or darkened by it—a multitude of ghosts rises to fill in the gaps in that hemisphere no European has yet seen with his own eyes but which exists nevertheless as a stage or a screen for the divinest comedy. Inertia conspires with these conditions to produce a new history, the one beginning in 1492, from the start a fabulous epic. And all of Europe, spellbound by such tales since her infancy, continues enchanted by the very events she generates. She starts out by inventing a fabulous Asia, the Asia of stupendous dragons and hybrid creatures. And then she believes in it all just as the Greeks believed in their gods and the Christians believe in their saints and their demons. Who is the brave soul, who is the harebrained skeptic, who can at once turn his back on the pressures of that atmosphere and yet find it all compelling?

Columbus and the Enchanted Sphere

The books Columbus knows—not many, mind you, apart from the Scriptures and fragmentary texts of the Church fathers—put his mind in a quixotic whirl. During the sleepless nights in which he prepares for the voyage, he experiences the wonderful omnipresence of the magical tale. He peers into the future through this mirage. Travelers who have explored Asia give accounts of what they have seen and not seen and, together with the real, describe the imaginary fauna, flora, mineral kingdoms. These, being the really new in their experience, are reproduced in bestiaries, mirrors, forests and gardens, lapidaries. Mandeville, Prester John, Marco Polo pave the way for legends that for hundreds of years circulate through courts, monasteries, universities—even today. More than all the rest of these volumes, one especially impresses Columbus. It sets his imagination on fire: *Imago Mundi*. The author, Cardinal Pierre d'Ailly, is known in Spain as Pedro de Aliaco, his name Castilianized (the fashion in those days).[1]

In the margins of Columbus's copy of *Imago Mundi* appear 898 notes in his own handwriting. On some pages, the annotations overwhelm the text. Columbus hardly ever argues with the cardinal's words. The book is his Bible. He underlines it. He uses it to convince himself that his projects have a solid base, or, as a source, something concrete to refer to when he discusses his plans with kings. D'Ailly is the wizard who, taking his hand, gently pushes him into the ships. Here is something charming to imagine: Columbus before the Great Voyage, a thinker sitting on the philosopher's stone, gazing upon the transparent sphere in his hand. It is not the earth he holds: it is the many-sphered celestial globe D'Ailly took from the astrologers. The most ancient books describe it as having seven or more transparent layers, one inside the other like a Chinese toy. Their colors are those of the seven heavens. They are rotating vaults over which the moon, the planets, the sun, and the stars move. The earth is at the center. Whoever looks from earth toward the spheres will see the celestial zoo passing overhead: the Ram, the Scorpion, Sagittarius . . . the Bear and the "seven little Goats." Columbus looks at his fate in this toy and contemplates the divine power that will give a turn to events, supernaturally, in a way unfathomable by reason. What if he were to be the arm of Divine Providence? And why not? He was already rubbing elbows with queens and kings. . . . In the end, he would answer for his work directly to the Creator.[2]

D'Ailly had lived one hundred years earlier. An academic, active in politics, he was a new wave philosopher, vehemently attacking magic and at the same time attracted by it. D'Ailly fought the first great battle for a calendar reform, and, had he triumphed, we would remember him today as we do Pope Gregory. He took up the defense of the dogma of Mary's Immaculate Conception. He reasoned and dreamed. He drew the greatest spiritual benefit from his dreams and the best material profit from his reasoning. Columbus was certainly dazzled with admiration for these qualities; but Columbus conquered that conqueror. With D'Ailly's toy in his hand—no Melancholy he!—Columbus witnessed the discovery of his own self and the powers that were to be the instrument of his ambition: an unrestrained desire for wealth and a limitless fantasy. D'Ailly also, like the practical man he was, had a flair for collecting wealth and, being a dreamer, broke spears for the cause of Church union. A political idealist, he praised the democratic power of the Church, represented in councils, and opposed the pope's monarchic authority. And when he spoke, he charged for his speeches. . . .

One of the pages of *Imago Mundi* presents D'Ailly's sphere as follows (we must read it as a model of medieval poetry):

In this figure are reproduced the nine celestial spheres which today embody the astrologers' theories. Aristotle admitted only eight. Saturn, which is naturally cold, has an effect on draughts: its sphere is white and its influence malignant. Jupiter is warm and humid: its sphere, in its purity and clearness, tempers Saturn's malignant character. Mars, warm and dry, is both fiery and radiant: a harmful sphere of bellicose influence. The Sun is warm and bright: the variety of the seasons operates in its sphere: it makes the stars glow, and its volume is greater than theirs. Venus's sphere is warm and humid: Venus is by its own light the brightest of the planets and always accompanies the Sun: as the Morning Star if it precedes it, the Evening Star if it follows. Mercury is radiant and always gravitates with the Sun at a constant distance of XXVII degrees: for this reason it is rarely visible. The Moon is humid and cold and the mother of the waters:

illuminated by the Sun, it shines by night. The astrologers believe that these signs and divisions of the zodiac have various and multiple properties and influences; they should neither be admitted with exceeding faith nor rejected in excessive disbelief.

This image of the world that falls into Columbus's hands is one of many that have been written (and illustrated) over the centuries; by no means is it the most celebrated. But what makes it different from the earlier ones is that it already shows a tremulous drift toward the Renaissance. D'Ailly is at the exact point of equilibrium: there should be neither too much faith nor too much skepticism, he writes. A factor: If his science comes from way back, it also is conditioned—as any summary made at that moment—by the magical age and the Greek anticipations. Astrologers and astronomers here work hand in hand. An even older *Imago Mundi* is that of Gautier de Metz in the thirteenth century. When Arthur Piaget unearthed the lost text, he wrote:

> In the vast encyclopedias that appear in the thirteenth century there are Bestiaries and Lapidaries and other works with titles like *Image of the World, World Map, Mirror of the World, Brief Philosophy, Layman's Light, Nature of Things, Property of Things.* These works, in Latin or in French, in verse or in prose, theological, philosophical, geographical, are for the most part devoid of originality, compilations of material collected here and there, from all manner of authors, sacred and profane: Aristotle, Pliny, Solon, Saint Isidore of Seville, Honorius of Autin, or from the Old and New Testaments, from the Fathers of the Church, from the physiologists, Palladius, Isaacs, Jacques de Vitry. . . . We have two versions of Gautier de Metz's *Imago Mundi,* one in 4000 verses, dated 1245, and a revised and enlarged one containing some 7000 verses, dated 1247.

The World Is a Fable: America "Made in Europe"

For the European, limited as he was by the scarce and difficult communications of his time, the great telescope was to look from the bottom of a well and see the stars as they passed over the well's mouth. Only those who lived in ports knew about strange lands, talked with the seamen, and heard travel yarns full of lies that people tended to believe because faith and credulity were part of the same mental process. It is possible, however, that the difference between the Greek and the medieval man may have had to do with the fact that the Greek was in contact with the sea whereas the medieval man was an inland creature. Only the Italian ports and cities looked toward the outside world. Wonders and miracles were plentiful enough in the European inland, but the truly extraordinary things were considered to be outside. There were tales of how in Sardinia a certain weed made people die of laughter (sardonic laughter). How in Ibiza there were no snakes and, on the other hand, how they abounded in Columbine Island. In Meroe there were no shadows: the sun shone steadily upon the bottom of wells a hundred feet deep and seven feet wide. Scylla was the island of the Cyclops. Plato placed—not far from Europe—an island bigger than Europe and Africa together. It sank into a raging sea. It was, people said, the island that Saint Brendan set out to find. In Ireland, birds grew out of trees. When they were ripe, they dropped off the branches by their bills as if they were fruit. There was a certain place there—a purgatory—which burned like a grill: unrepentant sinners who wandered in suddenly disappeared, and those who suffered in proportion to the sin they had committed returned without ever again being able to smile. In Thule, trees were always green, summer or winter. In Brittany, whenever water gushed from the top of a high rock, a sudden wind, rain, thunder, and the fury of the elements were loosed. That was the place where men's tails hung behind them. In the Alps, on Mount Saint Bernard, women lived whose chins grew down to their breasts, and this was considered a sign of beauty. Not to mention hermaphrodites, and men born with no hands and no feet . . .

Communication improved, but the images did not fade: instead, they traveled. Imagination would move them to whatever part of the world was still unexplored. In those days, that would have been the imagined "America." And there, beginning with the moment of his discovery, Columbus searched about for the fabled freaks.

An impressive variety of problems arose from the contemplation of nature. Why did the dove feed the young of other birds? Why did the nightingale die singing? Why was the swan white on the outside and black on the inside? Why did pebbles that sank to the bottom of water or of oil float upon quicksilver? Why did the rays of the sun blacken people and whiten clothes? Why did iron make flint give off sparks? Why did the earth, which was heavy, stay suspended in the sky with no foundations of columns to support it?

Such conundrums, preserved in thirteenth-century texts as an age-old heritage, remain unsolved. Gautier de Metz transfers them to his endless poems and more than a hundred years later D'Ailly adopts them. Another century goes by, and now we see Columbus turning them over. And the story does not end here. Fable continues to be the source of inspiration for books of chivalry published in Spain at a feverish pace as discoveries multiply. The conquistadors grew up listening to them. Irving Leonard has proven the point with many illustrations in his *Books of the Brave*. Pierre D'Ailly was the conduit of fantasy that sparked the motor that set in motion "the Admiral of the Oceanic Sea and Viceroy of Terra Firma." When Edmond Buros publishes, in 1930, the entire text of D'Ailly's book, translating it from the Latin and reproducing Columbus's marginalia, Buros comments: "D'Ailly, with his fascinating teachings, was the man who inspired Columbus and should be considered America's spiritual father." And to this father must we resort in order to know about an America prefabricated in the Western style—an America "Made in Europe"—and well known before Columbus ever began to unwrap her. To date, it's been a widespread practice to insist that Paolo dal Pozzo Toscanelli's letter was the most important document upon which Columbus based the project of his voyage. Far from it. Toscanelli was the pretext Columbus used to push on with the theories in D'Ailly. D'Ailly it was who quoted Aristotle: "Small is the sea that separates Spain from East India"; and Seneca: "The distance may be traversed in a few days if the wind is favorable"; and Pliny: "The Navigation of the globe, from

Arabia to the Pillars of Hercules, can be accomplished in a short time." When Toscanelli says that by sailing constantly toward the west one may reach the east, he is only the contemporary scholar who confirms the tradition for Columbus's time. Henry Harrise, in his study on Toscanelli, goes so far as to say that Toscanelli's letter may well have been fabricated, a forgery. D'Ailly is the imaginary bridge Columbus chanced upon, one that allowed him to envision a journey from the shores of Iberia to the islands of Japan— a theoretical bridge with one brace resting in the Middle Ages and the other in modern times.

Pierre D'Ailly, Eminent Personage

There is a lot to say about Pierre d'Ailly, but his biography has yet to be written. He was an encyclopedist. It has been remarked that he was ahead of Descartes as a philosopher of theory of knowledge. In his opinion, self-knowledge is more reliable than knowledge of the external. "I can never be wrong when I affirm that I exist; while, on the contrary, my belief in the existence of exterior objects could be mistaken." Politician, polemicist, theologian, professor, he was chancellor at the Sorbonne and of Notre-Dame, treasurer of the Sainte-Chapelle and the king's confessor. The king chose him to interview Pope Luna—the antipope Benedict XIII—and ask him to resign, as a starting point for Church unity, an aspiration that few men had expressed with D'Ailly's eloquence. It was the unity that the University of Paris and the clergy of France wanted. D'Ailly went to Avignon, and, instead of returning with the pope's resignation, came back with the title of archbishop of Cambray, bestowed upon him by the pope himself (one of the most lucrative positions to be had in France). To take possession of his archbishopric, D'Ailly had to resort to armed combat: it was neither the pope's will nor that of the empire. To reach Cambray, he had to evade the duke of Burgundy's troops, which had been mobilized to block him.

The same king sent D'Ailly to persuade the Roman antipope,

Clement VII, to resign as well. Clement remained immutable, but D'Ailly returned with a fuller purse. Bonifacio Ferrer judges D'Ailly as follows: "In order to silence this fire-spitting dragon [D'Ailly], Clement VII gave him a fat tid-bit: such a generous morsel was it, in fact, that it stuck in his gullet." And it was true. D'Ailly kept the most cautious silence until Clement VII's death. It's bad manners to speak with one's mouth full.

Finally, when the popes were no longer two, but three—the last straw in the schism of the West, D'Ailly went to Rome to ask John XXIII to resign. Three dignitaries accompanied him—an obvious precaution after the past experiences. The four returned from their delicate mission, each one a cardinal; and John XXIII was more solidly ensconced on his pontifical throne than ever. This cardinalship did not prevent D'Ailly from becoming, sometime later, one of the adversaries who dismissed John XXIII from the papacy when it became possible for D'Ailly to enforce his old doctrine—that the power of councils figures above the power of the pope, popes being mere church administrators.

The Earth Is Like an Egg: Columbus's Egg

In order to gain a clear concept of the Columbus that emerged with the discovery—the second Columbus—we must keep in mind the image of the first one: the man with the sphere of the seven heavens in his hand, gazing on the earth with medieval eyes. What was the planet like? In Pierre's *Mappemonde* (1217), we find the description: "The world is like an egg, where may be found, concentrically, the shell, the white, the yolk and a greasy drop, the germ, from which chicks are born. In that same manner does the sky enclose the world in its shell and contains, first, the starry firmament (the white), then, the air (the yolk) and, last, the germ (the earth)." This idea D'Ailly develops two hundred years later:

The philosophers place the fiery sphere under the moon: it is there that fire is purer, invisible because of its great subtlety. Just as water is cleaner than earth and air is cleaner than water, fire is more subtle and thinner than air, and heaven more subtle and thinner than fire, with the exception of the stars, which are the densest parts. For this reason the stars are bright and visible. . . . Then we have the airy sphere which surrounds the water and the earth. It comprises three zones: one—the supreme one, confining with fire—where there are no winds, or rains, or lightning, or similar phenomena. It is believed that certain mountains, like the Olympus, reach these zones, and, according to Aristotle, it is there that comets are formed. Furthermore, the fiery sphere, together with the highest zone of the air and with the comets formed therein, revolves in the same direction as the sky, that is to say: from east to west. . . .

Then comes the middle zone, where clouds and the different meteorological phenomena are formed because it is a zone perpetually cold. . . .

Then the lowest zone, which birds inhabit. And last of all, earth and water, as water does not surround the earth but leaves a part uncovered so that animals may live on it. One part of the earth is less heavy than the other—that which, due to its greater height, is farther away from the planet's center. The rest, except for the islands, is entirely covered with water, according to the philosophers. Earth, being the heaviest element, is the center of the world and constitutes, in fact, the world's center of gravity. According to others, the center of gravity for earth and water is the center of the globe itself.

Although the earth is carved into mountains and valleys, which are the cause of its imperfect roundness, it may be considered round, and this explains why lunar eclipses caused by the earth's projected shadow appear round. For this reason we say that the earth is round: its shape is almost round.

The first thing that strikes the reader about this description is its poetic quality. Poetry pervades all things: astronomy, geography, philosophy, religion. . . .

Was the unknown hemisphere fit to live in? Was it possible for the antipodes to exist? Could there be a terrestrial hell on the other side of the planet? When Christ affirmed that his message would reach the last corner of the earth, could he have ignored the antipodes—the people on the opposite side of the globe? Once, in the eighth century, the archbishop of Milan informed Pope Zachary that he had declared a bishop named Virgil to be a heretic for daring to assert that antipodes in fact existed. The pope wrote to the archbishop: "If it is proven as Virgil insists that there is another world and other men under the earth, another sun and another moon, convoke a council, condemn him and expel him from the Church, once he is deprived of his priestly investiture."

Saint Augustine, though he believed that the earth was round, rejected the existence of antipodes, and his doctrine prevailed for centuries. Under "antipodes" in Diderot's *Encyclopedia,* one reads: "Saint Augustine, according to Chapter IX, Book XVI of *The City of God,* after having discussed whether or not it might be true that there are Cyclopses, Pygmies, and nations that stand on their heads and have their feet in the air, treats the question of the antipodes and asks himself if the bottom of our earth is inhabited. He begins by agreeing that the world is round and that part of the globe is diametrically opposed to the part we inhabit, but he denies that it is inhabited; and the reasons he gives are not bad for a time in which the New World had not yet been discovered."

Great credit should go to Cardinal D'Ailly for remarking, in 1400: "It is not advisable to dwell on fanciful arguments, but rather to study facts based on experience or based on plausible theories." Not wishing to discard plausible theories, he accepts the existence of antipodes as a possibility. But what sort of creatures would live there? The answer would only be found by those who followed Columbus.

All speculations up to that point were based on the concept of a world only pocket-sized. Lacking the slightest idea or merest suspicion of the new continent and vast ocean before him, Columbus set out to find Japan on his tiny globe. What is more, his Japan turned out to be another India. Because of him, the natives of the continent he stumbled across find they still refer to themselves as Indians; the Caribbeans, as West Indians. The laws promulgated for America were known as "The Indian Laws." There was an Indian policy. "Indianos" (not "indios") were what the Spaniards who lived in America came to be called. For Columbus, the West Indies formed the westernmost part of the Asian continent, which was divided into many Indias. This is why he embraced the additional enterprise of finding those freaks so abundant in European literature about the Indies, for their existence would establish that he had indeed reached the land of Marco Polo.

The East Indies, or America Foreshadowed

The one document that best guides us as we advance over the new India is Prester John's letter, written in the eleventh century. It describes a fabulous fauna: white wolves and white camels; lions black, red, and spotted; enormous eaglelike birds able to carry huge oxen through the air in their talons, to feed their chicks. They brood forty days, and when the babies break their shells, they are as big as full-grown eagles. Their parents then fly out to sea, escorted by every bird in the sky, and there they kill themselves by plummeting into the water. Their retinue flies back to take care of the young nestlings.

In India, one could see the phoenix, as well as the red, white, and black unicorns. The white unicorn—the one depicted on tapestries—was the most powerful. It attacked lions and prevailed. It would wait for the lion, hidden in a flowery grove. When a lion passed, the unicorn plunged its ivory horn, steellike, directly into its entrails. Only then, wrote Prester John, could a unicorn be captured: as it struggled mightily to pull its horn from the vanquished lion's belly.

Prester John described men with horns and men with two eyes—one facing forward on their faces and one on the other side of their heads. And he told of anthropophagi. According to his account, Alexander of Macedonia placed the two nations of Gog and Magog between two mountains, with the city of Oriona as capital.

These nations had been announced by the prophet as outposts of the Antichrist. Ezekiel had said as much, and Saint John confirmed the story in Revelations, in The Apocalypse. The announcement that someday those two nations would set out to conquer the world created a fear of catastrophe that shook the heart of Russia. It was conceivable that the next duel would take place between Prester John's India, allied with the nations of Gog and Magog, and the Kingdom of Israel. Prester John signed a peace treaty with Israel, enforced by the weapons of the era: three thousand cavalrymen, five hundred halberdiers, ten thousand archers, and thirty sergeants placed on the border, plus the secret weapons: Gog and Magog. Upon surrendering, Israel pledged a tribute of one hundred loads of gold, silver, and precious gems contributed by two hundred kings and twenty-four hundred vassal princes. Two of the rivers of the Garden of Eden flowed through that same land. . . .

India's wealth was measureless. Prester John's palace glows like a magic lantern in the medieval night, sending out from the East a dazzling brilliance.

The majority of the walls are made of sardonyx and carnelian. Carnelian, taking its name from the serpent Corstis, has strange virtues: it warns against any visitor who might arrive at the palace bearing poison. The windows are of inlaid crystal. The dining table, of gold and amethyst. The sideboards, of ivory. In a vast hall, where knightly jousts are held, the walls are of onyx and precious stones—there are four carnelians to temper the onyx's ardent virtue. The bed is made of sapphire to preserve chastity. Once a day, dinner is served for thirty thousand, not counting the ushers and the servants. The table is emerald. Amethyst are the sideboards (a good stone for guarding against drunkenness). In front of the palace stretches a field for single combat. The contestants face one another with clubs and shields. There is a mirror of wondrous size, and to reach it one must climb a staircase of 125 steps, made of porphyry, serpentine and alabaster, of crystal, jasper and sardonyx, amber and yellow agate. "Your Majesty," writes Prester John in his report to the king, "you may not realize why I am called Brother John. Behold the reason: many individuals in my court enjoy great Church honors. My seneschal is king and primate. The servant in charge of my wine cellar is archbishop and king. My chamberlain is bishop and king. . . . For the sake of modesty, I am content to call myself "brother." My dominions extend over lands that would take four months to cross in a straight line. If you want some notion of my dominion, pray count the stars above or the grains of sand in the sea. . . . I have another palace, of greater size, that my father built for me when he knew that I would be born. A voice told him that God would bless it, granting that whosoever should enter the palace would feel neither cold nor hunger, nor fall sick, nor experience any discomfort. Whosoever crossed the threshold would be immediately healed.

Where should such ravings lead, such as they were: part European fantasy, part Arabian Nights? To Paradise! To the paradise that Columbus believed he had finally discovered in the Caribbean.

Liber Monstruorum

Myth traverses mountain and valley, spans mountain range, sea, and desert, lets the flow of time take it where it will. Centuries, instead of destroying it, inflate it. Distances do not erase it; they give it new, resplendent hues. The story of warlike queens in territories defended with the ardent impetuosity of feminine belligerence—where men could come but once a year—is a very ancient invention. Herodotus tells about such man-killing Amazons, and Plutarch places them in a vast Russian territory, framed between the Caucasus and the Volga. Others think that Amazons live perhaps around the Baltic or in Sweden or in Finland. Francisco Tamara places them in Africa, in Sierra Leone. Duarte López, in Ethiopia: the queen of the Ethiopian Amazons never knows a man and is venerated as a goddess. There is a tradition: The custom of sexual segregation was introduced to the Ethiopian Amazons by the queen of Sheba in the time of Solomon; because of the nobility of these origins, neighboring kings protected and assisted them from then on.

Whatever might be the point of this tale (an apologue seemingly invented by a union of henpecked husbands), the Middle Ages adopted such fictions and embellished them with international variations. The English first, in an eighth-century book, *Liber Monstruorum*. Prester John's letter follows. In it, he describes the province of Feminie, which men may enter only once a year and whose government is in the hands of three queens. The French story is more open. Compiled under the title of *Sidrac,* it relates that men may go to the Amazons' camp but four times a year, to participate in an eight-day period of banquets, dances, and pleasant sexual unions. After the parties, the men withdraw to wait for the next season. In Pierre's *Mappemonde* (thirteenth century), the Amazons are famous warriors: they contribute to the sack of Troy. In their province, he says, are two castles, and their lands border on Hircania, a realm rich in strange animals. In the forests are large, luminous birds with wings that shine in the night.

In its travels from one continent to another, the story falls, in 1440, into the hands of Cardinal D'Ailly. Columbus takes it from *Imago Mundi*. He sails forth with 'this legend as the figurehead for his ship the *Santa María*. The Amazons, he decides, cannot possibly dwell in Africa or in Scandinavia. They are in India, where he is headed. He sails into the Caribbean like a sorcerer, throws the news to the wind, and for years and years soldiers, captains, governors continue the quest after Amazons. The search is not restricted to the credulous Spanish: the story belongs to the rest of Europe even more than it belongs to Spain. Men of every tongue and nation—some because they have read the tales, others because the story has reached their ears—all hunt the same illusion.

The first to be convinced are the Italians, led by Columbus. From Columbus, the information is passed to another Italian, Peter Martyr, who puts it into his book *The Decades;* and so it is diffused all over the Latin world. Another Italian, Antonio Pigafetta, who accompanied Magellan, the Portuguese, on his voyage around the world, says that the Amazons are on the island of Ocoloro, to the south of Java, and that they are fertilized by the wind. Giovanni Botero Benesi, however, knows that they are on the great river of America. Italy is the ideal place to arrange the news into a grand chorale, and Ludovico Ariosto does just that in his *Orlando Furioso*.

Germany has always been the great country of magic. The Germans—the Wesler and Függer Families—entering upon the great American adventure, follow the dazzled multitude and fatten the fable. Nikolaus Federmann sets out from Coro in Venezuela in search of El Dorado and, on his way, learns that there are Amazons and Pygmies on the Orinoco Basin. To the south, in Río de la Plata, a countryman of his, Ulrich Schmidt, who has joined with the Spaniards in the discovery and conquest of Paraguay, records the same information as Federmann.

Then, once more it is the Englishmen's turn. Among their antecedents is Sir John Mandeville, who in 1356 held that the earth was round and made an account of his voyages in the East, the country of the Amazons included. Mandeville's voyages were originally published in French and translated into many languages, but in English they are a classic. The book is the first important one in English to occupy a distinguished place in literature. And Mandeville's voyages are related to Vespucci's works in an extraordinary way! The first editions of Vespucci's *Paesi Nuovi Ritrovati* bears a very curious illustration on the frontispiece. It represents an Oriental monarch, sitting on his throne, surrounded by an entourage of warriors. The sovereign is on the riverbank, an army stretching before him. "The scene takes place upon a field surrounded by a vast circle of walls, perhaps representing the Great Wall of China. The picture owes its most exotic character to the bridges, typically Chinese in style, which remind one of those described by Marco Polo." In the background, many sailing vessels, including caravels. What does the Oriental character of this engraving have to do with Vespucci? Leonardo Olschki discovered the relationship: it is the same picture that appears in the Italian edition of Mandeville's voyages, made in Milan. . . . Two hundred years after Mandeville, Sir Walter Raleigh includes an Amazon story in the account of his journey to Guiana.

Then came the Portuguese. The Amazon Basin becomes the start of their empire in America, and the legend of the Amazon women comes to figure even in Luis de Camões's Lusitanian epic *Os Lusíadas*.

The Spanish interest is obvious. The stage on which the story is to unfold is entirely theirs. Juan Díaz discovers Yucatán, home of the warrior-women, about whose fortress he has been informed. Diego Velázquez, governor of Cuba, when he makes his agreements with Hernán Cortés, stipulates: "Because it has been said that there are people whose ears are large and wide, and others who have faces like dogs, look for them . . . and also learn where and in what place are the Amazons of which the Indians tell." Cortés himself, usually so objective in his letters, writes to Charles V, telling him how he has been informed by the Indians of an island inhabited entirely by women, not one man among them. He entrusts his relative Francisco Cortés with the mission of exploring the land of the Amazons described in ancient narratives. Cristóbal de Olid on his way to Ceguatán and Nuño de Guzmán on his way to Michoacán are both searching for the Mexican Amazon, just as Jiménez de Quesada's brother, Hernán Pérez, in the New Kingdom of Granada, sets out on a quest for El Dorado. From Chile, Agustín de Zárate writes: "The Indians of Leuchugona told the Spaniards that between two of the realms is a province inhabited exclusively by women." In Paraguay, Hernando de Rivera transmits to Álvar Núñez Cabeza de Vaca the news he has just received: "Towards the Northeast live, in large towns, women who have made white and yellow metal: the chairs and tableware in their homes are all made of those metals. Their ruler is a woman. . . . Nearby is a nation of pygmy Indians."

Thus the Amazons heralded by Columbus begin to people the heart of South America, filter themselves into the imagination of those who first explore Chile, Paraguay, Peru, New Granada, Venezuela, Guiana. . . . And in North America, just as in the south, the largest river was named the "Amazon" and the name of California, queen of the Amazons, is given to a peninsula, a sea, a gulf, and two states, where today are found the last Mexican and Anglo-American descendants of the legend.

There might have been a slight ingredient of indigenous malice in the swift propagation of the myths of El Dorado and the Amazons. The Indians could see that what the Spaniards wanted most was gold and women. In order to rid themselves of the bothersome invaders and send them as far away as possible, they invariably pointed toward the horizon and spoke of distant lands where the conquistadors would find both the gold and the women. The chroniclers refer constantly to this native wile, which so readily deceived them.

When their function in the New World was exhausted, the legends returned to Europe. They were all the rage, and the books of chivalry multiplied furiously. Cromberg, the German printer who lived in Seville, published *The Exploits of Esplandian, Lisuarte of Greece*. . . . In Amsterdam were printed chronicles that confirmed the renaissance in America of every known freak that ever inhabited medieval fiction. A nonfactual geography persisted even after the discoverers should have fully realized that the Indians were fairly ordinary flesh and blood like themselves. But myth was made of stronger stuff than reality. Those who chronicled such histories had either lived in America, as in the case of Las Casas or Fernández de Oviedo, or had never set foot in America and did everything secondhand, like Antonio de Herrera or Juan Díaz de Solís, who never crossed an ocean. Into this mélange of Greek, Asian, and European invention, the American ingredients began to filter. Garcilaso de la Vega arrived in Spain with a treasure trove of Incan tall tales. It is curious that, being part Indian, he was so much more inclined than many white Europeans to delve into the complexities of Neoplatonic humanism. He introduced León Hebreo to Spain, producing the best Spanish version of his work.

The story of the Amazons was so vivid in Spanish minds that once, in 1533, one of Charles V's agents informed him that the ports of Santander and Laredo had witnessed the arrival of sixty ships with ten thousand Amazons on board, attracted by the rumor that the men of those regions were known to be "real men." The Amazons had come to reproduce: each one would pay fifteen ducats to any stud who made her pregnant. The story had strange but very real economic repercussions: even the price of meat in Valladolid was affected.

At the same time, illustrated geographies began to grow very popular. The first engravings of New World natives were made by the Germans. There is an illustration accompanying a letter of Vespucci's dated 1505 that comes with the following commentary: "The men wear precious stones on their faces and chests. No one of them possesses anything of his own, because all things are shared. The men can have as many women as they wish, be they mothers, sisters, or friends. When they make war among themselves, they eat one another—they kill them, then hang the meat to smoke. They live to a hundred years of age." According to the illustrations in Theodore de Bry's *American History* (1590–1634), the fabulous wealth described by Prester John is all located in America. Columbus disembarks, and the naked Indians come out to welcome him and render him homage, bringing chests, necklaces, chiseled gold chalices. Gold mines are depicted as marvelous spectacles. Gold dust is scooped up from the hillsides as if it were sand and poured into baskets that the natives place, one by one, at the admiral's feet. In other engravings, the Amazons are the center of attraction; especially so in the cannibal scenes. Curaçao is depicted as the Isle of the Giants. And the first maps are animated by similarly imaginative scenes.

The Earthly Paradise

On the one hand were the human monsters and mythological fauna of the New World; or animals no one had ever laid eyes on before, such as iguanas, those miniature living facsimiles of dinosaurs. . . . On the other, the delights: The Fountain of Eternal

Youth, the Garden of Eden. The garden, of course, drew every-one. The actual place where Adam and Eve had first dwelt existed: its reality was universally accepted. One only had to establish just which corner of the planet it occupied. Cardinal D'Ailly never doubted its existence, and Columbus set out to discover it. Paradise, or the Garden of Eden, said the cardinal, was at the source from which sprang the four rivers: the Phison, the Gehon, the Tigris, and the Euphrates. The last two had been identified. The existence of the first two was argued over by many authors, but they were all certain that the Phison, according to Genesis, was made of fine gold. Isidore of Seville, José Damaseno Estrabón, Herodotus, all agreed that Paradise was in some region of the East, at a great distance from the world they knew. Some supposed it to be in such a high place that it was at least partially located in the lunar sphere, to which the waters of the Deluge had not risen. The cardinal reduced all such discussion to its proper limits: there was no reason to conclude that the Earthly Paradise was as high as the lunar circle. That was clear hyperbole. The plain truth was that its altitude could not be compared with that of the low earth: it rose high into the serene air that capped the atmosphere. It was there that emanations and vapors—so Alexander had stated—formed an ebb and flow toward the moon. The waters that came down from that mountain formed a great lake. The rush downhill, it was said, made such a noise that the inhabitants of the region were born deaf: the din destroyed the newborn babies' eardrums. Such was the testimony of Basil and Ambrosius. And these were times in which testimonies by authorities counted far more than experiential proofs. It was an English source (Bartholomew Anglicus, as the French translator affirms) from which D'Ailly borrowed his information that the four rivers most probably were the Nile, the Ganges, the Euphrates, and the Tigris.

So what did Columbus go out to discover at the mouth of the Orinoco? The Garden of Eden! He arrived at the spot, saw its contours, was able to validate D'Ailly and all those who had come before. He admired the extraordinary mount that anyone today may see on the island of Marguerite, modeled like a perfect sculpture.

They call it María Guevara's Teats. Columbus: "Great signs are these of the Earthly Paradise, because the place conforms to the opinions of the saints and wisest of theologians and proves correct those who have said that the world—land and water—is spherical: I found that it was not round in the way they write about it; it is shaped like a pear, as if one had a very round ball and on it were the breast of a woman with the part of the nipple highest and nearest to Heaven."

What follows this encounter with Paradise is the acceptance of all things, possible and impossible. The Europeans perch in their theater stalls to watch as an unparalleled drama unfolds on the American stage. When the Catholic kings sign agreements with Alfonso Hojeda that allow him to explore the sea gardens of Cubagua, they grant him the right to keep whatever he may find, "be it gold or silver or copper or lead or tin or any other metal, and any or all gems or precious stones and also carbuncles and diamonds and rubies and emeralds or any manner or kind of precious stone, and likewise pearls of any kind or quality that there might be, and likewise monsters, animals or birds whatever be their kind or quality of form, and all and any serpents or fish that there be, and likewise all manner of spices and drugs."

Apologetic Commentary on the New World Paradise

One of the most erudite bibliophiles of the seventeenth century was Antonio León Pinelo, who wrote *El Paraíso del Nuevo Mundo, Comentario Apologético, Historia Natural y Peregrina de las Indias Occidentales e Islas de Tierra Firme del Mar Océano (The Paradise of the New World, Natural and Foreign History of the West Indies and the Isles of Terra Firma on the Oceanic Sea)*. Pinelo belonged to one of those families of Jewish origin who overflow in their public affirmations of their new Christian zeal. Although his father was Portuguese and he was born in Valladolid, he considered himself Peruvian: almost all of his works were written in Spain, upon his return there from Lima, where he had studied and where his parents had died. His paternal grandfather had been a Portuguese Jew who did business in Madeira. (He was burned alive in Lisbon, together with his wife.) His parents became Christians—what if they hadn't!—but no matter how eloquent were their protestations of faith, they felt they would be much safer away from Spain and Portugal and thus sought a somewhat less dangerous refuge in Lima—although, even there, myriad watchful eyes continued to spy on them. "From 1605 to 1637 the Inquisition convoked and tried Diego López [Pinelo's father], accusing him of trifling and ridiculous offenses, such as having a horse named Peter, having cast down his eyes when the host was raised, and having tied his mule to a cross." All these accusations gradually drifted away thanks to the most noteworthy Christianity of Diego López, who (as a widower) ended by becoming nothing less than a friar. His son became a passionate defender of Mary's Immaculate Conception, devoting himself to the most painstaking reading of the Old and the New Testaments, the fathers of the Church, and every book that his tireless diligence enabled him to find, till he arrived at the vehement conviction that the Garden of Eden could only be located in America. According to him, in Iquitos on the Amazon River were idyllic green mansions of timeless poetic beauty. Novelists of our own time paradoxically refer to them as the Green Hell. The four rivers mentioned by the ancients were, in his view, none other than the Amazon, the Plata, the Orinoco, and the Magdalena. The Earthly Paradise was not square, as the Frenchman Jacques d'Auzoles had drawn it. It was a circle, 160 leagues in diameter.

Nine hundred large-format pages did León Pinelo write to combat the seventeen most authorized hypotheses that placed Eden in the center of the moon, in the middle regions of the air, on top of the highest known mountain peaks, in the sky, in Libya, in India, in the world of the Hyperboreans, in the Moluccas, in Ceylon, in Sarmatia, in Charon, in Syria, on the Plain of Esdraelon in Palestine, in Damascus, in Canaan, on the Elysian Fields, on the Fortunate Isles. . . . For Pinelo, all this was groundless geography, and he argued: Where is the richest, most pleasant land, the most delicious and sweetly moderate in climate, if not in the magic bower of Amazonia with its exotic orchids and its butterflies winged with pearly iridescence and emerald?

One curious fact: As a Jew, León Pinelo was not the sort of poet who ignored the reality of his time. Together with Solórzano Pereyra, he was the most thorough compiler of the new laws on which the *Política Indiana* were based—an invaluable monument of colonial history—and, being an especially close friend of Lope de Vega, he provided the poet and playwright with information that the latter could and did use in his own literary pieces. Product of a culture, more than of an age, Pinelo moved in an environment where empirical fact and fantastic legend held equal sway. Raúl Porras Barranechea has rediscovered León Pinelo's book. He concludes: "Spurred on by a desire for erudition and documentation, Pinelo registers books and papers that refer to America; he delves into old folios of medieval geography and ancient cosmography—in Latin, Greek, and Hebrew; he initiates himself in Talmudic and Biblical science, devouring 680 Hebrew books from a rabbinical library in search of a quotation about the Garden of Eden. And to clear up any theological doubt, he submerges himself in the works of the Church Fathers, the Bible exegetes, and the doctors of scholastics."

As a complement to this preparatory work, Pinelo transferred to America—one by one—the monsters Europe had invented or adopted and, finally, sure that Peru was wealthier by far than India, sure that everything in divine and humanistic letters pointed to the inevitable conclusion that the Earthly Paradise lay somewhere in the vicinity of Iquitos, he wove with these elements the enchanted tapestry of his books. For those Occidentals who were weary of the hardships of the Old World, marvelous America was to be the Seat of Paradise.

3

•

Utopia:
Protest and
Illusion

A New Philosophy Is Born

Of all the philosophies of the West, no other possesses the fascinating charm of *Utopia,* the first joyful moment of the sixteenth century. With it the great sleeping expectation is fanned into awareness. The idea of such a place causes man, a captive of injustice for centuries, to become a rebel, to plunge into the most absurd of explorations and adventures. In the end, the idea mobilizes millions of Europeans in search of new worlds, places where they might begin to imagine conditions of well-being nonexistent in their native lands. The new movement—a hopeful one—is toward social justice, for centuries suppressed by the monarchy, the aristocracy, the Church, the powerful bourgeoisie.

Humanism brought together a group of select philosophers who tried, throughout Europe, to propagate a new gospel, born out of a radical revision of ideas. Erasmus, Luis Vives, Thomas More, with equal doses of finesse, subtlety, and reckless courage, challenge all manner of authority: monarchs as decided as England's Henry VIII (an emperor victorious in two hemispheres—first such case in history!), genial Machiavelli, Luther (formidable as a bull), even the Catholic Church, then in the hands of the most arrogant pontiffs. No small risk is involved in demanding a stricter moral conduct of the great ones, at a time when courts have become lax and self-indulgent; nor in advocating a theory of peace before an audience of ambitious and triumphant warriors—even when the pope had armies and used them; nor in proposing the idea of a just government for free men and in repudiating the policies of cold, unscrupulous calculation that then characterized the newly formed states; nor in rising against the power of a bourgeoisie that was growing wealthier every day with the aid of industrial machinery and causing others to sink hopelessly into poverty as a prelude to modern times. It was time to rediscover the Gospels, to restore their original powers, and to do that—in the case of Erasmus and More—without running headlong into the path taken by the rebellious friars who attacked Church unity. To try to bring into the struggle against injustice those very monarchs who were causing the injustice in the first place . . .

The books and discourses of those philosophers—who denounced the viciousness of contemporary society—provide the ideological foundations of Leftist thought. Even today, they are quoted by those who continue to cherish what seems to be only a fantastic hope, but a hope that maintains its eternal allure. Thomas More writes *Utopia* at the same time that his friend Erasmus writes *The Praise of Folly*. The twin works, conceived in the closest rapport, give us the exact measure of the belligerent idealism of those days. After which a vast literature, ushered in by those two volumes, penetrates the best currents of Western thought through hundreds of prototypes. Still, not one of all these authors, not even Erasmus himself, was able to invent such a fortunate word as More did with his *Utopia*.

It was probably an instant's flash of genius during a sleepless night. More, subtle and hypercritical, shuffling Greek words, fashioned a new term without imagining that it was destined to attract forever the aspirations of the most vehement revolutionists. "Utopia" means a nonexistent place; it is a name conceived in skepticism and reflecting the irony at the heart of every idealist who is afraid that the treacheries of destiny will mock the children of his imagination. More builds a castle in the air, a structure whose foundations are very much fixed, however, on solid ground. To be just, his *Utopia* is the work that sparks the mightiest exodus of all time. Utopians all, Europeans emigrate in a constant and massive flood, now four centuries long, to the continent of their hopes: America.

In 1516, More publishes his book, and if today we are to record the number of times that the word "Utopia" has been used ever since (in every language, by people from every nation, every continent), the most efficient computer would be unable to give us an approximate figure; its currency is universal and on the increase. In the notion of a Utopia remain fixed all the best and most noble things, the healthiest parts of Western thought. Utopia is a pure act of contrition and faith, one unmatched in any other school of thought born in Europe. In Utopia, the man who loves peace and justice reconciles himself to that old world corroded by imperialistic designs, scarred by the most devastating armed conflicts that humanity has known, arrogant before the races that it has enslaved or reduced to colonial servitude.

The Key Year, 1516

The idea in itself was not new. There have been Utopias ever since the first dreamer opened his eyes upon the world. In the history of Western thought, More's *Utopia* is related to schemes derived from Plato. But the difference is great: If we look back, the pre-More Utopias are really built on air, poetic abstractions without consequence, mere spells induced by magic means. More, on the contrary, places his island, homeland of modern socialism, in America—in the New World, on the continent and beyond the oceans just revealed by Amerigo Vespucci. He says and does not say—with an intellectual's characteristic blush—that Utopia is a nonexistent place, but he tacks it firmly on a real map; and, from then on, those who read him believe him and disbelieve him. They would rather believe, though. They are inclined to be positive, to acknowledge that the appearance of America alters circumstances, mandates a new perspective. Raising the Utopian banner, the European becomes more expansive, more ambitious than ever: he crosses the Atlantic. In other words, if for geographers—finally!—the Terra Firma that the persevering Genoese admiral Columbus was looking for in the vicinity of the Caribbean was confirmed as truly existent, philosophers could by all rights also claim the territory, from the time of Vespucci, as a landscape upon which to construct ideal republics. In the light of that promise, the announcement of continental America produces a profound change in the history of Western thought.

In fact, the difference wrought by the new Utopian philosophy is so great that an imaginary dividing line should be traced—at 1516—to show that prior to that year Utopia was fantasy; after 1516, something real. Plato invented his island as fantasy; and fantastically he himself sank it into a dark, terrifying sea. From that point onward, we have known what a Platonic "idea" is. Plato's "no place" was a device for transmitting his abstractions. One consequence: The legend remained imprinted in medieval fabulation. When More reads Vespucci's report, he finds what Plato could not have suspected, extracts the real news and resorts to the magic style in only one thing: the invention of names like Utopia. The Saint-Dié geographers had launched another happy word: America. And here is the marvel that can be worked with just two words!

The Great Western Protest

Let's begin by thinking about how Utopias originate: theirs is a rebellion against a contemporary reality. Whoever enters their world inscribes himself in the philosophy of protest. Starting with Plato. That Greek was in absolute revolt against the Athenian government and its vices. His *Republic* and his *Atlantis* are simply his way of condemning all the evils he saw around him—of condemning a reality to exalt a possibility: a just society, aiming to make men happy, not predicated on their enslavement and submission. The fifteenth-century humanists were not unfamiliar with Plato's ironic mode of protest. The new academy further stimulated it. From here stems a new critical confrontation, one especially effective in times when ambitions are greatest. Although Martin Luther claimed the word "protestant" for his own movement, protestant is what they all were. Everyone protested—Erasmus and Vives, More and Saint Teresa, Jan Hus, Calvin, Savonarola, Ignatius of Loyola. If Luther denounced the corruption of Rome—and he was not the first to do so, Teresa fought as vehemently against the weakening moral standards in Spanish convents; and men like Vives were by no means lacking in courage when they proposed a Christian philosophy of peace to take the place of the imperial arrogance of the Spanish courtier, especially since he was saying this at the very moment when Charles V had just triumphed over Rome. Machiavelli had anticipated that sort of might when he wrote about Ferdinand the Catholic, his model for princes.

Thomas More was convinced that he could guide the new English sovereign, Henry VIII, in a revolutionary direction. Everything about the young king made him think so: he was gallant and enlightened above all other princes. He could easily be a trendsetter. He would be capable of setting right the legislation that was turning the kingdom into a deplorably unhappy society. His world view was broad. He spoke Latin as fluently as Spanish, Italian, and French. He had read choice books in all those languages. The lute and the harpsichord he played like a virtuoso. He had invited Erasmus to teach at Cambridge and appointed More himself as his chancellor. So Thomas More—with complete loyalty and no little illusion—set before the new king a whole English panorama exactly as his rebel Christian eyes were seeing it. *Utopia* is a book with two faces in dialectical contradiction. It denounces a crude European reality—in particular, England—by contrasting it to an ideal republic. As always happens in such cases, the essay presents a precise and felicitous exposé of the miseries of the day and age, but is less successful in its proposal for a cure. In his analysis, More proceeds over the solid ground of tangible, concrete facts. The redeeming fantasy remains at the mercy of the human condition. *Utopia* presupposes a government in the hands of good men. . . .

Kings, says an indisputably courageous More, dream only of promoting war—and neglect the beneficial arts of peace. Ever ambitious to annex new realms, they pay little attention to the governance of their own states. Their ministers and counselors say nothing, either because they are inept or because they are cowardly parasites whose sole aim is to win the king's favor by flattery. What else might one expect of courtiers dominated by their own vanity, jealousy, and selfish interests? In England, the infamous massacre of Cornwall had just taken place. Captured leaders were summarily executed; two thousand rebels lay dead on the battlefield. More raises his voice against the death penalty. It is, he asserts, a barbarous routine that "passes the limits of justice and is always hurtful to the commonwealth. For it is too extreme and cruel a punishment for theft, and yet not sufficient to restrain a man from theft. . . . In this point you are like evil schoolmasters, readier to beat than to teach the scholars." He blames this misery on "a great number of gentlemen who cannot be content to live idle themselves, like drones, on that which others have labored for: their tenants, I mean, whom they shave and cut to the quick by raising their rents. . . . They carry at their tails a great flock of idle, loitering servingmen who never learn any craft whereby to get their livings. . . . When the master is dead or they are sick themselves, they are . . . thrust out of doors . . . to either starve, or manfully play the thieves."

With the rise of industrial capitalism, England entered one of its periods of greatest poverty. Having artfully appropriated the Flemish manufacture of woolens, the wealthy multiplied their herds of sheep and their looms. Small farmers were driven off their fields so as to convert their croplands into pastures. Whole villages disappeared. The displaced farmers and farmhands poured into the city slums, "thrust out of their own . . . by cunning and fraud . . . or by wrongs and injuries so wearied that they are compelled to sell it all." Such injustices—and at this More's indignation grew—were not committed for the benefit of the state, but only of the new, rich bourgeoisie. The wool industry was not a legal monopoly: only a few derived benefits from it. "Sheep . . . that were wont to be so meek and tame, and such small eaters . . . now eat up the very men themselves. . . . They pluck down towns, leave nothing standing, but only the church, to make of it a sheep-house."

And as for arms, sad, too, was their destiny! Thieves multiplied for the glory and the benefit of the armies. The best soldiers ended up as thieves, and thieves became the most redoubtable soldiers. Luxury and senseless waste spawned gambling and prostitution everywhere. Divine justice was subordinated to human justification, which ironically legalized and authorized itself. The rumors of future wars were bandied about in order to levy new taxes and decrease the value of currency. There was no cause, no matter how heinous, that could not find a judge capable of decreeing it a good one. And the Church! Preachers softened the Gospel's injunctions to accommodate them to man's bad habits.

Anticipating Don Quixote

Don Quixote is anticipated in the underlying meaning of the dialogue between the two parts of More's book. Alongside the raw reality that he exposes with a voice of common sense, he evokes a Cervantian illusion: the dream of a marvelous island whose culture might well serve as the model for a good government. The juxtaposition of the two discourses doubles the book's force and its charm. Four centuries after its appearance as a sort of novel about England, it continues to be read and used, on the one hand, to make a critical, historic evaluation of sixteenth-century European society and, on the other hand, to stimulate the invention of nobly idealistic political reform. Utopia, as many have noted, is the theoretical antecedent of modern socialism and communism.

Socialism and Communism

More points to private property as the cause of the dire poverty he sees all around him. He speaks of the gold by means of which the wealth of nations is measured; of the laws that regulate commerce; of nascent capitalism. And he turns his eyes to the primitive Church, where, as is stated in Acts of the Apostles, "the believers were of one heart and soul, and . . . they had all things in common. . . . Those who owned lands or houses would sell them and bring the price of what they sold . . . and distribution was made according as anyone had need." The faithful deposited what sums they had obtained at the feet of the Apostles, who would then distribute the wealth. Marx,[1] Lenin, and Stalin[2] either quoted More or referred to his words. He has so often been called a precursor that in the most recent Polish edition of *Utopia,* a comparison is made between what he wrote and what the founders of modern communism set down. In other socialist currents, allusions to the English saint are even more frequent. The difference lies in the contrast that might be made between the atheistic communism of Marx and More's conceptualizations, which are steeped in Christian principle.

More's political conception does not differ much from that of Erasmus or of Vives. The three were very close friends, and Erasmus was not unaware of the publication of *Utopia.* In Erasmus's opinion, "People build cities, and the folly of princes destroys them." In *Utopia,* a king is elected for life by the people, but he may be removed from his position if he tries to reduce them to bondage. The people elect their Parliament. The object of the government is not to accumulate wealth for a few, or to provide for the king's pleasure, but to secure happiness for all. More saw the social order of his time as a permanent conspiracy of the rich against the poor.

Vives, in turn, says: "Just as it would be disgraceful for a rich father to tolerate that in his home anyone should starve or go naked or dressed in rags, it is equally unacceptable that in Bruges—which is anything but poor—magistrates should tolerate that some citizens be victims of hunger and misery." To quote Alain Guy: "Vives was not only a determined democrat—hostile to tyrants, in favor of public consensus—and a tireless pacifist, but also a true collectivist, a severe critic of incipient capitalism, who recalled frequently that the appropriation of goods is a degeneration, in relation to primitive common property."[3]

Like More, he turns to the New World to point out the difference between a corrupt European society and the noble savages of the other hemisphere, whose kind and generous ways contrast so vividly with those of the Old World.

In 1520, Erasmus, More, and Vives met in Bruges; no doubt, the general panorama of their times must have been the highlight of their conversation—especially the revelation of the New World. It inspired their books, their famous discourses, their teaching. We have an excellent record of these friendships in the letters they wrote to each other. It suffices to read the portrait of More in Erasmus's letter to Ulrich von Hutten to be reminded up to what point the written word may rival the paintbrush, even that of Holbein, the immortal painter of these peerless figures.[4]

Why in America?

When he placed Utopia in the New World, was More being arbitrary? What inspired him to make that geographical choice? Did America really have anything to do with the genesis of his book? From his own words, we learn the answers. Henry VIII—or, to be more exact, the London tradesmen who were interested in wool—had sent him together with Cuthbert Tunstall (former ambassador to the king of France, and later bishop in London) as emissaries to negotiate commercial agreements between the two kingdoms with Archduke Charles's envoys. Charles would soon become Charles I of Spain and Charles V of the empire.[5] The meetings took place in Bruges. One day, when conversations were interrupted because the Archduke's envoy had to return to Brussels for instructions, More went to Antwerp. The port attracted him for many reasons. In Antwerp, in those days, art had reached peaks of excellence, like the genius of Quentin Metsys. Erasmus and his friends could always be found in Bruges or Louvain or Antwerp. Fortune smiled on Thomas More: the unexpected came out to meet him. In Antwerp, he made the discovery of America! Vespucci's America, not Columbus's islands: the *new continent* reported by Vespucci in his letters, published in Antwerp eight years before, in Latin and Dutch. It is probably on that occasion that More learned about other letters: those of Peter Martyr. But his curiosity was especially captivated by Vespucci's accounts, and *Utopia* came forth.

The Printing Press

One of the great strokes of good fortune that favored the discovery of America and its ensuing intellectual activity was the invention of the printing press. So fresh is this invention that in London it was introduced just one year after More's birth; and More's acquaintance with Vespucci's letters was brought about by his friendship with those who worked in publishing houses. These were the happy days when a proofreader could be, and was, Erasmus. *He,* of course, worked on the Greek-language editions. The proofreaders were like a family, a family dwelling in the highest spheres of humanism. Another proofreader was Peter Giles, whom we may see next to Erasmus in a canvas by Quentin Metsys. (Metsys was, together with Holbein, painter of the most outstanding portraits of Erasmus.) The great editorial centers were Antwerp, Louvain, and Bruges. Peter Giles worked with Thierry Marren's printing office in Louvain. But Giles was in Antwerp in the days when More visited that city. "Nothing gave me greater joy than meeting him," writes More to Erasmus, and in *Utopia* he writes: "It is hard to say whether the young man be in learning or in honesty more excellent. . . . In no man is more prudent simplicity . . . and conversation so merry and pleasant."

More was not disproportionate in his praise. It was Peter Giles who put him on the road to the discovery of America, and *Utopia* is dedicated to him.

The English humanist saw himself before a group of editors who were to be the best promoters of the American book whatever its form: whether it be, say, accounts by the king's chroniclers or Las Casas's tract denouncing the conquistadors' decimation of Indians. With the rise of Charles V to the Spanish throne, Antwerp became Spain's printing press. The first picture of an American potato plant was printed in Antwerp, long before anyone could imagine eating, as the Indians did, the tubercles that fattened on its roots.

Among all this literature, no other book would ever have the resonance of *Utopia;* and, among the most important events shaping European intellectual history and the destiny of America, we must place very high on the list the casual meeting in that port city of Thomas More and the proofreader Peter Giles.

From Vespucci to Thomas More

Two of the words More coins in his book are highly significant: the name "Utopia" and that of "Hythloday." A supposed sailor, Raphael Hythloday is said to be one of the twenty-four companions of Vespucci who stayed in Brazil. But the name "Hythloday" is taken from two Greek words, which mean "skillful storyteller." Could More's intention have been to allude to Vespucci himself? Has it not been said that the Florentine owes part of his glory to the piquant quality of his narratives? The name "Raphael" could refer to the vessel *São Rafael*—Vasco da Gama's—which opened a new passage to India by sailing around the Cape of Good Hope.

More tells us that Peter Giles, pointing to Raphael Hythloday, said: "See you this man? . . . I was minded to bring him straight home to you. . . . There is no man this day living that can tell you the sorts of things he knows; he has just come from the New World. He is unique: in addition to his travels he has studied Greek. He did this for the love of philosophy, whereas the Latins have limited themselves to memorizing bits of Seneca and Cicero, as if in these, the whole of ancient wisdom is accessible."

From "Raphael" More gets the idea of Utopia: the island of the New World, in Brazilian waters. A Brazilian scholar, Alfonso Arinos de Mello Franco, reading More's text, has identified the location of Utopia.[6] It is Cabo Frío, where Vespucci left twenty-four of his companions. Vespucci's description of our Noble Savages is transformed by More into the first principle of the philosophy that he presents, whose ramifications in time go as far as the Romantics of the nineteenth century, and even farther. America becomes for all time the continent that dissatisfied Europeans will turn to in every age.

More selects from Vespucci's information those items that best suit his Platonic aims and his Christian feelings. He eliminates everything to do with cannibalism, tones down certain passages in which Vespucci expresses himself with crude realism; still, his painstaking care to accommodate the American story in his way of thinking jumps out at us. Despite the omissions, his debts are apparent.

More says: "On this point they seem almost too much inclined to the opinion of those who defend pleasure, in which they say all or the chief part of man's felicity rests. . . . For they define virtue as a life ordered according to nature and say that we are hereonto ordained by God. . . . For when nature bids thee to be good and gentle to others, she commands thee not to be cruel and ungentle to thyself."

Vespucci says: "The people of the New World live according to nature and could be called Epicureans rather than Stoics."

With these words, More and Vespucci unleash a trend of thought whose projections will go as far as Rousseau. When Vespucci balances the old Stoic formula—live according to nature—with the Epicurean one, which emphasizes sensuality and pleasure, he gives More the opportunity to speculate on the good points in each of these philosophies; and in one of the most extensive parts of his book, he expounds on the idea of sensual pleasures, which Vespucci had described in his own very particular style:

The women, as I have told you [he wrote to the Medici], although they go naked and are libidinous, have no defect in their bodies, which are graceful and clean, nor are they coarse, as some may suppose, for, although they are fleshy, there is no ugliness in them, as this is compensated by their good stature. One thing we have thought miraculous: that not one of them has sagging breasts, and those who had already given birth were no different from the virgins in the shape of their stomachs or their waists, nor in any other parts of the body, which I will not mention out of decency. When they could unite with the Christians, driven by their exceeding lust, they overcame the others' modesty. . . . They make their husbands' penises swell in such a manner as to make them seem misshapen and brutal, and this they do with a certain artifice of theirs and the bite of certain poisonous animals. . . . The men take as many women for themselves as they wish.

More, for his part, says: "The Utopians count diverse kinds of true pleasures. Some they attribute to the soul, and some to the body. . . . The pleasures of the body they divide into two parts. The first is when delight is felt and perceived by the senses. . . . The second part of bodily pleasure, they say, is that which consists and rests in the harmonious state of the body. And that truly is every man's proper health, intermingled by and disturbed with no pain. . . . All the Utopians grant it be a right great pleasure." He refers to outward and external pleasures that restore the body: eating and drinking to refurbish strength, animal functions that expel whatever substance is superabundant. These are "pleasures not greatly to be prized, but in so far as they are necessary. Nevertheless, they enjoy them too and thankfully acknowledge mother nature, who with her tender love combines pleasant delights with functions indispensable to life."

Vespucci says in *Mundus Novus:* "No kind of metal is found there except gold, which abounds in those countries, although none have we brought on our first navigation. And of this the inhabitants gave us news, affirming that towards the interior there was very great abundance of gold, which they hold in no esteem or appreciate in any way." In another place, he repeats: "Its inhabitants do not regard gold or silver or any other jewel as precious, preferring jewels made of feathers or bone." More finds in these lines the realization of the Platonic ideal, as expressed in *The Republic:* "Wealth engenders luxury, laziness, fickleness; poverty engenders vileness and wickedness. . . . In the ideal state, those who rule are the truly rich, not in gold, but in such wealth as man really needs in order to be happy: a wise and virtuous life." Now here is More, in *Utopia:* "They have found a means, which, as it is agreeable to all their other laws and customs, so it is very different from ours, where gold is so much prized and so diligently kept, and is therefore incredible except to those that are wise. . . . They eat and drink in earthen and glass vessels, which are indeed elaborately and handsomely made. Of gold and silver they commonly make chamber pots, and other like vessels that serve for most base uses." And Lenin, in an article published in *Pravda,* wrote: "When we will have triumphed on a world-wide scale, I believe that we will build public urinals out of gold in the main streets of the world's greatest cities."

The communistic idea is already expressed in Vespucci's letter: "They have nothing that they may call their own, but all things are in common. They live together without a king, without authority, and each one of them is his own lord. . . . Their dwellings are in common and their houses made like cottages, but very strong, built of enormously large tree trunks and resistant against storms and winds. In some places they build them so large and wide that in a single house we found six hundred souls . . . every eight or ten years they move to another place." More locates his republic in a city, but at the same time preserves the contact with nature that goes with American life. His Utopians live by the principle of common possession; and, in order to do away with the idea of individual and absolute property, they change their dwellings every ten years, drawing lots to decide who should have which house. "On the back side of the houses, through the whole length of the street, lie large gardens. . . . Every house has two doors, one into the street, and a postern door on the back side into the garden. These doors are made with two leaves, never locked or bolted, so easy to be opened that they will follow the least drawing of a finger, and shut again by themselves. Every man that wills may go in."

The idea of religious freedom among the inhabitants of the New World made Erasmus and More very enthusiastic, for both were as dismayed over the religious wars as they were disgusted by the degeneration of the monastic orders. Vespucci: "We did not see in these people any law, nor may they be called Moors or Jews; they are worse than gentiles, for we saw not that they made any sacrifice, nor do they have houses destined for worship. I judge that their life is Epicurean." In *Utopia,* there are "diverse kinds of religion," and "no man shall be blamed for reasoning in the support of his own religion . . . still, he should use no kind of violence . . . No image of any god is seen in the church, to the intent that it may be free for every man to conceive God by his religion after what likeness and similitude he will." More referred to friars as "the greatest and veriest vagabonds that are." Erasmus wrote to a friend: "I would not wish you to give a mistaken interpretation of what I am going to say, supposing that it goes against theology, for which, as you know, I have always had the greatest respect. I only wish to amuse myself at the expense of certain theologians of our time, whose brains are moth-eaten, whose language is barbarian, whose intelligence is blunt, whose learning is a patchwork quilt, whose ways are uncouth, whose life is pure hypocrisy and whose hearts are black as hell." More calls the justice that is founded on European law hypocritical and stupid.

The American Novel Begins?

Up to this point, everything could just as easily have been a novel. Isn't there a trace of Platonic fantasy in Vespucci's narratives? At home, in the Florence of his youth, hadn't Plato's ideas been Vespucci's daily bread? His uncle and teacher, Giorgio Antonio, was sought by German humanists such as Johann Reuchlin, who were eager to make contact with Florentine philosophers. Amerigo Vespucci was not an ordinary adventurer or seaman like so many others. A cultivated man, he remembered the philosopher-uncle's lessons; and, as he approached the New World, he recalled Dante's verses, which he knew by heart. In the same way that monsters and magic legends and Pierre D'Ailly's fancies made up part of Columbus's mental baggage (his vision of the mouth of the Orinoco is filled with fabulous medieval inventions), Vespucci brought with him the idealism of the Neoplatonics. When he thought that he had found the Earthly Paradise in the New World, he traced it from the immortal poem in which Politian sang to the charms of the Fair Simonetta—Simonetta Vespucci, Botticelli's dancer in the *Primavera*.

It is hard to tell fact from fiction in the first accounts of America. More's *Utopia* may have provided the Inca Garcilaso de la Vega with ways to make his narrative about the Peruvian kings more attractive. It is true that many of the highly detailed descriptions contained in the *Royal Commentaries* have been confirmed as true in our days through a great variety of sources and archaeological studies. But it is also a well-known fact that the genial mestizo had quite a remarkable imagination. The authenticity of a great part of his account of the kings of Peru does not preclude the possibility—which would have to be proven by researchers—that More's *Utopia* exerted an influence upon his description of the Utopian Inca government.

Were that true, aren't we making a novel out of this whole American labyrinth? No, for many of Vespucci's descriptions in *Mundus Novus* coincide with those of later chroniclers who made the same travels. But there *is* something else. While it is difficult to know up to what point More, in the creation of his marvelous island, depended on Vespucci's facts, or on his fantasy, something is positive and evident: destiny began to turn his Utopia into a reality. At first, solitary adventurers crossed the Atlantic full of the conviction that they were going to come upon El Dorados and other chimeras, striving at the same time to free themselves from an old continent that was too narrow and oppressive for them. They crossed the ocean and put down roots into the terra firma. After this came the multitudes, millions of Europeans embarking for America on the same quests. Whether it was truth that triumphed or fantasy that materialized, finally it makes little difference.

The first to become independent from Europe and plunge into the American Utopia were the Spaniards and the Portuguese. Toward 1570, the number of those who had settled on the Atlantic coast reached 140,000. It is interesting to note that, with the passage of time, not only does the idea of Utopia not fade, it affirms itself more and more in millions of Europeans who continue to see in their native countries the same miseries that More exposed, and in America the same hopes. What may have been begun as a quixotic Iberian adventure becomes a universal contagion in the Old World, and those who are most enthralled are the English, the Dutch, the Flemish: those who had been closest to the world of More, Erasmus, and Vives. It has been estimated that by 1650 250,000 English settlers were already in North America (the number rose to 1,500,000 in the eighteenth century); 200,000 Germans, Swiss, Scandinavians; 200,000 Dutch, Belgians, Frenchmen. This is only the beginning. The massive European immigration takes place in the nineteenth century. Between 1865 and 1914, 65,000,000 Europeans move to America. In the long run, those who stay behind are the Spaniards. Between 1820 and 1930, those who are at the head of the exodus are the Germans, coming to the United States. During that period, 5,000,000 Germans arrive there, as well as 4,300,000 Italians, 4,200,000 Austro-Hungarians, 3,500,000 Englishmen, 3,400,000 Irishmen, 2,000,000 Scandinavians. In Latin America, Brazil alone absorbs 5,000,000 immigrants between 1820 and 1940. The Italians arriving in Argentina between 1860 and 1925 total 5,300,000.[7] Millions and millions believe in *Utopia*.

Real and Imaginary Utopias

Social experiments had already been imagined by dreamers or actually attempted long before More published his *Utopia*. And they continue to this day. It was only natural to conceive of new styles of colonization at a time when humanism was prevalent in Europe and Vespucci was describing a Platonic society in the New World. More is not altogether an inventor. He discovers something that is part of the reality inherent in the news that arrives from the other side of the ocean and is in the minds of those who wish to reform Church and State. America comes as an opportune ferment. Already, in More's own home, a plan for colonizing North America had been discussed and resolved six months before the publication of *Utopia*.[8] If More was present during those preparations, surely great consideration must have been given to the noble qualities of the inhabitants of the New World and to the corrupt ways that prevailed in England. When Thomas More sent over his son-in-law, John Rastell, to carry out a colonization project in the lands discovered by John Cabot in 1497, Rastell had failed because of a mutiny on board. With these antecedents, *Utopia* appears like an opportune expression of what More saw as a reality of superior moral values on the other side of the Atlantic, a theme that later would be expounded by Bartholomew de Las Casas, Francisco de Vitoria, Montaigne. . . . Perhaps all this was discussed around More's fireside, when Vespucci's letters were read.

On exactly the same date as John Rastell's voyage, Bartholomew de Las Casas was engaged upon a similar enterprise: his own plan for colonial reform, tried out in fact from 1516 (the year *Utopia* was published) to 1518. His plan has been called "utopian" by Marcel Bataillon. As Bataillon put it:

> The project of peasant colonization was presented by Las Casas to the Council of the Indies with a new exactness and a wealth of detail which permits us to label it utopian. He calls each social cell a *family,* and it is comprised of a Spanish married couple and six Indian ones. At the head is the *father of the family.* These terms resemble the *rustic family* of some forty members which More, in his famous book, then only recently appeared, presents as a basic element in the society of *Utopia*. Actually this concept tended to make the little families into successful *encomiendas,* en-

trusted to a Spanish farmer, perhaps a modest *hidalgo,* tempted by the grant of lands and Indians in exchange for his service in administering their family community and teaching them the practices of the Catholic faith.[9]

After *Utopia* was published, many Spaniards either produced parallel works or tried to reproduce the experiment in America. All the Utopias, no matter where in particular they are envisioned, look toward America as the land where such dreams may become reality. Bataillon has rediscovered a book by Juan Maldonado of Burgos, where, again, a practical parallel is established between the passions and vices of the Europeans and the good disposition of the Indians. In Maldonado's account, a dreamer who has just made a short trip to the moon (where people live in a Golden Age) descends to a certain region of America that had been visited before by Spaniards. These had taught the inhabitants the Spanish tongue and the Christian doctrine. After some time, because of disputes among the chiefs, they had killed each other; and the soldiers, who were anything but temperate, had died of dysentery. The Indians continued to practice the Christian religion under the direction of a small number who acted as priests. They went to Mass every day before beginning their work, were baptized, confessed their sins, and received Communion. They married after going through a prenuptial examination that each one passed before a person of his own sex. Fraud as well as oaths were unknown. There were beauty contests in which the women did not hide their charms. There was great liberty, and no hypocrisy. The land was fertile. There was neither commerce nor currency.[10]

More's Voyage to the New World

One passage in *Utopia* is notable for registering a debate-like conversation among More, Peter Giles, and Raphael (More's fictional companion to Vespucci). Raphael has insisted on the uselessness of discussing these matters in kings' councils, where all that is ever said is false and deceitful. More tries to dissuade him: "You must not forsake the ship in a tempest . . . nor must you labor to drive into their heads new and strange information, which you know well will be disregarded. . . . But you must with a crafty wile and subtle art endeavor to handle the matter wisely and handsomely." He refers to "the kind of philosophy . . . which knows her own stage . . . playing her part accordingly, uttering nothing out of order or fashion." Raphael replies: "If indeed I should speak of those things that Plato imagined in his Republic, or that the Utopians do in theirs, these things, even though they were, as they are indeed, better, yet they might seem spoken out of place. Forasmuch as here amongst us, every man has his possessions separate to himself, and there all things are common. . . . Master More, to speak truly as my mind moves me, wheresoever possessions are private, where money wields all the influence, it is hard and almost impossible that there the commonwealth be justly governed. . . . Unless you think that justice is there executed where all things come into the hands of evil men; or that prosperity there where all is divided among a few . . . and the rest live miserably wretched and beggarly . . . and for the most part . . . this latter sort are more worthy to enjoy that state of wealth than the others are, because the rich men are covetous, crafty and worthless." More (Socratically) provokes Raphael: "Methinks men shall never live wealthily where all things are held in common." And Raphael: "If you had been with me in Utopia, and had personally seen their fashions and laws, as I did, who lived there five years and more, and would never have come away, but only to make that new land known here, then doubtless you would grant that you never saw people so well ordered but only there." Peter Giles then contradicts: "Surely, it will be hard for you to make me believe that there is better order in that new land than is here in these countries that we know. For good wits are here as well as there, and I think our commonwealths are ancienter than theirs." And Raphael: "As touching ancientness of commonwealths, you might better judge if you had read the histories and chronicles of that land."

Utopia had been circulating in Spain slightly less than twenty years when Vasco de Quiroga was nominated member of the royal *Audiencia* in Mexico and traveled there imbued with More's ideas. The ideal essence of that philosophy crosses the Atlantic with him. If Spain is going to rule Indian peoples, she must do so following their ways and customs. "The laws and ordinances should adapt themselves to the quality and manner of the land and its natives, so that they may be able to know, understand, use and keep them, and be capable of them . . . without the intricacies and obscurity of our own laws. . . . Because not in vain, but with much cause and reason is this called the New World . . . not because it was newly found, but because in its people and in almost everything it is like that of the first and Golden Age, that through our malice and the great covetousness of our nation has for us become the Iron Age or worse."

Vasco de Quiroga follows More not only in what concerns Utopia, but also in his translation of Lucianus's *Saturnials*. The *Saturnials* are a paradisal representation of the Golden Age that Quiroga—somewhat in the manner of Vespucci—finds in America. Quiroga decides to transform the Spanish style of colonization into an American style. He follows, word for word, the description of Utopian institutions and applies them to the settlements that he founds in Michoacán, where he has just been made bishop. For Vasco de Quiroga, *Utopia* should be the New World's Magna Carta. Although he was only able to realize his ideal in a small Mexican territory, his experiment is memorable because of the prodigious contrast that it presents compared with the systems that Spain imposed in almost all the rest of her empire. Paradoxically, for two centuries no one took the time to compare Vasco de Quiroga's experiment with Thomas More's *Utopia*, in spite of the constant references the bishop made to it. Not until 1937 did the Mexican historian Silvio Zavala discover this source.[11]

It's fascinating to see how—through the English humanist's book and the experiences of the Spanish bishop—the image of America presented by the Florentine Amerigo Vespucci in his justly famous letter (an image embellished with Platonic flourishes) comes to be embodied in literature and then in practice. The new ingredient that the presence of America contributed to the literature, philosophy, and politics of the most select men of the European 1500s may be poetically admired in the marvels that Quiroga describes when he reports from America on the new Golden Age resurrected for the enchantment of Castilian letters.[12]

At the other end of America, the Jesuits of Paraguay created another republic, whose sources of inspiration—Plato, More, or the Incas—have yet to be established. The famous Guaraní missions are hybrids of them all, favored by the disposition of the natives themselves, to judge (if we might) through the eyes of Montaigne. In the missions, cities were built, houses distributed, schools and workshops organized; and the people dined, got married, and ruled themselves all in the manner of Plato's *Republic* or *Atlantis*. The rituals are described in an extensive study by one of the expelled Jesuits, José María Peramás, in his book *De Administratione Guaranica Comparate ad Republicam Platonis Comentarius*. That curious work, written in Faenza, would have delighted Montesquieu, who saw in the Jesuit missions the true realization of Plato's dream.[13]

Utopias in Saxon America

The most curious movements toward the continent of hope that resulted from European Utopianism were those in England, Holland, Scandinavia, Poland, and France. The Nordics turned out to be no less credulous than the Spaniards. The result, ultimately, was the birth of modern democracy. The leaven of Utopian thinking was destined to produce republics in America that in time transformed the time-honored political foundations of the Old World.[14]

The desire to make American-style governments, following the model left by Thomas More, was reproduced many times, not merely under the enthusiasm of the humanist renaissance but also during the time of flourishing industrial expansion and great mercantile enterprises. The reasons for protesting against European systems were still there, and remain today. We have recognized that same desire more recently, motivating the exoduses determined by

Nazism, Fascism, Spanish Falangism, and the Russian occupation of countries on her periphery. Since the seventeenth century, the groups of free men crossing the ocean in a gesture of emancipation have been very many, beginning with the founders of the New England colonies.

By 1683, the Dutch Mennonites had established in North America their first communistic colony, and the seed fell on such fertile soil that by 1885 130 more such colonies had sprung up. A German, Johann Conrad Beissel, founded the Ephrata colony in Pennsylvania. It had no written constitution, no rituals of any kind. The celibatarians wore white garments and lived in cloisters, the married members in nearby houses; and they all worked in the fields, mills, tanning factories, and bakeries. Benjamin Franklin wrote a hymnal for their religious ceremonies. Voltaire included the news of their communistic creation in his philosophical dictionary. In 1794, two young men from Oxford, Samuel Taylor Coleridge and Robert Southey, launched the idea of a Utopian colony, pantisocracy, which many groups of immigrants followed across the sea. In 1803, George Rapp unleashed a passionate campaign against the Lutheran Church's rationalism and proposed an exodus to America. Six hundred followers went with him to found the community of equality. In 1843, a tailor, a carpenter, and a chambermaid founded a society in Europe; together with eight hundred followers, they went to America, where they founded a communistic colony in Oneida, near Buffalo. The German Pietists, the English Methodists, the French Prophetists and Fourrierists—all went, each in due time, to the New World. Perhaps what Thomas More had unearthed was a secret illusion lying dormant in every dissatisfied European. He awakened it and blazed the trail. We may still read in Giovanni Papini's memoirs how, in his youth, he had envisioned crossing the Atlantic and founding in the United States his own Platonic society.[15]

4

•

America in the Spirit of Doubt and Adventure

The Mother of Doubts

———————

1507. The old monastery of Saint-Dié, at the foot of the lofty mountain peaks of Lorraine (green, green, green they rise into the sky), is a solitary refuge. Four or five houses to shelter farmers and cows, a church, the abbey, the bell, the wet light of dawn, the night's starry silence . . . What more can twelve canons ask for, if they are dreamers and almost sages, almost mad, almost poets? From the depths of the gigantic amphitheater of fragrant pine, on days that are open and blue with radiance, one sees delicate tufts of ermine clouds traveling overhead. Everything that man has built here is made of stone. Walls protect from the wolf, from the vagabond bear: not from men in armor. Warriors never come to such an out-of-the-way place. This—nothing more, nothing less—is Saint-Dié, the baptismal font where the New World received the name of America.[1]

It happened this way. The abbey's clergymen are a symbol—condensed, in miniature—of what Europe was in those days, engrossed in revising medieval knowledge, in resurrecting Greek philosophy, in opening paths for the humanists. The canons of Saint-Dié were as studious as they were idealistic. One—draftsman and engraver—came from the school of Dürer. He drew fantastical maps and embellished them with borders of portraits, mythological figures, clouds (swollen with winds and blowing announcements with full cheeks). Another was an erudite. He had published his own translation of Julius Caesar's *Commentaries,* hailed from Strasbourg, had spent months in Paris, Heidelberg, Florence. . . . Another was a poet (they all were) who in Italy had listened to Pico della Mirandola. . . . Apart from prayers, the canons took no heed of time. They had long dialogues on the same issues that were being revived in the Germany of Reuchlin and Paracelsus, in the Florence of Lorenzo the Magnificent and Marsilio Ficino. Ideally ambitious, they wanted to create lasting works. They turned the monastery into a publishing house. They printed an illustrated grammar, which was a pedagogical revolution more in keeping with our own time, and they were determined to do something completely out of proportion to the material instruments they had: a new edition of Ptolemy's *Geography.*

Ptolemy is, for the Europe of those days, the great treasure trove of ancient science. The Arabs had preserved his *Geography* like a hidden jewel, and now the Christians had found and rescued it. It is the epitome of what man had learned about the planet throughout the centuries. (A planet, quite still, in the middle of the sky, ever so small.) The canons of Saint-Dié are going to print the new Ptolemy, polishing away a few errors that they have been able to detect in the better-known editions. And so, possessed by the most impetuous Renaissance fervor, they go about putting the project together . . . when they receive a piece of information that contradicts their science and announces the awakening of a new era: it is Amerigo Vespucci's letter. The unknown Florentine tells about a new continent; a "New World" he has seen with his own eyes. Revolution in the monastery.

Ptolemy drops from the canons' hands, and, together with Ptolemy, drops everything by the scholars of ancient times. Instead of continuing to work on the old geography, the canons dedicate their time to the Florentine's revelation: they will make an edition of Amerigo Vespucci's letter and present the new world map with great display.[2] They intend to venture still farther: disregarding Amerigo's request that the continent revealed by him be given the name of New World, they are going to christen it with his own name, coining a new phonetic combination: *America*. The canons are imaginative, enthusiastic, ingenious. When they register the appearance of the new continent, they recognize the collapse of the nearly sacred obstacle that had been standing between man and science. Vespucci's news sweeps away Saint Augustine's affirmations, Aristotle's theories, their own myth of Ptolemy: in other words, all those things that the day before were still taken to be unquestionable truths. The new truth destroys the authority of centuries. America thus becomes the mother of doubt. Perhaps the canons are unable to foresee all this exactly, but it is so: from now on, what is there that a critical spirit will not question?

How has that doubt, that skepticism, which had never gone so deep, been gradually growing? Already, on a certain April day in 1495, something had happened in Spain that was to have incredible repercussions. On that day—who could have whispered the doubt in his ear?—King Ferdinand the Catholic halted the normal course of history to ask himself if the American people—the aborigines of which Columbus spoke, the ones he had seen arriving in Barcelona—might not be useful as slaves. Hadn't all those who had been vanquished in similar circumstances been slaves? The answer he received (or that was given to them from whom he had sought advice) is bewildering: No. This "no" is destined to change the fate of the largest group of nations conquered by one empire since the time of the Romans. The doubt that ensues is enough to stop Columbus from capturing Indians in the Antilles to sell in Seville, as he had arranged so well in advance with those who managed his business affairs in Spain. The Catholic king's first decision materializes and soon becomes the topic of universal argument when Fray Bartholomew de Las Casas makes his Savonarolian entrance—when quietly but deeply, Francisco de Vitoria touches the heart of the problem. They impose on the world a most unexpected thing: America is not a land for slaves. Her settlers will consider themselves free men and a new international law will make rules unprecedented in the Western world. The way would be long, but here was the beginning. Even the Africans would some day become emancipated in America.

In another sense, after the purely geographical discovery, doubt expanded rapidly to pervade an entire cosmographic system as old as the known world. The science upon which Western man's philosophy rested was gravely challenged. At a critical hour, the West was going to free itself from principles that were until then nearly sacred. Each piece of news coming from the New World contradicted some part of what had up to then been taken for granted. The following passage, written by Father José Acosta when he arrived in Panama, is quite typical:

> I confess that I laughed and made game of Aristotle's meteors and his philosophy, seeing that at the time and place where, according to his rules, everything had to burn and be made of fire, I and all my companions were cold. . . . The ancients were so far from thinking that there could be people in this world that many of them refused to believe there was land on this side; and what is still more wondrous, not a few also denied that there could be sky here. Because it is true that the best and the greatest number of philosophers sensed that the sky was completely round, as indeed it is, and that therefore it surrounded the earth on every side, and contained it; still others, and not few nor the least respected among the Holy Doctors, had a different opinion, imagining a world shaped like a house, where the roof that covers it does so only at the top.

Copernicus versus Saint Augustine

In the Greek and medieval world everything led toward purely imaginative adventures, especially in the field of cosmography.

Writing in the air, men turned their prow toward the stars. They lacked the information that later Columbus, Vespucci, Magellan and others would provide; and, having no solid scientific base, even these great investigators had to depend on fantastic speculations to create their working hypotheses. Once the dark Atlantic was crossed, once the new continent and the other ocean had been revealed, once the world had been proven round, science abandoned the stars and came back down to earth. Geomagic became geography. Each step taken westward was an invitation to be part of the adventure of great explorations.

The social sciences, the study of man's customs and relation to the environment, were born in America. Anthropology and sociology were written on the western side of the Atlantic Ocean centuries before the sociologist philosophers Auguste Comte and Herbert Spencer make their mark. As soon as the Latin alphabet is used in America, Fray Ramón Pane embarks (by order of Columbus) on the systematic study of the uses and customs of the Indians in Haiti. The Catalonian friar's treatise is an extraordinary groundbreaker, a work that makes him the precursor of anthropologists, something said as well of Bartholomew de Las Casas, who arrived years later, or of Sahagún, who surpasses all the others. The study of a new man, whose image is going to project itself in such unexpected descriptions as that of the Noble Savage, contradicts an old and false concept of the human being. On one occasion, caustic Florentine tongues began to question the news given by Amerigo Vespucci to his Tuscan correspondents. The verbal shredding of his letters animated many an entertaining soirée. He learned about that and a letter of reply exists, full of wit, sarcasm, and irony directed at his critics—who had proved themselves indeed accomplished, but accomplished in a science that reality had proved altogether false.

For Copernicus, it was essential to have lived at the time of Columbus and Vespucci.[3] In 1492—the year of the landing in Guanahani—he is a nineteen-year-old student at the University of Krakow. His uncle is a bishop, and the boy is persuaded to seek an ecclesiastical career; but he matriculates in the College of Arts and begins to study mathematics and astronomy. Everything follows the patterns of the period. His uncle does not waste the opportunity offered by a canon's vacancy in Warmia, and Copernicus, having learned all there is to learn in Krakow, goes on to Warmia in search of the canonship. The uncle is ambitious. In order to settle his nephew more comfortably in his ecclesiastical career, he sends him on to Bologna. In 1497, when Columbus has completed two voyages to the other hemisphere and Vespucci is on his first, Copernicus matriculates in canon law. In 1500, the Church celebrates a jubilee. Copernicus, the canon, attracted by the religious feast, goes to Rome, and there he discovers something very different from what his uncle had hoped he would; very different, too, from what he himself expected. He comes face to face with Columbus's story. He returns briefly to Poland and comes back to Padua with a license to study medicine. It was thought that he could become "a useful medical advisor to the Most Reverent Superior and the gentlemen of the Cathedral Chapter." From Padua, he goes to Ferrara. In Ferrara, his doctorate in canon law is confirmed. In 1503, he returns home. That same year, Amerigo's letter arrives in Florence to announce the existence of a new continent. Now the expression "New World" does have real meaning. This, the navigator himself proclaims. Copernicus is not exactly the assistant doctor that the gentlemen of the chapter were expecting, nor is he the doctor of canon law, attested to by the Ferrara diploma. He is, rather, a kind of Saint Christopher who comes back to Poland carrying the globe of the world on his shoulder. He directs himself to Lidzbark Castle, where his uncle the bishop lives: it is the remotest spot on earth. At night, he looks at the stars. The only news that commands his attention is that which concerns Vespucci. For years and years, he loses himself in the study of cosmography. Now he can finally construct a solid system to explain the universe and reduce to fantasy every bit that he had been taught in Krakow. A bold ambition, because Copernicus, who in theory brings about the end of astrology (as Hermann Kesten, his biographer, declares with remarkable optimism), appears at the very same time that Nostradamus is becoming an outstanding figure (1503–66).

If Copernicus takes thirty years to verify his system, his delay is not due to mere perfectionism. He has to convince himself.[4] It is not easy for him, a devout Catholic, to oppose his theories to those of such authorities as Saint Augustine, who not only denied the existence of the antipodes, but placed the problems that preoccupied Copernicus outside the margin of what a good Christian should be concerned with:

> When the only thing that man really wishes to know is What should we believe in matters of religion? it is not necessary to test the nature of things as did those whom the Greeks called *physicists;* nor should we be alarmed if Christians do not know the power or the number of the elements, the movement, the order, the eclipses of the heavenly bodies; the species and nature of animals, plants, stones, rivers, springs and mountains; or know of chronology and distances, or be able to recognize the signs of a coming storm, or a thousand other things that those philosophers found, or thought they had found. . . . For the Christian, it suffices to believe that the only cause of all created things, on earth or Heaven, visible or invisible, comes from the infinite goodness of the Creator, the one true God; and that only He exists, He whose existence derives only from Himself.

Such a peremptory affirmation had not kept the father of the Church from entering upon scientific territory and erring. Only the presence of America could render his scientific authority groundless. "Now we know," writes Copernicus in the first pages of his book, "that the earth is inhabited in greater proportion than what is left to the ocean. This is still more evident if we add all the islands that have been placed recently under the flags of the princes of Spain and Portugal, especially that place known as America, a land so named by the captain who discovered it, and which is, by reason of its unexplored size, recognized as the mainland. Nearby are many other islands, so far unknown. For this reason we are no longer surprised at the so-called antipodes or antichthones. By geometric reasoning we know that the American mainland lies in a position diametrically opposed to the Ganges basin in India."

Copernicus, A Child of America

From Copernicus himself, we may conclude that Amerigo or America made the formulation of his system possible. Without the revelation of the New World, Copernicus would have lived a life like his uncle's, the life of a bishop, or of a professor in Krakow; and his name would not have gone beyond the tombstone of a local cemetery. Thus, Copernicus becomes a child of America, one of the many illustrious sons who found their cradles in Plato's Atlantis-made-real. Like Columbus, like Thomas More, like so many others . . .

The Risk in Revolutions

It is impossible to ignore the risk involved in confrontations like that of Copernicus and Saint Augustine—not just in the Middle Ages or the Renaissance, but in every age. It is even worse when control over ideas is assumed by inquisitions that have always existed, that continue to exist, from the time of Aristarchus of Samos in ancient Greece to Alexander Solzhenitsyn under the Soviets. We must not forget that the Spanish and Italian inquisitions were contemporary with the flowering of humanism and of the Renaissance.

The idea that Copernicus presented was not original. Two thousand years before him, Philolaus had questioned the earth's immobility and its central position. Two centuries later, in an open and definite form, Aristarchus of Samos formulated the hypothesis that the earth was a planet like all the others and revolved around the sun. Aristarchus of Samos was the brilliant astronomer who directed the library of Alexandria. How did the learned ones of *his* time take his ideas? They called them a sacrilege. Cleanthes, speaking for the Stoics, accused Aristarchus of impiety. To deprive the earth of the privilege and hierarchy of being the center of the universe, to reduce it to one of the many spheres turning about the sun, was too hard for man—who then, as in the days of Saint Augustine, considered himself the king of Creation, master of the great stage of the world, the sun circling around him. Thus, no one followed the sacrilegious Aristarchus in his extravagance. No one, whether in ancient times or in the Middle Ages, wanted to share in such a humble position, to give up the throne on which the child of the gods sat so proudly, with sun and heavenly bodies moving around him on crystal spheres.[5] Copernicus knew the risk that he was taking; and because of this, not only did he wait thirty years to publish his book—he wanted to be absolutely sure of his calculations—but also, when he finally launched it, he placed it under the protection of Pope Paul III, saying in his dedication: "I realize quite clearly, Holy Father, that there will be persons who, having learned about what I say in my book about the revolutions of the spheres in the universe and that I attribute certain movements to the terrestrial globe, will raise a hue and cry and demand that I be condemned together with my convictions." Copernicus knew that Paul III was a humanist, open to many things: his correspondents in Rome assured him of this, and it was true. But let us not forget that Paul III never opened a consistory or set out on a journey without first studying the constellations. He refused to celebrate a peace and friendship treaty with France because he considered that the dates of his own birth and that of the king of France were incompatible, under cabalistic signs.

So evident was the risk that the editor, Andreas Osiander, less brave, cautious as befitted the circumstances, introduced a change that most certainly Copernicus never knew about. The book only reached his hands on the day of his death—when he had already lost his memory and understanding. Osiander changed the original title *De Revolutionibus*—a splendid one, for Copernicus had revolutionized the foundations of science as a whole—and gave it a more limited one: *De Revolutionibus Orbium Coelestium*. Not content with this, the editor wrote a prologue, where he made it clear that the work was only the hypothesis of a "fictitious mathematical scheme."[6]

The book was published in 1543. The system was admitted by

the Catholic Church only 277 years later, in 1820. But we must not think that blocking Copernicus was an exclusive Catholic privilege. Even before the book appeared in print, when the Polish astronomer's beliefs were already known, Luther said, in 1539: "There has been mention of a new astrologer who endeavors to prove that the earth, and not the firmament, moves and revolves in circles. . . . This crackpot wants to disrupt the whole art of astronomy. Nonetheless, as the Holy Scriptures indicate, Joshua ordered the sun, and not the earth, to stay still." John Calvin asked himself: "Who can dare place the authority of Copernicus above that of the Holy Scriptures?" And the illustrious German humanist Philip Melanchton: "A certain man, eager for novelty, or wishing to make ostentation of his ingeniousness, has come to the conclusion that the earth moves, and proclaims that the sun and the heavenly spheres do not move. To assert such a thing publicly is to be lacking in honesty and decency."

The universities agreed. In 1553, the theory was condemned by the University of Zurich, in 1573 in Rostock, in 1776 by the Sorbonne in Paris, in 1582 in Tübingen. Pope Urban VII considered that the Copernican theory had done greater harm than Calvin's and Luther's teachings. . . .[7]

Galileo Thinks of Succeeding Vespucci

Galileo picks up the Copernican heritage and the results are familiar to all of us.[8] His trial brings to mind the debates Columbus sustained against the scholars of Salamanca. Columbus's first projects were repudiated using texts from the Holy Scriptures and from the fathers of the Church, proving how absurd it would be to sail to the antipodes. Only through his stubbornness and cunning was Columbus able to win support. It was then proven beyond a doubt that the world was spherical and its two hemispheres inhabited. But, even so, why should Galileo try to do as Copernicus had done? This exceeded everything that the Inquisition was prepared to tolerate. So important is Galileo's trial that in Bertrand Russell's opinion its date marks the birth of science in the modern world. Actually, the year in which *De Revolutionibus* was published would be a better choice. But the repercussions of Galileo's trial dramatized the theory and thus fixed the date.

More than a century had elapsed since Columbus's voyages, and more than half a century since the publication of the book by Copernicus, when the Inquisition prepared the trial against Galileo. In possession of the best intelligence service in the world, the Inquisition fell upon the Florentine sage and applied its well-known mental tortures in the most famous brainwashing case of that century. The theologians had to examine the two propositions that the court had submitted: (1) That the sun is the center of the universe and does not move. (2) That the earth is not the center of the world and has two movements: displacement and rotation. After a five-day discussion, the theologians gave their answer: That (1) the first proposition is false and philosophically absurd. Furthermore, it is formally heretical, inasmuch as it expressly contradicts many texts of the Scriptures, in their own sense as well as in the interpretations given by the fathers of the Church and the doctors. And (2) that the second proposition calls for equal censure from a philosophical point of view. From the point of view of theology, it is least erroneous.

When the trial was concluded, not only was silence imposed on Galileo, Forcarini's book was also condemned; and those of Copernicus and Zúñiga were placed on the Index for examination. A general decree was issued forbidding all books in which the sun was held to be immobile. The sun would continue to turn about the motionless earth. . . .[9]

Galileo among the theologians and Jesus among the doctors! In the fifteen centuries elapsing from one scene to the other, the danger of saying things that offended the guardians of the law had increased. Galileo offered to keep quiet. After an interview with the pope, he returned to Florence. Eighteen years later, the Jesuit Grassi formulated a new accusation, and the second trial was held: 1633, the twenty-first of June. The Inquisition asks Galileo: "Do you believe, or have you believed at any time, in the movement of the earth?" The answer: "Before 1616 I considered the two systems, the Ptolemaic and the Copernican, to be scientifically equivalent: after the orders that I received at that time, I have always held Ptolemy's system to be true beyond any doubt." The Inquisition: "Your works show positively the contrary; tell the truth, and we will not have to resort to torture."

Galileo repeated his thoughts in the same terms, and the session was closed. Since the threat of torture had produced no effect, the inquisitors had to comply with Pope Urban VIII's instructions. If Galileo insisted on the faultlessness of his intentions, he could not be considered a *formal heretic,* but would remain only *vehemently suspected of heresy.* On June 22, he was taken to the Dominican convent of Santa Maria della Minerva and heard the sentence in the presence of the cardinals of the Inquisition. The book *Dialogue* was forbidden by public decree; its author, confined to prison upon orders of the congregation. He was to recite for three years, once a week, the penitential psalms. After the sentence was pronounced, Galileo read and signed the abjuration act, where he declared himself justly suspect of heresy, detested his errors, promised to submit to the penances that had been imposed on him and not to support condemned opinions.

But when the Inquisition began to concern itself with Galileo, he saw a way out: America. Apparently, the Spanish ambassador in Florence had become a friend of Galileo. Documents have been found by Raúl Porras Barranechea that bring to light this unknown part of Galileo's life. Galileo wrote to the ambassador asking him to inform the Spanish government about the invention of the telescope, which could be extremely useful on the ships that traveled to America. Sailors would be able to see enemy ships from ten times the normal distance. If Spain named Galileo "pilot major," he could go there and acquaint the seamen with his invention. There was a favorable antecedent for Galileo's request: the first pilot major to be named, inaugurating that position with immense benefits during the reign of the Catholic kings and at the time of the Discovery, had been just as Florentine as he was: Amerigo Vespucci. Did Galileo think he could, from Spain, go to

Lima? But . . . As his bad luck would have it, he did not go, nor had his affairs at the Spanish court moved with the swiftness of the Inquisition.

Enter Descartes

Descartes is in Holland, where he has just returned from a short trip to Italy and France, when he hears of Galileo's sentence. He writes a revealing letter to his old friend Marin Marsenne. He tells Marsenne that, as soon as Descartes learned that the Florentine astronomer's book had been thrown in the fire and that he had been forced to retract, the news "almost led me to burn my papers, or at least not to let anyone see them. I must confess that, if what Galileo has written is false, so are all the bases of my philosophy." Later he writes again: "They tell me that the Jesuits have contributed to Galileo's condemnation, and truly, all of Father Schneider's book shows that they are really no friends of his. But the observations that appear in the book provide so many proofs demonstrating that the sun moves as Galileo says that I refuse to believe that Schneider himself, in the bottom of his heart, does not accept the Copernican theory."[10]

Thus skepticism was imposing itself as the principle of intellectual liberation. One by one, the authorities were crumbling. There were voyages that made the maps change every day. Yesterday's astronomy was already worthless. No one could cling to the principles considered immutable the day before. Everything must be submitted to unceasing revision. An urgent need for freedom led Europeans to proclaim the right to contradict even that which was apparently haloed with beatific sacredness. The free man pitted against the totalitarian power of the Inquisition was the protagonist of a symbolic duel. The duel would repeat itself as long as on one side there were men who wanted to think aloud and on the other authorities determined to smother their voices.

In the midst of all this, René Descartes lays the foundations for modern thought in his *Discourse on Method*, proposing methodic doubt as an essential basis for conduct in persons claiming the right to think. For him, to think, think, think, freely, straightforwardly, with full rights of contradiction, was like touching one's self and knowing that one was alive. To doubt is to think. In his "I think, therefore I am," there is a personal expression as deep as a soul-rending cry in a night dense with the darkness of centuries. *Cogito ergo sum* is the motto of the new man who rises out of the most dramatic experiences and reflections.

If the crisis of authority begins on October 12, 1492, up to what point can we perceive a reminiscence of Columbus's voyage in the *Discourse on Method*? In the first place comes the ardent defense of travel as the first principle for doing away with a bookish schooling: "At the age in which I was permitted to break away from my teachers, I completely abandoned the study of letters. And having decided not to look for any science other than that which I could find within myself or in the open book of the world, I spent the rest of my youth in travel . . . and after some years spent studying the great book that is the world and trying to acquire experience, one day I made the resolution to study within myself and to use all the energies of my spirit to choose the ways that I should follow. That, I believe, produced for me better results than if I had never left my country or my books."

Regarding Descartes's interest in America we have indirect testimonies, such as the letters he exchanged in 1646 with Father Mesland, when the latter was about to embark for the missions in Martinique. The priest felt that to go to Martinique was no different from going to his death. And Descartes: "I have read your 'farewell forever' with great emotion . . . and it would have impressed me even more did I not live in a country where every day I see persons who have come back from the Antipodes. Such frequent examples keep me from losing the hope of seeing you again in Europe." He let his friend know that he understood very well how much zeal and patience were needed for an enterprise like the one he intended to realize in America, working among savages, but this did not mean that the same virtues would not be necessary when he returned, for he would have to exercise them in France as well, converting atheists, who were no less difficult in their nationalistic arrogance than the Americans in their ignorance.[11]

How the Spirit of Adventure Is Born

The temptation to see the other side of the globe and the growing need for individual emancipation gradually form a new spirit of adventure that lures millions of Europeans to try their luck in America. The fact that Spain and Portugal have created empires incites England, Holland, France, and Denmark to follow their example. A change occurs in policies regarding development and expansion and the desire to keep up with the others is expressed openly. Modern science owes an important part of its progress to these migrations of spirited men, creative intellects, who widened the horizons of universal thought. Not without reason do the French derive the two words *avenir,* "future," and *aventure,* "adventure," from the same root. During the sixteenth and seventeenth centuries, Spain and Portugal, but especially Spain, are the heralds of the new spirit; but the coming of the Enlightenment in the eighteenth century precipitates a second discovery of America.

In 1702, the Frenchman Louis Feuillée begins to reexplore the Colombian and Venezuelan coasts; in 1711, those of Argentina, Chile, and Peru. From then on, the catalogue of names grows constantly, and a great variety of countries are represented in explorations. Amédée Frezier, who is French, goes to Lima; Pehr Kalm, Swedish, to North America; La Condamine and his colleagues of the Paris Academy of Sciences, to Ecuador, together with the Spaniards Jorge Juan and Antonio de Ulloa; Peter Loefling, Swedish, to Venezuela; Nikolaus Jacquin, the Dutch director of the Vienna Botanical Garden, to the Caribbean; José Mutis, Spanish, to New Granada; Louis de Bougainville, French, to Montevideo; Piso and Marcgrave, Dutch, to Brazil; José Pavón and Hipólito Ruiz, Spanish, to Peru; Aublet, French, to Guiana; Felix Azara, Spanish, to Río de la Plata; Comte de La Pérouse, French, as far as the Easter Islands. Alessandro Malaspina, Italian, travels over the Pacific coast from Chile to Alaska; Humboldt, German, goes to Cuba, Mexico, the United States, and explores a large part of South America. . . .

As the general idea was rediscovery, a chief consideration was to revive the problem Columbus and Vespucci had raised: the size of the globe. More than three centuries had gone by since Magellan voyaged around the world, and so far neither the size nor the exact shape of the planet was known. Scientists and thinkers from many nations had considered the problem without ever solving it, and in Paris, in 1735, the members of the Academy were divided into two schools of thought: Gian Domenico Cassini, director of the observatory, thought the earth was melon-shaped, growing longer at the poles; Sir Isaac Newton held that the earth was as round as an orange, flattened at the two poles. Voltaire burst in, favoring Newton's opinion, and what had begun as an academic discussion became an impassioned polemic. From the king down, everybody had something to say about it. Two commissions were chosen to go and measure, over the meridians themselves, their respective arcs. One was to go to Lapland, headed by Malpertuis. The other, presided over by La Condamine, would go to the equator. La Condamine had Voltaire's full support. If the facts obtained in Lapland remained a cold document, those of La Condamine—who with his companions spent ten years in the Quito area (which was then christened Ecuador)—provoked debates at the Academy, made their way into the conversations of the Encyclopedists and were found extremely interesting by the general public. La Condamine's report to the Academy had human as well as scientific interest because of the dramatic incidents that befell the expedition. The physician Jean Seniegues was murdered by an enraged mob in Cuenca because of a woman; Joseph Jussieu, professor at the University of Paris, lost his memory during the same riot in which the doctor lost his life, and the commission lost a large part of the scientific material that had been collected; the botanist Mabillon lost his mind, but in the last analysis . . . no one had lost time.

The essential importance of La Condamine's mission lies in the fact that it was the first group of scientists who remained for some time in America. Some stayed as long as fifteen years; in the case of the youngest member of the expedition, Jean Goudin des Odonais, twenty. Together with astronomers and mathematicians were botanists and naturalists, and even sociologists and political experts like Jorge Juán and Antonio de Ulloa, who, although engineers by profession, wrote the *Memorias Secretas* for the use of the Spanish crown, a shocking document on the errors of the colonial administration. La Condamine's return serves to expand America's image so effectively that hundreds of terms are entered in the *Encyclopedia*—mountains, rivers, plants, animals, tribes, cities—opening new perspectives for the work of Diderot and D'Alembert.

A fascinating conversationalist, La Condamine turned many an academic evening into a seminar on America. Through him, European philosophers learned the virtues of Peruvian bark (quinine), of the communication between the Orinoco and Amazon rivers through a branch of the Casiquiare, and of a thousand such curious facts that awakened, in Humboldt, for instance, the wish to explore those regions. La Condamine reintroduces the discovery of rubber, a novelty that had been forgotten since the time Montaigne interviewed the Guaranís. He told about the usefulness of curare as an antidote for snakebite. . . .

During the first discovery, gold had been the distinguishing feature of the New World in the European's imagination. Now it was natural history, much richer and more mysterious, original and revolutionary in medicine, in daily life, in organic chemistry. Hadn't potatoes, tobacco, chocolate, and corn changed European habits? Hadn't the Iberians of the fifteenth century braved the ocean in search of brazilwood? Hadn't pepper and cinnamon been more decisive in the voyages to the Orient and the discovery of America than gold itself? The Swedish botanist Carolus Linnaeus began to sense that the New World was a storehouse (as unknown as it was fabulous) of herbs, barks, roots, and flowers which would transform pharmacology, medicine, food, industry.

Loefling Rediscovers an Herbal from the Time of Philip II

One of La Condamine's companions, Joseph Jussieu, went to Lima to "herborize." Another, Goudin, upon his return to Spain, met a young disciple of Linnaeus, Peter Loefling, and kindled in him the desire to see America for himself. Among the treasures from the time of Philip II in the Escorial library was Francisco Hernández's herbal with drawings of the Mexican flora. Hernández had spent seven years in Mexico, gathering material for *Historia de las Plantas de la Nueva España*. His book had been all but forgotten; but in the great adventure of the rediscovery it became invaluable. Under the sponsorship of the Spanish authorities, Loefling planned a voyage to Havana and the mainland: he would go up the Orinoco and Meta rivers and continue as far as Bogotá, he would go on to Quito, Lima, Buenos Aires. . . . The project was realized only in part. Loefling died in Guiana.

Collecting Loefling's drawings and writings, Linnaeus compiled a book to honor his memory. The work created a little local resonance in Sweden; the news of Loefling's incomplete mission was stirring enough to persuade José Celestino Mutis of Cádiz to continue the exploration. The result was the Botanical Expedition of the New Kingdom of Granada, the most ambitious and successful of all such projects in Spanish America.

Linnaeus and the American Flora

When visiting Linnaeus's house in Uppsala, one is impressed by the number of drawings of American plants with which the walls are literally papered. It is as if the plants of America, turned into images, had crossed the sea and all stopped at the magic circle of the Nordic land. The Swedish scientist had disciples and correspondents in Canada, Mexico, New Granada, Brazil, Lima. He saw in Venezuela the most marvelous country under the sun. If Loefling had lived longer and had been able to carry out his expedi-

‹90›

tion as he had planned it, "going to Río Negro, the Orinoco, the Amazon, crossing the border into Brazil and the lakes that nourish the Plata River, through Paraguay, Quito, Peru—places that no other foreigner had been able to reach, it is easy to imagine all the new and extraordinary things that he would have discovered and that the world of science, after his death, had to miss for years and years." The passionate disorder with which the praises of Loefling are written is the best testimony of Linnaeus's fascination with America.

From the study of plants to a scientific revolution . . . The movement is difficult to visualize in all its vastness. It begins with the discovery and classification of Swedish flora and extends to China and the East Indies, to Japan and South Africa, to Western Africa and the Near East, goes around the world with James Cook, arrives in Canada with Kalm, in Guiana with Rolander, in Patagonia with Solander. . . .

Humboldt, America's First Ambassador

Better known than the images left by Linnaeus are Baron Alexander von Humboldt's descriptions of America. His voyage to the Spanish colonies was a chance event. On his way to Africa with Bonpland, he was detained by fortuitous circumstances and yielded to the temptation of going to America. La Condamine's and Bougainville's recent experiences had impressed him greatly. Today we are used to imagining the German scientist as he appears in two of his best-known portraits, which may be seen in his house near Berlin: in one, he is holding a flower, and is in the middle of a jungle, near the Orinoco River; in the other, he is at the foot of the Chimborazo, beside an Indian hut. He had, in fact, gone there to explore the land, the plants, the minerals, the zoology. But his great, unexpected discovery was of the Americans themselves.

In the eighteenth century, after three centuries of continuous immigration, the Europeans had found, from Alaska to Patagonia, the largest field for expansion and adaptation that they could ever imagine. Unmixed with the natives in the English colonies, mixed with Indians and blacks in the Spanish and Portuguese colonies, the European was the white ingredient in the formation of nations destined to introduce a new social concept in the world. Independence extended from the United States to the south. But when Humboldt arrived in these lands at the turn of the nineteenth century, independence was still less than a dim possibility.

Humboldt, on his way through Caracas, Bogotá, Quito, Lima, Havana, and Mexico, found small literary and scientific centers composed of very active and enlightened men. Together with the white Spaniards, there were Indians, mestizos, Creoles. Illiterate natives initiated their Latin professors into the secrets of plants and their medicinal properties. Then they became the creators of the finest flower drawings in the world. They revived and restored the validity of Mayan, Aztec, and Inca astronomy. They took part in the building and directing of the observatories, studied the stars, predicted eclipses. Humboldt saw in this vast territory of the Spanish colonies a group of nations ripe for the same revolution that had been triumphant in the United States. He had the good fortune to live many years and see the fulfillment of his predictions.

The United States that Humboldt visited was that of Thomas Jefferson. He was present at the preparation of the Lewis and Clark expeditions to explore the Missouri Basin. The youthful impetus of the first republic of the modern world gave Humboldt the measure of what emancipated men might be able to accomplish. But his favorite subject was the other America, the one that was still preparing its independence under the protective shadow of the renewed university, aided by the Indians who had kept quiet for centuries, by the blacks who defeated Napoleon's army in Haiti to the rhythm of voodoo drums.

In Paris, for twenty years, Humboldt devoted himself to organizing and publishing the great report of his American experience. The outstanding men of his time—Goethe, Jussieu, Napoleon—found him full of surprises. Europe began to take an interest in matters like the Panama Canal, which Humboldt and Goethe discussed. Napoleon was rather annoyed at first with this man who competed with him in captivating salon audiences; but in the end he accepted the rights of this other empire—of science, of the geography of plants—within whose territory the Prussian moved as confidently as Napoleon himself did in Austerlitz or Marengo.

Humboldt's voyages to Asia and Africa, his stay in Saint Petersburg with the chemist Valentin Rose and the engineer Menchenin, his visits to the most out-of-the-way places, made him remember and present America as the theme of his time in Saint Petersburg and Berlin and Rome or London or Paris. He met Bolívar in Paris, then only a young man with strong ideas and a predilection for discussions, saw him as a tourist in Italy, and kept up a correspondence with him when he was already the Libertador and president of the emancipated republics. Thus, Humboldt was able to help other scientists to visit the Bolivarian states.

All this produced Humboldt's definitive work, *Kosmos,* where the America of the second discovery finds its place on the map as the focal point in the new Western society.

In the Galápagos, Darwin Discovers the Origin of the Species

In 1830, something happens in England that brings to mind the arrival of the Guaranís in Rouen in the days of Montaigne: Captain Robert Fitzroy, astronomer and seaman, brings along some natives with him from a voyage to Tierra del Fuego. He keeps them under his care for a year, in part studying them and in part teaching them European civilization. He goes back to Tierra del Fuego to return them to their homeland and to continue his studies on Patagonia, passing through the Strait of Magellan and visiting the Pacific coast from Chile to Peru. A young naturalist is with him, the twenty-three-year-old Charles Darwin, recently graduated from Cambridge. The ship is the H.M.S. *Beagle.*

"When Darwin left England in 1831," says Victor von Hagen, "nothing seemed so immutable in his mind as the belief in the immutability of the species." This was the impasse into which Western science had fallen and these were the platitudes that, for the young man, were going to be dispelled in America. An enthusiastic reader of Humboldt, Darwin considered him the greatest traveler of all time. The natives of Tierra del Fuego, who accompanied them on the *Beagle,* first inspired Darwin to reflect on the American race. Some months later, he saw them living in their own country; and this was to inspire his first anthropological observations, the first surprise of his writings. His notes on the culture and civilization of these people show that he considered them to be the purest descendants of the remote immigrants that had crossed the Bering Strait in prehistoric times.

On February 29, 1832, Darwin arrives in Rio. His stay in South America will last four years. When he comes in contact with nature in Brazil, he gives himself over to the passionate study of an environment in dramatic contrast to everything that his eyes had seen in the Old World. Leaving his companions, he loses himself in the wilderness, looking for birds, insects, flowers, trees—all the brilliant flora of the tropics, all the strange fauna unknown elsewhere. At the Socêgo plantation—his new university, his transfigured Cambridge—he lays the foundation for a new science. From Brazil he goes on to Patagonia. When there, he studies bone deposits geologically, his mind plunges deep into the totally unforeseen past. The grand finale is going to be the Galápagos Islands. There, science takes the sudden turn destined to produce the greatest change imaginable. In his diary, Darwin says himself that his journey to Galápagos is the source of those reflections that brought him to the origin of the species.

When Darwin goes back to London and begins to publish his books, he is the first one to be surprised. His life and destiny had turned 180 degrees. And to close the circle of marvels in his career, Humboldt comes to his aid! It is Humboldt who takes the first steps toward ensuring the translation into French of his book, opening thereby the way for Darwin's worldwide apotheosis.

Humboldt and Darwin went to America on the spur of the occasion. They made discoveries and discovered themselves. As they gradually revealed what they had seen, not only was it the revelation of a new land and the preview of a society that would have a leading role in the twentieth century; it was the death knell to many old ideas. Doubt grew, and the most positive political results of this new intellectual freedom may be seen in the ongoing revolution that freed the whole American continent—the most extensive revolution before the Russian and Chinese revolutions in this century.

5

•

The True Story of
the Noble Savage

A Revolution Whispered in the Ear

Something happened—providentially?—between the twelfth and
the sixteenth of April, 1495. These two dates mark the start and
finish of a revolution that began secretly and ended by turning
Western thought upside down. On April 12, the Catholic monarchs, King Ferdinand and Queen Isabella, wrote a letter to the
bishop of Badajoz with instructions regarding the sale of Indians
that Columbus had sent from the Antilles. The transport of Indians was meant to mark the beginning of a slave trade in which the
admiral was placing his highest hopes. Up to that day, the monarchs had only one preoccupation: how to make the best profit.
"With respect to what you wrote us about the Indians that came
in the caravels, it seems to us that they could be sold there, in An-
dalucía, for a better price than anywhere else: You must sell them
as seems best to you."

Four days later, the monarchs give the countermand. Why? What
caused their sudden qualm of conscience? Who whispered the first
doubt in their ear? Who troubled their peace of mind?

Until the twelfth of April, everyone in the West understood that whenever one set out to conquer barbarian lands or defeated a nation that had been purposely declared an enemy so as to subjugate it, the invader could obtain reimbursement for his war expenses and celebrate the glories of his adventure by enslaving his victims. It is what we see in high relief on the Arch of Titus in Rome, where the Imperial Army returns with candelabra from the Jewish temples and a multitude of vanquished peoples reduced to slavery. . . . But on April 16, 1495, an unexpected moral obstacle arises. The monarchs hurriedly annul the original order:

> By another letter we had written you that you should put up for sale the Indians sent by the Admiral Christopher Columbus, arriving in the caravels, and because we wish to consult about the matter with lawyers, theologians and specialists in canon law, to see whether or not they may be sold in good conscience, and this cannot be decided until we see the letters that the Admiral sends us, to learn the reason why he sends them here as captives. . . . In the sale of those Indians, keep the money that was paid for them apart for some time, because . . . till we know whether they may or may not be sold, and that those who would buy them ought not pay a thing; still, those who have already bought the Indians should know nothing of this.[1]

The letter is worded with such delicate cautions that one might think it written by the Indians themselves. . . . What was going to happen? The bishop must have been very perplexed as he waited. For poor Columbus, a business that had been well planned on the basis of traditional practices was falling to pieces behind his back. On June 20, the monarchs resolved their doubts in favor of the Indians. Their Majesties signed a decree ordering that the Indians brought over in the caravels and sold by order of the admiral be freed and returned to their native countries. It was the first important deprivation of authority that Columbus was to suffer in his business ventures. So early had the problem been posed, that it would be another eight years before Bartholomew de Las Casas would depart for the first time, as colonist, to the New World, and sixteen years before the accusations preached by Fray Antonio Montesinos converted him into a defender of Indians.

In those four to eight days of that most surprising month of April, it was concluded that the American could not be subjected to slavery. Aristotle had affirmed that nature designated a portion of humanity for slavery; and Europe, beginning with the Church, had decided that having slaves was implied in the moral law of the institutions. What then could have inspired the boon that placed the inhabitants of the New World outside a tradition that had survived so many centuries? At this moment the oldest Western notion, inherited from Roman law, begins to waver. One may well say that more outstanding than the discovery of America is the discovery that the American is a free man, or that he *should* be one. With this discovery is reborn a long-lost regard for human dignity.

For many people, this second discovery must have come as a greater surprise and awakened worse controversies than the first. The Old World was not prepared to imagine a whole continent of free men. For centuries—or at least since the time of the Romans—slavery had had nothing to do with race. The word itself indicates it: "slave" comes from "Slav." In the tenth and thirteenth centuries, many Slavic peoples were captured and taken to Germany to be sold as slaves. White slaves were frequently donated to churches and monasteries by the rich as a pious offering that was very well accepted. Some centuries later, the Europeans tended to have servants instead of slaves, but all around the Mediterranean the war between Moors and Christians continued to set the standard for the organization of society according to the moral law of armed conflict. The Arabs enslaved their prisoners and the Christians made slaves of Moslems and Saracens. In this international market, blacks were singularly lacking. Venetians and Genoese and tradesmen from the north of Europe, from the Baltic countries, bought Syrian, Serb, Bulgarian, or Armenian slaves from the Turks to resell them in every port. There were closed markets where the merchandise was exhibited: beautiful women to serve as concubines, eunuchs for guard services, men to do farm work and domestic tasks.

The black man comes into the general scheme of slavery as a

consequence of the Portuguese expansion in Africa, which is a recent event. Henry the Navigator is the first to be responsible for this trade, which began fifty years before America was discovered. Columbus probably learned the particulars of this business during his stay in Portugal. In a letter to Pedro Sánchez, he had proposed importing slaves from America for the Castilian navy. Portugal maintained her slave-trading policy for a long time. Nobody had whispered anything in the ears of the Lusitanian kings. Arinos de Mello Franco notes that, before sugar, slaves provided Brazil's most valuable commercial link with Europe. Only around 1570, when more hands were needed for work in the plantations, did Brazil begin to import Africans. At the time of the Spanish discovery of America, Lisbon was a city of exotic colors. The streets teemed with black Africans, Indians from Asia, Chinese, Japanese—and finally Brazilians. All of them—wearing native dress, speaking their own languages, maintaining their customs—were slaves. Men were bought to share in the work of beasts. And women—chambermaids—to alternate with legitimate wives.

Within this traditional framework, it must have been confusing to come upon the Catholic monarchs' preposterous reservations, the impassioned words of Bartholomew de Las Casas, the new Spanish laws that favored the Indians . . . and Pope Paul III's declaration: "With apostolic authority, by the tenor of the present bull, we determine and declare that those Indians (of America) and all those which Christians shall henceforth discover, even though they do not belong to the Faith of Christ, cannot be deprived of their liberty by any means . . . and they shall not be slaves."[2]

Blacks, Slaves; Indians, Free

Never, so far as we know, has a document been written in Europe to defend the black man of Africa that was at all comparable in its vehemence or its results to the defense that Bartholomew de Las Casas made of the American Indian in his *Very Brief Relation of the Destruction of the Indies.* Paradoxically enough, from this *Relation* stems the black legend that tarnishes Spain's history regarding the crimes committed during the Conquest and at the beginning of the colonial period when the Indians were subdued. Before this time, equally inhuman things had occurred within the boundaries of Europe, but no one had raised his voice in such indignant terms as those of the Spanish friar. And Spain had to submit to his accusing evidence, dictating Christian laws destined to protect the Indians, not only from the threat of slavery, already kept in check by the secret revolution of 1495, but also from abuse at the hands of the *encomenderos,* "commanderies." There was, however, an unfortunate distinction at the beginning of Las Casas's tirades—which he was to regret later—when he suggested that black slaves be bought to America. The consequences were fatal, because he gave his blessings to a policy that was to last for two centuries: whenever people thought of America, their minds pictured a continent of free Indians; but the name "Africa" brought to mind a storehouse of slave reserves. If we wish to simplify Las Casas's original thought, we could say that he visualized America as the place for a revival of Christian ideals. One could continue to think of Africa in terms of "the just war," which of course implied the right to hunt blacks and enslave them. America was the new land, open to the gospel; Africa the land of slave trade.

These ideas project themselves dramatically into the centuries that follow. Great Britain emerges as an industrial power—because of the African slave industry. Liverpool's greatness and the development of its navy start with the hunting and selling of Africans. Liverpool controlled half of the world's slave business. Humboldt, in his day, wrote:

It is known with certainty that the English West Indies alone have received during the one hundred and six years prior to 1786 more than 2,130,000 negroes, torn away from the African shores. At the time of the French Revolution, slave trade provided 74,000 a year (of which 38,000 were for the English colonies and 20,000 for the French ones). It would be easy to prove that in the en-

tire Antillean archipelago, where there are only 2,400,000 negroes and mulattos—counting free men and slaves—from 1670
to 1825, 5,000,000 negroes, fresh out of Africa, have entered. In
these shocking calculations on the consumption of the human
species, we have not take into account the number of unfortunate slaves who died in the crossing or were thrown into the sea
as damaged merchandise.[3]

When Humboldt wrote this, the second part of the liberation
process in America was on its way: the abolition of black slavery.
"Legislation in the Spanish American republics," wrote Humboldt, "can never be praised too highly for its prudence. From its
early beginnings it has applied itself seriously to the total extinc-
tion of slavery. In this sense, this dilated part of the world presents
a great advantage with respect to the southern part of the United
States, where the whites, during the war against England, established liberty for their own benefit, and the slave population, which
was already approaching 1,600,000, grows at an even greater rate
than the white population."

The Progress of a Doubt

The doubt that made the Catholic monarchs stop Columbus's
slave project evolved, as we have seen, into an indignant protest in
the West Indies against the *encomenderos*. The Dominican Fray
Antonio Montesinos raised a hue and cry against the Spaniards to
whom Indians had been commended for evangelization but who
exploited them without mercy in the mines. Montesinos was succeeded by Las Casas—who had started out as an *encomendero* himself and became an evangelist instead—thus causing a transformation in the laws of the New World. Finally, with Francisco de
Vitoria, "human rights" acquires a new orientation—in fact it is
born as a new idea—and pontifical Rome returns to forgotten
Christian ideas, delving into evangelic archaeology for treasures that
the passage of centuries had buried. Among the treatises of Las

Casas, one takes on special importance—*Treatise on the Indians Transformed into Slaves*—because it denounces the diabolic mutation through which the *encomendero* made a mockery of the ethical policy born from the Catholic monarchs' secret revolution.

If Salamanca is to be considered one of the mother universities of the West, Vitoria's magisterial lesson, or *re-lesson,* marks the beginning—universally understood—of a new Western political philosophy. Works like Vitoria's were written every year in Bologna, Montpellier, Avignon, but Vitoria's is exceptional in that it sets new norms for international law. What in the Spanish court had been a whisper, in Montesinos a roar, and in Las Casas an explosion, with Vitoria becomes a reasoned process of justice. Its origin lies in the American people. (By a peculiar coincidence, Vitoria was born the same year Columbus first crossed the Atlantic.) If the discovery of America had brought no other consequence, Vitoria's famous "re-lesson" would have been quite enough for us to consider the voyage of Columbus a most fortunate event.

The case of America motivated Vitoria's entire philosophy. In untangling the justifications for "just" wars, he gets to the heart of the matter. As if everything he has said in his lectures at the university were not enough, he tilts at Portuguese kings and Spanish *encomenderos* alike. "The blood freezes in my body," he writes to Father Miguel de Arcos, referring to the Peruvian case.

> I do not question whether the Emperor may or may not conquer the Indies: I presuppose that it is his strictest right. But, according to what I have heard from those who were present at the battle against Tabalipa [Atahualpa], never had Tabalipa or his men offended the Christians in any way, nor had they done anything that would justify a war against them. . . . The defenders of the Peruleros reply that to examine such things is not the soldiers' duty, their only obligation being to follow the captain's orders. *Accipio responsum* for those who did not know that there was no cause for war. But were they not all, or most of them, moved by the desire to steal? And I believe that the conquests that have followed after have been still baser. . . .[4]

A general readjustment of ideas is thus beginning to take place. In the meeting between Las Casas and Sepúlveda the point in dispute is Aristotle's truth. Those who affirm the Indians' bestiality refuse to believe that the Indians have souls; they embrace an economic system based on slavery—a good business all around—arming the fervent impetus of their passions and interests with theological arguments. Their adversaries argue with corresponding evangelical zeal. Who would win? Would the traditional norms left in place by the Renaissance continue to govern customs, or be modified? Victory, if attained, would belong to the American Indian. To the Noble Savage . . .

1550: *The Noble Savage Appears in France*

The discovery of America may itself have slipped out of France's hands, but the conquest and partition of it made by the Spanish pope Alexander VI—all land west of a fixed meridian would belong to Spain; east, to Portugal—compelled Francis I to make his famous protest: "Let me see the clause in Adam's will stating that France is deprived of her rightful portion in the New World." Then, he sent Jacques Cartier to colonize Canada—a matter in which Rabelais took great interest. In addition, the king granted letters of marque and reprisal to vessels bearing the French flag, so that they might maraud and privateer on the new Atlantic. At the time of Francis I's death, quite a few French seamen could be seen around the West Indies and up and down the coasts of Brazil, and one could see Indians from the New World in Bordeaux and The Hague.

Henry II is crowned and makes his triumphal entry to Rouen on October 1, 1547. An extraordinary spectacle is organized for the celebration: lawns bordering the Seine are transformed into Brazilian jungles. Tree bark is painted red, like the fiery embers of brazilwood. As backdrop there are fake palm trees. Hammocks hang from trunk to trunk. Macaws on the branches. Three hundred naked Indians—of which fifty are authentic; the rest, "costumed"

French sailors returned from the other world and acquainted with its ways and habits—all dancing to the accompaniment of maracas and drums, playing soccer with American rubber balls, bartering objects, holding mock battles, smoking as they loll on the hammocks . . . Such a theater of freedom and nature unleashes some unprecedented literature: that of the poets of the Pléiade, a name that still resounds in France, among the best in her literary treasury.

It is a pity that by now no one remembers how the Pléiade obtained her highest glory—that it was based on these Brazilian celebrations. Ronsard wrote a poem, "The Fortunate Isles," describing an idyllic land that entices one to leave a France torn by religious wars and to find peace in America, dreaming away like the Indians who drowse in their hammocks and know not the trail of flames that His Most Christian Majesty of France leaves in his wake as he burns away the Protestants. . . .

With Ronsard, the Fortunate Islands move gradually toward the West: they cease to be the Canary Islands and become interchangeable with paradisal America, Vespucci's world, the world of the Rouen festivities. Everything was conforming to that mobile, fluid geography that was the stage for More's *Utopia* . . . and for Erasmus.[5] Brazil, land of happy men, where harvests come without having to plant seeds or till or toil or suffer from old age and sickness; where the meadows are sweet, not with such common flowers as mallow, asphodel, lupine, and lima beans, but with the white and fragrant blossoms that Mercury gave Ulysses to preserve him from Circe's magic, and with panacea, nepenthe, ambrosia, sweet marjoram, lotus, rose, hyacinth: as many beauties as ever adorned and perfumed Adonis's gardens.

Ronsard's Brazilian poem inspires La Boétie to compose one in Latin. The subject is tempting: France has become an unbearable place to live in. Let's abandon it! Where to? To the newly discovered regions where land is not divided and men live in harmony, sharing the common soil. The continent that rises on the other side of the Atlantic! Its population is not pressed and crowded together, and life there is easy. It is there we should emigrate to!

This wild world of La Boétie's poetry invades Montaigne's spirit and inspires some of the best pages in his *Essays*. The Noble Savage is immortalized in them. Montaigne, in the chapter "The Cannibals," praises the American so highly that he shifts to purest poetic language. Centuries later, Romanticism will take inspiration from those pages. Thus it happens that a Carioca carnival on the banks of the Seine determines a profound current in French literature.

Montaigne, American

Montaigne kept to himself in his Périgordian castle, ruminating on the conversations that he was able to hold along roads and cities with men of all levels and extractions. Surrounded by books, memories, and silence, he wrote. A handful of objects decorated the walls of this room in American style: hammocks, Indian flutes, wooden swords and shields, maracas, different kinds of cassava.[6] In Rouen, he had met three Guaraní Indians. One of them entered his service, accompanied him for ten years, and became more useful than any of the books on America. Apparently, Montaigne never read Bartholomew de Las Casas, but he was well versed in López de Gómara and, most certainly, Vespucci. He was familiar with the life of Hernán Cortés, knew about Atahualpa and Moctezuma. But he was closest to Brazil, the country of his Guaranís. He possessed André Thevet's *Les Singularités de la France Antarctique* and Jean de Lery's *Histoire d'un Voyage Fait en la Terre du Brésil*. He also had Ossorio's history *De Rebus Regis Emmanuelis*. But more than on books, Montaigne (true to Descartes's theory) relied on direct observation, on dialogue with the unlettered. His interest in America begins with his friendship with Étienne de La Boétie, a relationship that has come to be considered excessively close for what is natural among men. Perhaps this was so. Attracted by the same subjects, drawn to each other by a mutual overflowing admiration, for four years they maintained one of those inseparable unions that remain imprinted in universal history. Montaigne was twenty-one years old when he met La Boétie, who was twenty-eight. La Boétie died at the age of thirty-two, and Montaigne honored his memory with utmost devotion. "I loved Monsieur de La Boétie above everything else. He was, in my opinion, the greatest man in our century." Why? How? "If I were to force myself to say why I loved him, I would not know how to express it." Then he reflects, and adds these words that no one in Périgord or in France has ever forgotten: "I can only express it by saying: because he was he and I was I. . . ."

The first to discover the Noble Savage, if not Vespucci, if not Montaigne, would be La Boétie. In his *Discours de la Servitude Volontaire,* he puts it in these words, that remained fixed in Montaigne's mind: "If by chance different people are born today, who are not accustomed to servitude nor fear liberty, and they are bidden to choose between being slaves or living in freedom . . . there is no doubt that they will be more inclined to obey reason than to serve other men." It was what he had concluded after seeing the free Guaranís in the Brazilian carnival in Rouen.

Two streets in Paris end at the Champs-Élysées, a short distance from each other: *avenue Montaigne* and *rue La Boétie*. Ideally, each one evokes the first images of the Good Savage, who is—in the world of letters—now four centuries old and still a viable notion. Montaigne goes out to find the savages his friend had praised and discovers in them a series of virtues in sharp contrast to the European vices of his day. In his opinion, if Plato himself had known them, he would have found that they had even higher qualities than the ideal humanity he had invented.

For it seems to me that what we are seeing in the New World surpasses, not only all the images with which poetry beautified the Golden Age, and all the inventions destined to present a happy condition of Man, but also the concepts and hopes of philosophy. We cannot imagine a purer candor than theirs. . . . It is a nation, I would say to Plato, where there is no commerce of any kind nor knowledge of letters nor science of numbers nor magistrates nor political hierarchy nor servants nor rich nor poor nor contracts nor estate liquidations nor partition of lands nor any occupation that interferes with idleness nor any respect due other than family ties; no clothing nor agriculture nor metals nor wine. The very words that mean treachery, dissimulation, avarice, accusation, pardon are unknown. How far from such perfection is Plato's imagined republic!

In his Noble Savage, Montaigne found a sense of human dignity that in Europe was unknown. He remembered the interview that King Charles had had with the Indians during the famous encounter in Rouen. The monarch thought he had impressed the Indians, dazzling them with the splendor of his court, with the grandeurs of the city. And he asked their opinion. They made three comments, of which Montaigne was only able to remember two when he wrote his *Essays*. In the first place, they found it strange that so many older men, bearded and well armed, like the ones who make up His Majesty's entourage, rendered obedience to the monarch, who was a child, and that they should not choose instead the eldest among them to command them. Secondly, that among the people there should be a privileged half that enjoyed every luxury and comfort, while the other half were beggars who implored at the doors, wasting away from hunger and poverty. It seemed strange to them that this half that suffered such great injustice should not fly at the rich ones' throats and set fire to their houses.

In the chronicles of Francisco López de Gómara, Montaigne found many pages of recent American history that confirmed his conversations with the Guaranís. In the essay "The Carriages," Montaigne reproduces in his own way the declaration *(requerimiento)* imposed by the kings of Castile, who ordered that the conquistadors read it aloud to the Indians before exercising any authority over them. The conquistadors were to say that they had come in the name of a prince greater than any other in the known world; that the pope, God's representative on earth, had given him powers over the Indies; that they would be treated kindly, asked only for food for nourishment and gold for the state treasury; and that, in passing, the conquistadors would teach them about the existence of the one God and the truth of their religion, which they advised them to accept—under threats.

The Indians' answer is transcribed by Montaigne as follows: That if the Spaniards had come with peaceful intentions, they were not showing it by their attitude; as to their king, judging from what he asked of them, it was clear that he was destitute and needy. It was fine for the Spaniards if they wished to believe in a single god, splendid for them. . . . "As for us, we do not wish to change our religion. As for the threats, we consider it lack of good judgment to address them to persons whom you do not know. The most advisable thing for you would be to leave this country as soon as you can, for we are not used to thinking well of a show of force with weapons and by foreigners, and we would have to do with you what we have already done to others." And they showed them the heads that were hung as ornaments in their camp.

It is curious that Montaigne did not take examples of American greatness from Las Casas but from an official chronicler for the crown: Gómara. In the conduct of Aztec princes, of the Inca kings and the caciques of Bogotá, and in the treachery of which they were the victims, he founded the theory of the Noble Savage. He observed in the Guaranís' songs a sweet, pleasant language that reminded him of Greece. Among the Guaraní poems that he reproduces in his *Essays* are these, of which he says: "There is no barbarity here; and, if anything, they resemble Anacreon":

Come everyone to the feast
to devour a valiant man
for the laws of war are these.

I also have feasted on your people:
in my entrails you will find the taste
of your forefathers and their mighty deeds.

Stop, little viper, stop,
I want to copy your beauty

in a belt that I will paint
for the woman that I love.
Think what a gift—like no other!—
From one serpent to another.

Calvin's Brazilian World

The idea of a continent—of an island!—where one might live freely, surrounded by nature, brings together two words: "America" and "Liberty." If there is a part of the world—and it would not be unjust and fanatical Europe, or mysterious and despotic Asia, or Africa of the slaves—if there be a portion of the world where man can be free, that portion would have to be America. That is the conclusion, a hasty one, perhaps, to which the sixteenth-century European arrives. In his eagerness to emancipate himself and to bring that new ideal of the Noble Savage into his life, the man who departs for America thinks, like Ronsard,[7] like La Boétie, in terms of radiant optimism. Among those who first turn their eyes to the New World are the dissidents from an inflexible Catholic Church, dissidents who proclaim a Christendom with no ties to Rome. Those who seek the expression of their faith outside the old dogmatic congregation. Fanatics of liberty. There is a moment when such hopes are confused with those of the Calvinists. The Noble Savage could be—in fact, was to be—a European seeking in the New World the freedom that the Old World treated with scorn.

The great Calvinist adventure in America is born in the mind of Admiral Gaspard de Coligny. His idea is to found an Antarctic France in Guanabara—Rio de Janeiro Bay. Coligny entrusts this mission in 1555 to Vice Admiral Durand de Villegagnon. Though Catholics and Protestants both are to be counted among the first of these settlers—not to mention criminals who obtain their release from jail in exchange for participation in the project—Villegagnon gets started by contacting Calvin and enticing him into organizing Calvinism in the New World.

The correspondence between Villegagnon and Calvin makes a curious chapter in the history of Calvinism. Villegagnon arrives in Brazil and does not find the promised land he expects. In a long letter, written in Latin with brazilwood ink, all he describes are the difficulties continually blocking efforts to achieve good rapport between Frenchmen and savages. He had hoped, he says, to find rich, fertile lands; but all he sees around him are wastelands, desert, not a single roof or dwelling; and the natives, ferocious and wild, devoid of any religion, make him think that he has come to a place where some of the beasts happen to look like humans. There is no agriculture, and to find grain one has to wander from one place to another. But "as I had assured my friends that I was leaving France for the purpose of extending Christ's Kingdom, that for its sake I had abandoned the care and diligence hitherto dedicated to the things of this world, I persisted." Indeed he does, against tremendous odds; for, if the American natives seemed wild to him, his fellow Frenchmen are would-be murderers. He tells Calvin how some of his own companions conspired to assassinate him. The timely word of an informer saved his life. Villegagnon seized the conspirators, put them in chains, and brought them immediately to trial. The first one, as soon as his chains were removed so that he could speak freely, made a break and, hurling himself from a high rock, committed suicide. Villegagnon sentenced the chief instigator to death: everyone could see him hanging from a tree as warning. Prayers from then on were said with trembling lips, inspired by fear. Justice was forevermore symbolized by the gallows tree. And thus, he explains, "we were able to live quite restfully for what remained of that year."

But not everything was as grim as the vice admiral's letter. With Villegagnon there was a Franciscan, André Thevet, a tireless traveler of whom it has been said that, had newspapers existed then, he would have been immortalized as the father of the feature story. He wrote books that became famous: *Géographie du Levant, La Cosmographie Universelle,* and, especially, *Les Singularités de la France Antarctique,* which was a source of valuable information for Montaigne. Contemporary poets and writers praised Thevet's work highly: Ronsard, Du Belley, Baïf, Joselle, the poet laureate Dorat. Thevet "was acclaimed as if he had greater merits than Ulysses, and eulogies were written in his praise in French, Latin, Greek, and even Hebrew, assuring him immortal glory. . . . He introduced tobacco and redeemed the Indians. He is the father of the Noble Savage. In the *Singularités* Ronsard found his dreamed-of Golden Age."

Jean de Lery was the bearer of Calvin's answer to Villegagnon. To consolidate the founding of the colony it called Coligny, France had sent three hundred settlers (Villegagnon had asked for three thousand) and de Lery was one of them. A Frenchman and a Calvinist, he came with fourteen Genevans, Calvinists like himself. He was staunchly religious, and a famous book emerged from his experiences in Brazil: *Histoire d'un Voyage Fait en la Terre du Brésil.* It was written after his return to France, where he miraculously escaped the Saint Bartholomew's Day massacre. De Lery confirms Vespucci's paradisal news stories. His description of the way the Indians live naked is quite famous. In answering the perennial questions about how it might have been possible to have social contacts with these naked savages, whose wives most assuredly must have excited lust, he replies that such nakedness was much less dangerous than the cosmetics, garments, jewels, and infinite bagatelles with which European women led men into temptation. For this zealous Calvinist, to leave France for Rio de Janeiro was like moving from Hell to Paradise. The savages lived in peace, a state edifying in contrast to the constant religious wars of the French. Paul Gaffard, in his prologue to de Lery's book, observes: "It would be impossible to relate the cruelties committed in France by both parties. Where the Huguenot is master, he destroys tombs and sepulchers, even those of kings; he steals sacred property and sacks churches. The Catholic, in turn, kills, murders, drowns anyone that he knows to be professing the new faith."

Europe's Noble Savages

The Europeans, with the Spaniards in the lead, go to the New World to practice their own theory of the Noble Savage, taking with them the spark of independence. They become Americans. Cortés, Balboa, Jiménez de Quesada, the colonists of Paraguay de Asunción—all rise up and refuse to accept the king's authority to become masters of their own conquests. Democratically supported by their communities—their fellow insurrectionists—they begin to enjoy a liberty that does not recognize the bounds of law. They establish their own hierarchies. All this reaches a nearly sacrilegious extreme in the tyrant Aguirre, who in the Amazonian solitudes revolts directly against the king of Spain, signing the letter he sends him, "Francisco Aguirre, traitor to the King."

This type of revolutionary, who finds in America the ideal territory for his emancipation, begins as a white man from Europe. By contagion, or by natural disposition, the Indian looks for support from him to free himself from paying tribute to the king. Eventually, a new man is born and enters fully into the new Western philosophy: a white Indian, a European immigrant who settles down in America, adjusts to his natural surroundings, makes them his, and feels quite capable both of attacking what in the land of his origin he would have considered sacred and of enjoying, as the natives do, his second homeland. European by birth, he is a Noble Savage in the same right as the Indian Benito Juárez, who at the age of twelve did not know a word of Spanish, who had not a drop of blood in his veins that was not American, and who gave the world the most nobly conceived philosophical formula, peerless in the literature of centuries: "Respect for the rights of others is peace." Noble Savage also is Simon Bolívar, who, with not a drop of American blood in his veins, is still as much a part of his country as Cuauhtémoc is a part of Mexico, and proves marvelously enlightened when he exclaims: "America's liberty is the hope of the universe."

When Benjamin Franklin informed the London Parliament that the English colonies were refusing to pay new taxes, thereby throwing the card of independence on the table, William Pitt saw the countenance of a prophet in this white savage from Philadelphia: "I rejoice that America has resisted," he said in Parliament, adding that three million men so insensitive to every notion of liberty as to submit to being slaves would have been the "adequate instrument to reduce us all to slavery." Diderot believed that emancipation would mean the recuperation of the virtues inherent in the Noble Savage and that emancipation would redeem mankind from the prevailing corruption of his time.

Enlightenment and early Romantic engravings show the Noble Savage trampling royal crowns. Similar pictures could have had as protagonists American-born heroes or the Indians who fought for independence . . . or the blacks. As Diderot tells us in one of his novels:

> I was passing a square in a New World city, when I looked to my right and saw, on a magnificent pedestal, the statue of a black man, his head uncovered, raising his arm, with fierce pride in his eyes and a noble and imposing attitude. All around him one could see the vestiges of twenty scepters. At his feet, the following inscription: "To the avenger of the New World." I was unable to restrain a cry of surprise and gladness. Yes, I said to myself, with as much warmth of feeling as surprise: at least Nature has created an admirable man, this immortal man who should free the world from the most atrocious of tyrannies, the oldest and most ignominious. . . .

The Noble Savage is essentially the American, whether native or originally from one of the four corners of the earth, a man of any color whatsoever, representing the liberated man to the Europeans. From the time of Montaigne, to the time of Diderot and, of course, beyond . . .

6
•

The Invention
of Independence

Is the Encyclopedia *Reactionary?*

If Diderot's and D'Alembert's *Encyclopedia* is the antechamber of the French Revolution and the crowning glory of the Age of Enlightenment, the treatment it gives the word "independence" comes as a surprise. It does not take into account the political implications of the word; and as for its moral meaning, the idea is rejected as arrogant boldness on the part of man, who, wishing to declare himself independent, refuses to acknowledge government authority, obedience to the law, or the respect due to religion. Assuming that such statements do not cloak a dissimulation . . . whatever happened to the spirit of the revolution?

On this point, the *Encyclopedia* is not different from any other contemporaneous European dictionary. Politically, the concept of independence is inoperative until the day of America's emancipation. Then, and only then, does it become the revolutionary—the triumphantly revolutionary—term that we know. The spark is struck in the New World, the result of natural causes. Europe, who had conquered, and was absolute mistress of her colonies, is startled to discover the subversiveness of those who would shake off their foreign yoke. The existing lexicographic monuments were unprepared for a gesture of this kind. Just 50 years had elapsed after the first edition of the *Encyclopedia,* and the world had already changed; but 150 years after it, when the idea of independence will have expanded from America to Asia and Africa, the greatest transformation of all time will be well under way.

Every time an English, French, Spanish, Italian, or Portuguese dictionary defines the word "independence" as part of the accepted political language in a Western tongue, reference is made to America. A Spanish dictionary would have had to be prophetic and ill-boding to speak of political independence before the emancipation of the colonies. In Sebastián de Covarrubias's *Tesoro de la Lengua Castellana* (1611–74), the word is ignored. . . . When the French Academy dictionary records it for the first time, an explanation follows: "United States War of Independence." In the Italian dictionary of Tommaseo (1869), it becomes "American War of Independence." In the English tongue, "independence" means the American case; and *The Century Dictionary,* after defining it as the liberation of a state by removing the control that another state exercises over it so that it may become self-governing, gives by way of explanation a précis of the United States Declaration of Independence.

All this, in substance, is obvious. Europe was the empire, America the colony. While such a state of affairs lasted, to talk in Europe of independence was absurd, to anticipate collapse. But Diderot's *Encyclopedia* provides interesting insights. Independence of a moral sort was condemned. It went against the prevailing order of things, which Diderot's own friends dared not contradict in their ideology. Today, a page like this would seem reactionary: "*Independence.* The philosopher's stone of human pride; the chimera that self-esteem blindly pursues. The goal which men invariably set for themselves and never attain." For the Encyclopedists, the human being is simply a ring on a chain whose final link is in the Creator's hands. Everything in the universe is subject to something else:

the heavenly bodies depend on each other for their movements; the earth is attracted by other planets, and likewise attracts them; the ebb and flow of the sea comes from the moon; the fields' fertility comes from the sun's radiance, the earth's humidity and the abundance of salts. . . . All nature must participate to produce the growth of a single blade of grass. . . . This chain formation in the physical order is reproduced in the moral and political order: the soul depends on the body and the body on the soul and on every exterior object. How can man, who is composed of these two parts, they themselves subordinated, consider himself independent? Likewise, the society into which we are born has given us laws that we must obey and imposed duties that we must fulfill. Whatsoever our position or rank, our destiny is to be dependent. There is only one kind of independence to which man may aspire: that which is given by philosophy. But philosophy does not liberate him from all the links: it preserves those that reason has given him. It does not make him independent at all, for he does not cease to be dependent on his obligations. For this reason, philosophical independence is not dangerous. It can never infringe on the government's authority, on the obedience that laws demand, or on the respect due to religion.

With the triumph of the American Revolution, such cautious discourses were destined to become groundless. The French philosopher Marquis de Condorcet describes how the insurrection on the other side of the Atlantic produced a revolution in European thinking:

For the first time, a great nation was seen to break away from every chain that bound it and serenely to give itself the constitution and the laws that it deemed suitable for the attainment of its happiness. This great cause was defended before the court of public opinion, in the presence of all Europe; the rights of man were fervently upheld and exposed without reserve or restriction in writings that circulated with total freedom from the banks of the Neva to those of the Guadalquivir. All this penetrated deep into the most oppressed regions, reached the most backward nations, and the men who lived there were astounded to hear that they had rights, learned to know them and learned about other men who had dared to reconquer and keep them. The American revolution would soon expand to encompass all of Europe.

America, Continent of European Emancipation

There is no reason to imagine that this feeling of independence was something that suddenly sprang up in Philadelphia. The experience of three centuries was needed to define it. America had emerged as the continent of European liberation from the moment that the first immigrant occupied it. The Spaniards, Portuguese, Englishmen, or Frenchmen that, in one way of another, discovered a land where they could feel free had gone in search of their own emancipation. John Adams observed this during the days of the revolution in Philadelphia. He was amazed to see how his countrymen immediately responded, enlisting without a moment's hesitation in the republican armies; and he asked himself: How can this miracle happen? To which he found his own answer: Because the revolution is in the hearts and minds of the people. The very founding of the colony had been a declaration of independence. Those who one day decided to shake off the yoke of the Church of England had transferred themselves to Holland and from there emigrated to the New World. They had thought initially of Guiana and other places before deciding on the territory that had been adjudged to London's Colony of Virginia. When they embarked on the *Mayflower,* they were already morally independent and ready for adventure. Rebelling against the official Church, although they invoked the king's name, they fled to elude his determination to subjugate the Puritans. They were bound for a colony that they themselves would have to organize, giving themselves their own laws, ordinances, acts, constitutions, and establishing their own government positions, for which they celebrated a pact: their social pact. The first wave of immigrants brought together by similar convictions could only grow: 14,000 arrived in Massachusetts; 18,600 in Barbados; 18,000 in other Caribbean islands; 4,000 in New England. They freely elected their deputies so that the community council would decree their taxes. By 1680, the New England settlers were already governing themselves; and if they formally looked to the king as their sovereign, they nevertheless had their own laws, traded according to their own norms, raised forces to defend themselves from the Indians. "Their link with England was more sentimental than imposed, and they developed in complete liberty."

The insubordination of the colonies came about when England attempted to recover her lost sovereignty, the sovereignty she had in fact earlier abandoned. Her inevitable error brought to light the depth of the estrangement that had accompanied the initial departure of subjects. The same circumstance may be found throughout America, from the time of the Spanish settlers. These, by one of those coincidences that seem providential, embarked on the great adventure of conquest at the same time that the uprising of the Castilian Comuneros was taking place under Charles V. Although the king was able to defeat Juan de Padilla's followers, the Comunero seed flew to America and maintained its vigor till independence was proclaimed in 1810.[1]

From the moment Columbus opened up the Atlantic for European navigation, millions—not just the passengers of the *May-flower*—have been pilgrims compelled to leave the Old World in search of a land of emancipation, their Utopia. Spanish younger sons, reduced to an underprivileged situation because of laws that favored the firstborn, Jews who concealed their identity to escape the Inquisition, English Puritans persecuted by James, Huguenots from France . . . and in our own time, Spanish republicans, Jews escaped from Germany, Russia, Poland, Austria, Czechoslovakia— all are human beings who on a certain day decided to proclaim their independence and to find it, or at least to look for it, in America. Europe has been—from the time of Alexander, and more so under the Romans—imperial by vocation. Even the smallest countries (in modern times: Holland, Belgium, Denmark) have followed in the steps of the larger ones. Castile, England, Portugal grew disproportionately, reducing to colonies whatever their weapons could subdue. This has been the Old World's "manifest destiny." At the same time, in the spirit of contradiction, the seed of emancipation was germinating in the New World. First the rebellious conquistadors affirmed their independence: Cortés, Balboa, Jiménez de Quesada, Lope de Aguirre; then, blacks, Indians, men of mixed blood, Creoles—all fought in turn to become independent in the Spanish colonies. The blacks of Cartagena became strong in Palenque in 1602, proclaimed a free republic and kept it so for a hundred years. They became invulnerable to such a degree that the king of Spain, at a certain moment, recognized their claims.[2] Haiti was ahead of the Spanish and Portuguese Americas, with the blacks there proclaiming their independence from France. The Indians of Tupac Amarú in their insurrection against Spain were forty years ahead of the whites. In this way, John Adams's reflection may be extended to encompass a range much wider than that of the English colonies, of which he was principally thinking. What he recognizes coincides with Amerindian and African ideas and imposes itself as a movement that, in America, brings together all the races.

In the field of pure ideology and its sources, the writers of the *Encyclopedia* willfully ignored all the writing that came from Bartholomew de Las Casas or the *Mayflower* pilgrims or Thomas More, and they failed to recognize many incidents that took place during the Spanish Conquest and the creation of the North American colonies, incidents in which they could have easily perceived the first signs of the uprising that so surprised Condorcet. Why was it so easy to forget the antecedents? In the sixteenth century, Europe is a disintegrated continent; and empire but a memory of ancient history. It is the discovery of America that produces the development of Europe's imperial policy in modern times. Where immigrants sought liberty, those who stayed home and ruled sought an empire. Politically, the discovery awakens sleeping ambitions. These impose themselves so effectively that, when the hour of the *Encyclopedia* comes, the emancipating spirit of rebellion does not count, is unforeseen. The most significant event that will be registered some years later is this: When the most powerful man in Europe—Napoleon—crowns himself emperor, his counterpart—Bolívar—who embodies America, is proclaimed Libertador, "liberator." Between those two extremes, the independence of all America, destined to cause the greatest damage to empires, sparks off a revolution between two worlds. Its origin and the extent of its projections make it more universal and decisive than the French Revolution. A liberated continent is worth far more than any declaration of principles or new constitution, even if these are as radical as those of eighteenth-century France.

Discovery of Political America

Europe begins her political discovery of America in 1766. Something of America's possibilities had already been sensed by scholars interested in the scientific exploration of that continent. But in 1766, with the revolution of the English colonies, it was demonstrated that from there, from the neighborhood of the antipodes, a new political philosophy could emerge. To what extent the presence of America was a formative influence on the precursors of the French Revolution was, at the time, a subject French authors treated quite clearly.

One of the first to make out the way was, obviously, Voltaire. In the *Encyclopedia* itself, it is easy to pick out his signals of discovery. The article referring to the Quakers, although it is signed Le Chevalier de Jancourt, may be considered his. It is written in 1765. Once more a golden age was arising in a promised land. The article begins with a nutshell biography of William Penn. William, who was the son of Vice Admiral Penn, became a Quaker as soon as he completed his studies at Oxford. "When he went to visit his father," Voltaire tells us, "he did not take off his hat, and invited him to thou him and become a Quaker." "Has he gone mad?" thought the vice admiral. He threw him out. Undaunted, the young rebel devoted himself to preaching the new faith, first in England, then in Holland. Upon his father's death, the crown informed him that some accounts had remained on the books, payable to the admiral's heirs; that a province in America could be given to the son in payment. . . . William sailed off to take possession of the land, named it Pennsylvania, and founded a Quaker state. In a short time, the spectacle offered by the colony was unique. The Indians—the so-called savages—had as their king a man who addressed them as "thee" and received them wearing his hat. No priests. The people had no weapons. All citizens were alike. Anyone could be a magistrate, and there were no rivalries between neighbors. William Penn could be proud of himself for bringing a golden age to earth. The age that was always on everybody's tongue but in fact existed only in democratic Pennsylvania. "Only Lycurgus had succeeded in doing something like this, once, in the olden days."

The European gazettes—*Journal d'Agriculture, Gazette de France, Gazette de Leyde, Mercure de France*—began to publish a series of articles on American life. In The Hague, a booklet dedicated to Pennsylvania describes "the haven where man can live in peace and plenty, a refuge for the poor and the oppressed of Europe, an ideal place for ingenious men of low position. . . . Pennsylvania offers something more than an open door for escape: It assures liberty, representative government with secret vote, taxes that may only be decreed by previous consent of the people, the right to formulate one's own laws and, above all, religious freedom."[3]

The day the English colonies definitively obtain their emancipation, everything in France is prepared to divulge the fundamental principles of that first rebellion, which, thirteen years later, would serve as the basis for a French revolution. Diderot speaks of the United States as a haven for those who are victims of fanaticism and tyranny in Europe. Richard Price declares that the Americans are the hope of the human race. Many Frenchmen go to America to take part in the war, fighting in the great battles for independence. The first of these is the Marquis de Lafayette.[4] Roland de la Platière, husband of Mme. Roland, predicts that English, because of the United States, will become the universal language. A few years later, a young French aristocrat decides to set out at once to discover America: his name is Alexis de Tocqueville. He is aware that France learned everything it knows about liberty after the American War of Independence—from it. Intrigued, he wants to see for himself how the idea of democracy came to renovate itself in the modern world. He finds that the United States has solved the problems that make so difficult the change in Europe—from monarchy and government by the aristocracy—to a republican system. "I believe beyond all doubt," he declares in the prologue to his famous book, "that sooner or later we will arrive, like the Americans, at an almost complete equality."

Franklin, Jefferson, Paine

If the image of America is the decisive stimulus that provokes revolution in France, then Benjamin Franklin, Thomas Jefferson, and Thomas Paine must be inscribed among the makers of that great European event. The French Revolution will close the turbulent Age of Enlightenment with a clasp of fire. The inclusion in the American Constitution of a Bill of Rights (human rights!) was the decisive example that enabled France to continue her reforms.

The scene that prepared the French Revolution is partly dominated by a foreigner. Half scientific genius, half extravagant provincial in heavy country boots, he comes from the already well-known state of Pennsylvania, from Philadelphia, where Voltaire says that he would like to spend his last days. Everything in Benjamin Franklin's biography tends to make this man (who looks like an eccentric professor or a good-natured bourgeois liberal) the idol that France will exalt for years to come. A Leonardo of universality, he learned Spanish, Italian, and Latin without teachers, in the land of the Quakers. He experimented with electricity, discovered the principle of lightning rods, invented a stove, created a better system for chimneys. He was a newspaperman and the author of excellent books. He gave Philadelphia her first itinerant library, the first fire and police departments. As postmaster, he put into words the motto (reproduced in countless United States post offices) for the postman's heroic mission, which requires him to deliver the mail by day or by night, through storm or fair weather, through cities or through deserts . . . that "correspondence" may exist among men. Famous for his playful wit, Franklin was capable of taking venomous messages to the British: he proposed that snakes from America be sent over and let loose in London parks in repayment for British injustices.

In Paris, Franklin embodied America's democratic greatness. He was the man of humble extraction, capable of speaking like a sage at the Academy of Sciences, or occupying the tribune in Masonic temples, alternating with Voltaire or Helvétius, his admirers. Georges Buffon in the end rectified his theory about American degeneration, reducing this unhappy privilege to South America. The naturalist considered that Franklin's presence alone was enough to redeem the United States. Franklin's likeness became the most popular thing in France. It was seen on etchings and handkerchiefs; on medals and lockets; in marble, plaster, bronze, wood; on snuffbox covers and watches; on cups, dishes, trays; on silver and ivory cane handles, glass paperweights; on knife handles, pocketknife sheaths, and the cockades of hats. Mme. de Pompadour, at the center of her collection of medallions, displayed one that bore the American's profile. Gazettes extolled Franklin in poems. Songs about him were heard on street and square, in theaters and cafés.

When Franklin is received at the Masonic lodge, it is Voltaire who presents him and everyone who is anyone in Paris is there. The same occurs when D'Alembert presents him at the Academy of Sciences. So often was the name "Franklin" repeated that soon the royalists had had enough. The Marquise de Polignac talked so much about him to Louis XVI that the king finally sent her a chamber pot bearing Franklin's image on the bottom and the famous sentence: "He snatched the thunderbolt from heaven and the scepter from the tyrants."

Franklin's works—published in French translation fourteen years before the Bastille was taken—were widely read during the years preceding the French Revolution. The edition is adorned with a steel engraving bearing the unmistakable countenance of the most popular American and a poem that ends: "L'Amérique le place à

la tête des sages—La Grèce l'aurait mis au nombre de ses dieux"—
"America places him at the head of its wise, Greece would have
numbered him among its gods."

When the news of his death arrived, Mirabeau announced at the
National Assembly: "Gentlemen, Franklin is dead. America's liberating genius, who flooded Europe with light, has returned to the
Divinity's bosom. . . ." At the Café Procope, across the way from
La Comédie, a meeting place for the Encyclopedists (Diderot,
D'Alembert), political men (Danton, Marat), and writers, artists,
and theater enthusiasts, where Voltaire held his gatherings (the café
still exists), the Friends of the Revolution and of Humanity hung
the sign "Franklin est mort" ("Franklin is dead"). Inside the café,
the bust of the distinguished American was covered with black crepe
for two weeks.

When Franklin was in London, a Quaker's son went to see him.
He wished to ask him about electricity. His name was Thomas
Paine. His enthusiasm was obviously more than scientific curiosity. He was passionately interested in liberty. He wished to travel
to New England. Franklin gave him a letter of introduction to the
editor of *Pennsylvania Magazine*. There, in 1775, Paine published
some pages that have been considered forerunners of the War of
Independence.

He accuses the British of committing horrendous acts of cruelty
in the West Indies, of causing the death of thousands by starvation, of sacrificing honor and decency to pride and luxury. He holds
Britons responsible for the misery and death of Indians, whom they
forced to fight for the empire, and refers to countless other examples of "similar barbarities," hoping that "the Almighty, moved
to compassion for Mankind, will take away the power from the
British." Indignant at the crime of slavery in America, he makes an
affirmation pronouncing the word "independence" in the American sense that, in the end, would find its way into the European
dictionaries: "I do not doubt for one moment that the Almighty
will finally separate America from England. Call it Independence
or what you will, if this is the cause of God and Mankind, it will
triumph."

When Paine returns to the Old World in 1781, he is already the

American of the revolution, and Paris is ready to follow the example of American democracy. Three years later, his friend Thomas Jefferson, who wrote the Philadelphia Constitution, is ambassador to France. Lafayette has come back from the great war in North America. He had gone there to fight against England; he returns a republican. He is received in triumph in the salons, he keeps a large framed copy of the text of the Bill of Rights from the Constitution of the United States of America, which fills one column, while the column on the other side is left blank: he hopes that the corresponding French declaration will soon fill the empty space. When will that be? The Almighty knows. . . .

As for Paine, he has come back from America with great illusions. He plans to patent a bridge that he has invented. But just as he begins his electrical experiments, he is nearly swept away by the current of the revolution. It is the French revolution this time. The key individuals who must write the constitution turn out to be the the Americans! Jefferson is the first to be chosen; but, because of his official position, he abstains officially. Today, a recent study of his private papers has shown how actively he was participating all along.[5]

The French National Assembly decrees Washington, Hamilton, Madison, and, of course, Thomas Paine, who is in attendance, to be French citizens. Paine then writes his appeal to the French people:

> I have had the opportunity to take part at the outset and in the victory of the American Revolution. The success and the events in that revolution have given me courage, and the prosperity and happiness henceforth reigning in that country amply compensate the hardships and dangers that had to be faced. The principles upon which the revolution was founded have extended to Europe, and a bountiful Providence is renewing the Old World with the New World's principles. The distance that separates America from the other parts of the planet so far has not permitted her to take those principles farther than her own boundaries. It is a privileged honor for France to raise today the en-

sign of liberty for all nations and to know that in fighting its battles it is doing so for the rights of all humanity.

The Americans' Singular Destiny

Enthusiastic for liberty, the Americans did not always approve of the way the revolution in France was developing, and they suffered the consequences. Those occasions when the movement strayed from its trilogy of basic principles—Liberty, Equality, and Fraternity—or simply ignored it were not few.[6] In discerning such discrepancies, South Americans shared, especially the Venezuelan Francisco de Miranda. Paine and Miranda were two uncomfortable witnesses to the men of the Reign of Terror. For the Committee of Public Safety—whose most expressive tongue was the guillotine—the ideas that both men had voiced about the meaning of human rights were too serious to be heard.

Paine would have preferred—and so he expressed it before the Assembly—that the king and queen, instead of being put to death, be exiled, if possible to America. There they might learn of that liberty which to them was unknown. He proposed, as well, the abolition of the death penalty and demonstrated the futility of condemning Louis XVI to die when the heirs to the throne—his two brothers—were still alive and would be most interested in the monarch's death.[7]

Miranda deplored the revolution's excesses, declaring: "Because I love liberty, because I want to see my homeland redeemed from the yoke of the Inquisition and the influence of the favorites who shame the people more than they do their own kings, do you think I am bloodthirsty? No! I love liberty, but not the blood-stained liberty that kills with no regard for sex or age and that has prevailed in your country. No! No permanent scaffolds, or France is lost!"

These Americanisms sealed the fate of both noble thinkers. Traps were laid to silence them . . . or to stop their lips with death. In Paris, a distrust for the British arose to the extent that a resolution was introduced in the National Assembly to exclude all foreign persons belonging to enemy countries. Paine, an Englishman by birth, was expelled, although he had been a member of the Constituent Assembly. In fact, he was arrested. In England, the news was received with glee. For Great Britain, too, Paine's existence was an awkward fact, to say the least. He had proclaimed America's independence. When London thought that he had been guillotined, his "last words" were published. False hopes. James Monroe, Minister to France at the time, asked for Paine's release, and Paine was returned to England very much alive. Jefferson gave him the keys of the Bastille to take to George Washington. A doubly symbolic gift: besides whatever the capture of the Bastille meant to the people, the old prison had been the place where the most illustrious writers had suffered abuses under the monarchy. The keys are still at Mount Vernon, Washington's house in Virginia.

Miranda's imprisonment was planned with the basest intentions by General Charles-François Dumouriez, who accused him of defeats that, through Dumouriez's fault and not Miranda's, the French army had suffered in Belgium. The Jacobins and *sans-culottes,* united against the Girondins, wanted to silence the South American general famous for being so ardent a defender of freedom. The Venezuelan's career had been fabulous so far. He shone with equal brilliance in the salons of famous ladies—among writers, artists, statesmen, and generals—or on the tribunes of the Assembly. He was more than a deputy: he was a general in the French Army. His name may still be seen among those engraved on the Arc de Triomphe.

Miranda and Paine had known each other in the United States and met again later in London where Paine was publishing *The Rights of Man.* When Miranda was imprisoned, Paine, as a member of the Assembly, declared: "It is impossible for a man to be able to understand another's heart as well as he understands his own, but, from what I know about General Miranda, I cannot believe that he would have any intention of betraying the trust that the French Republic had placed in him, especially because the French Republic's fate is closely linked with his heart's most cherished purpose, which is the emancipation of Spanish America, a cause for which he has suffered persecution by the Spanish court for many years."

Monroe took as great an interest in freeing Miranda as he had taken trouble for Paine. But Miranda took up his own defense. His eloquence, whether on the Assembly tribune or the Court of Justice, achieved the impossible, what not even Robespierre was able to do: he was set free. And still more: the trial that had been calculated to send him to the scaffold—the routine finale to trials—became instead his glory. The *Moniteur* informed: "The people applauded Miranda's sentence as well as his speech; they embraced him, carried him off in triumph and crowned him."

The subtleties with which Paine and Miranda wanted to endow the French Revolution, even if they were rejected by the agents of the Reign of Terror, were not proposed in vain. They became a living ingredient in the literature that was to culminate with Victor Hugo, and their thoughts are infused into the French Declaration of the Rights of Man.

In England, Switzerland, Poland, Italy

France gave such prestige to the publication of *The Rights of Man* that people often attribute their origin to Paris. But for the Europeans, the great revolution was the American one. They all knew which text first appended the famous charter. And if a whole continent's independence was a more important consequence than even the upheaval of the European conscience, the new political formula for democratic republics (in current use today) became the rule first in America. At the same time that the United States created a republic that has survived uninterruptedly since 1787, in France the first republic was proclaimed in 1792 and died in 1804; the second was proclaimed in 1848 and ended in 1852; the third, in 1870 and sank beneath German occupation in 1940; the fourth was a fleeting essay in 1946, and the fifth had its beginning in 1958. In the land of very ancient monarchic and imperial traditions, it is not easy to implant a representative and democratic system. Historical circumstances in America do not create a like obstacle. The artificial system there—and this has been proven—would be a king or an emperor, as we saw in Brazil or in Mexico. In spite of all their anarchies and dictatorships, the Spanish American republics are older than any of those in Europe, with the exception of Switzerland. But the case of Switzerland is an example. When it is said over there that the Swiss republic was a consequence of the French Revolution, an implicit reference to the American antecedent is understood. In 1777, in a series of letters between Peter Ochs (the author of Swiss independence and of the Swiss constitution, including its own bill of rights) and the Physiocratic philosopher Isaac Iselin, Ochs asked his friend: "What do you think of the Americans' success? Can it be true that on that side, on the other continent, we may see realized all that you have taught on the history of humanity?" And Iselin replied: "I am tempted to think that North America is the country where reason and humanity have developed faster than anywhere else."

In all these processes, ideas come and go. For we should also keep in mind America's European antecedents. Did not the Abbé de Saint-Pierre publish in 1713 the *Projet pour Rendre la Paix Perpétuelle en Europe (The Project for Lasting Peace in Europe)*, whose philosophical projections are discovered in the American constitution seventy-four years later? Did not Rousseau infuse new life into the abbot's book when he wrote his commentaries on it? Did not Montesquieu already possess the essential elements that Jefferson was to incorporate into his philosophy thirty-nine years after *L'Esprit des Lois* was published? Were not all the Encyclopedists represented in Bolívar's library? And, in Spain, were there not precursory works like those of Feijóo? All this is true, but it is also true that this explosive material, if it was to explode into an example for Europe, needed the conditions existing on the American continent. England's case is the most eloquent. In London, the seeds for the revolutionary movement that was to sweep through two continents had been planted already. When King William III approved the Bill of Rights in 1689, he recognized Parliament's right to meet, vote on taxes, control the carrying out of the laws, give every citizen the right to be represented. Locke preceded Montesquieu and Rousseau. Diderot's *Encyclopedia* was simply the French counterpart of what Ephraim Chambers had already done in London with his *Cyclopaedia, or Universal Dictionary of Arts and Sciences*. Voltaire used to say: "If I were to follow my inclinations, I would fix my residence in England, where one can learn to think." And Feijóo: "The beginning of the new philosophy is in England, but we have to wait till the French write it so that we can understand it clearly." What had not been reckoned with was the American consequences of the philosophy, which Benjamin Franklin finally exposed before the London Parliament—just before the revolution exploded—determining the creation of an important political trend. As soon as independence was won and Paine returned to London (where he published his book on human rights), the book became a best-seller. Toward 1792, 200,000 copies had been sold. To date, a total of 1,500,000 copies have been published in England. The American bible! The reaction against it was proportionate to its success. Beginning with the month of August, 1793, at least 320 communications against *The Rights of Man,* inspired by the English government, were published in different cities of that kingdom. The aristocracy became aware of the poison that was filtering into England and saw the danger of bringing the English people, who were protected by their insularity, closer to the revolutionary French. In a speech before the National Assembly, French statesman Jacques Brissot explained how, for that reason and not because of Louis XVI's trial, England had broken off peace negotiations with France. Still more expressive is Lord Fortescue's letter to his agent in Paris, Mr. Miles, when he learns that Paine has become a member of the National Assembly: "Tom Paine has arrived exactly where he had to arrive: he is member of a concentration of Cannibals. One would think it impossible that any kind of society, before the eyes of the world, would dare receive such a person. Now the most recent actions of the National Assembly have shown him to be the most qualified of them all. His vocation, or that of the others, will not be satisfied until his head finds its way to a pike, which will probably be soon."

Lafayette and the Independence of South America

The fortune of democracies in Europe was fragile, and eyes turned naturally to the New World. Not only to the United States, but also to Spanish America. The southern heroes left their imprint on the European imagination as deeply as did the British Americans before them. Bolívar's name was on everyone's tongue for many years. Lord Byron had thought of going to Venezuela; and Englishmen, Frenchmen, Italians, Poles, and Irishmen joined the republican armies in Spanish America or sent their sons. Ireland alone formed a legion among the Colombian troops, and one of the most outstanding patriots of that island, Daniel O'Connell, sent his son to Simon Bolívar, so that "affirming and imitating your example, he may serve under your command." Another Irishman, Daniel O'Leary, became Bolívar's escort. A nephew of Thaddeus Kosciuszko, the Pole, presented himself with these words: "I have crossed the globe's diameter exalted by the glories of the New World's hero so as to have the honor of serving him." Agostino Codazzi, an Italian who had served as artilleryman in Napoleon's armies, left his country to offer Bolívar his service. Many Frenchmen joined the liberation armies. They believed this land to be more solid for democracy and republicanism than Europe. Lafayette's case symbolizes these attitudes. The wealth of ideas and experience that he had acquired fighting alongside George Washington, what initially served to make him the most popular of the French revolutionists, soon met with great disappointment in Europe. Jacques Debû-Bridel, in his book *Lafayette, une Vie au Service de la Liberté,* writes:

> Everywhere around him he saw his friends' failures—the Italian liberals defeated in Naples by the Austrians; the Spanish constitutionalists swept away by Louis XVIII's armies, which had come to the rescue of Ferdinand VII's absolutism; the Polish patriots massacred by the Czar's cossacks; the Greek insurgents tortured by the Turks, with the complicity of the courts that were in sol-

idarity with the sultan's claim of legitimacy; when all over Europe freedom was outlawed by the forces of the Holy Alliance, in America the entire New World was shaking off the chains of oppression. The Catholic Monarchies' tutelage in America was coming to an end. The empire which Charles V had founded beyond the sea was giving way to young, ardent republics: the Republic of Mexico, the Republic of Guatemala, the Republic of El Plata, the Republic of Colombia. Lafayette was in constant communication with all the liberators of Latin America (Bolívar, Alvear, Rivadavia). In his retreat at La Gange, Lafayette received liberal conspirators from the two worlds, to whom he there gave hospitality, advice, and help. Bolívar and Lafayette were united by bonds of friendship. In the French House of Representatives, Lafayette had protested against the short-sighted policy of Louis XVIII's government, which refused to recognize the young republics, following the advice of the legitimists who considered them rebel colonies of His Majesty the King of Spain. The Holy Alliance had dreamed of a punitive expedition against the rebels of South America. This was one of Richelieu's fixed ideas, and he was nevertheless accused by the ultras of excessive moderation. Their aspiration was to restore in South America the legitimate authority of the Spanish Bourbons.

Within that framework must we place the initiative taken by Washington's family: they asked Lafayette to write Bolívar a letter; it was placed in Bolívar's hands together with a gold medal bearing Washington's image. The descendants of the Anglo-American liberator sent it as a token of their admiration for "the second Washington of the New World." Touched by this distinction, Bolívar wrote a letter to the United States chargé d'affaires, in which he links together the entire movement for American independence: "The United States of America were the first to have a Minister Plenipotentiary in Colombia: they have been and still are the exemplary nation: they are the sum of the greatest quantity of social happiness in power that order produces; . . . that liberty produces . . . They were the first to show us the path to independence." Lafayette, who, if he was ever close to anyone was certainly close to Washington, must have been delighted to know that Bolívar wore on his chest the medal of the North American general—"the saintliest of men," as Bolívar called him in his letter, and as many contemporary portraits bear witness.

But when Bolívar the Liberator accepted the dictatorship in 1828, he disillusioned the majority of the Europeans. Lafayette, who had become General Francisco Santander's friend when the latter was exiled to Europe after the September Conspiracy in Bogotá, thought that the moment had come to do something about the destiny of the South American republics. The Frenchman and the Colombian met at a funeral: the Colombian ambassador, José María Salazar, had just died; and both Lafayette and Santander had arrived early for the ceremony. From that moment on, Santander was invited to Lafayette's house every week, and Lafayette presented him to the same people who had once introduced Franklin at the Academy as well as to the social groups of Paris. One day, to his surprise, Santander read in the *Courrier Français* that Lafayette had decided to bring about his reconciliation with Bolívar, for Lafayette considered it extremely important. That was in April 1830. Lafayette could hardly have imagined that during those very days the Libertador had renounced the Colombian presidency and left Bogotá, intending to end his days somewhere in Europe. Bolívar died as he was preparing to embark, in December. Santander was called back to assume the presidency. When Santander was president, Lafayette once more expressed his faith in the American republics and his disenchantment with the European monarchies. Because he was an observer of the European and the American worlds, his words in a letter to Santander illustrate many things:

> The news that you give me about your country, apart from the interest that this nation has aroused in me ever since its first marvelous insurrection, and the American feelings that have always stirred my heart are for me motives of European satisfaction as well. You may have read in the papers about all that has been done, and is being prepared, against the reasonable and

necessary results of the July revolution. Indeed, out of consideration for the circumstances of the moment and respect for the national will and prejudices, we placed the system of our constitution under the protection of an alliance of the popular sovereignty. The aristocratic-monarchic principle has not agreed with this . . . and I believe that in the end there will be an open conflict between divine right and popular sovereignty. North America has already shown us that in its institutions lies the best guarantee for liberty, security and prosperity that has ever existed on the face of the earth. It is necessary now that the other part of America give the world another similar example: it is the best answer that we can give here to the reasons that intrigue puts forth or to the stubbornness of prejudices. . . . I suppose you are receiving newspapers from France, England, etc. . . . The Muscovite despotism commits unprecedented cruelties: three dozen conventions have just ended in a miserable way. The courts of Vienna and Berlin dominate the Frankfurt Assembly, have allied themselves to oppress Germany. Austria is permitted to lord it over Italy, and the July agreements have not been kept. But our revolution of the municipalities has aroused people and shaken down thrones. . . . The Polish nation, scattered like the Jews, preserves in itself the elements of its unification. The constitutional principles successfully fight St. Michael's tyranny and threaten that of Ferdinand VII; French patriotism maintains itself better than we could have hoped, because of the predominance of a reasonable middle course; the national sovereignty and the people nominate their officials. . . . The platform and the press are undefeatable. . . . This means that there is hope for European civilization and independence. . . . Send us news about you and about everything that concerns that beautiful part of the world where republican liberty and the union between patriots will be happy reasons for filling the American soul with joy.

The Independence of Haiti and of Spanish America

The expulsion of the Jesuits from Portugal, Spain, France, and Spanish and Portuguese America—followed by the suspension of the order—was caused by incidents in the Guaraní missions. The Portuguese minister, Sebastião Pombal, took the initiative. From the kings to the pope, everyone followed him. The far-reaching political consequences of his movement are well known in Europe. In America, the Jesuits expelled from their old homelands gave new life to the feelings of independence already latent in Creoles, Indians, and blacks. In European cities like Bologna, small colonies of exiles settled and devoted themselves to writing books that exalted the ancient Indian cultures and presented a new image of America, an image constantly ignored centuries after the discovery of the New World. A careful observer would have been able to predict that these other Americas were going to follow the example of the English colonies. It would have given a new dimension to the issues raised by Franklin or Jefferson. Not limited to the United States, such issues could embrace the whole continent.

The Venezuelan Francisco de Miranda took the anticipated news everywhere. He went to England, Holland, Prussia, Saxony, Austria, Italy, Turkey, Switzerland, Russia, Norway, Sweden, Denmark, Belgium . . . besides France. He aroused Pitt's interest (in London) and that of Catherine of Russia; he talked to kings, philosophers, statesmen, famous women, writers of renown in every nation. Miranda was the best qualified to tell about the results of the North American revolution. He was its living courier. He had had long conversations with Washington, Adams, Hamilton, Knox, and Paine in Philadelphia. During these, he informed them of the revolutionary plans in the Spanish colonies and introduced, to the salons, many of the American activists who passed through Paris and London—Bolívar from Venezuela, Antonio Nariño from New Granada, or the Argentine Manuel Belgráno, the Chilean Bernardo O'Higgins. . . . The Masonic lodges became centers for propaganda. Increasingly, gazettes began to print information about the other Americas. From 1810 on, news regarding insurrection in that other hemisphere alerted the European to another surprising reality.

The greatest surprise, and the first, was sprung by the mulattoes and the blacks of Haiti who had seats at the Paris National Assembly. One afternoon, a former slave who had bought his freedom stood up and asked for the abolition of slavery. As soon as the black man had finished his appeal, a mulatto asked for the floor and exclaimed: "When the Constitution of France was created, the French people ignored the unfortunate blacks. For this neglect, posterity will look on us with reproach. Let us repair the error and proclaim the blacks' liberty. Citizen President: let us not submit the Convention to the shame of debating on the step that we are going to take!" Everyone rose to his feet, and in the midst of uproarious applause, the proposal was approved. The black man and the mulatto who had taken the initiative were carried in triumph from their seats to the president's place. This was only the beginning. In Haiti, a black man, Pierre Toussaint L'Ouverture, assumed the government of the island, proclaiming a French protectorate that would permit the state to make its own laws, administer its finances, and see that the citizens received an education. In the Fundamental Charter that the state gave itself, the declaration reads: "All men in Haiti are born, live and die free and French."

Once the enthusiasm of the first day passed, France advanced into the Napoleonic era, and the National Assembly retreated. A new law decreed: "1st. In the colonies restored to France in exercise of the Treaty of Amiens of 6 Germinal, year X, slavery shall be maintained in accordance with the laws and regulations that existed prior to 1789. . . . 2nd. The Negro trade in said colonies will take place in accordance with the laws and regulations that existed prior to 1789." The French Revolution is over. Napoleon's reply to the liberal constitution produced by Toussaint L'Ouverture was to send an army of thirty-five thousand men, commanded by General Charles Leclerc. His troops succumbed to the blacks and to the yellow fever. Leclerc's only visible victory consisted in arresting Toussaint, who died in prison in France. Justice was done to his name afterwards, in literature, and Auguste Comte included him in his Positivist Calendar. . . . France experienced in her own colonial empire the meaning of the word "independence": the blacks of Haiti would never again come under her flag.

Toussaint was a learned man. He had read the Encyclopedists (having learned to read at forty). In his writings as a statesman, this is immediately perceptible. But years before, the illiterate ones had already invented their "Marseillaise" and proclaimed their freedom. The only new thing that the reaction at the General Assembly accomplished was to reinsert the paragraphs on slavery in a law . . . so that once more they would have to be eliminated. The blacks that had failed to escape the white hunters in Africa found in America the formulas for liberty that their brothers are testing even today, in their efforts at independence in the old continent. America's presence, in this case, has even reached Africa.

7

·

Between the
Dithyramb and
the Diatribe

From the Sixteenth Century to the Eighteenth the Style Is Unchanged

In the sixteenth century Friar Tomás Ortiz, a Dominican, wrote:

> The men of the mainland eat human flesh and are worse sodom-
> ites than any generation. . . . They go naked, have no love or
> shame; they are like donkeys, silly, mad, unreasonable. They think
> nothing of killing themselves or killing others; they keep not the
> truth unless it be to their advantage; they are inconstant; they
> know not the meaning of counsel; they are exceedingly ungrate-
> ful and frivolous; they pride themselves on their drunkenness;
> they do also inebriate themselves with smoke and with certain
> herbs which make them go out of their minds; they are bestial
> in their vices; no obedience or courtesy do young men have to-
> ward their elders, nor sons toward their fathers; they are inca-
> pable of teachings or punishments; they are treacherous, cruel
> and vengeful; have the greatest enmity toward religion; they are
> indolent, thievish, false; base and timid in their judgments; they

are sorcerers, believers in omens, necromancers; they are cowardly as hares, dirty as dogs; they eat lice, spiders and raw worms; in their ways they are not like men; they have no beards, and, if any happen to grow, they pull them out; as they grow older they get worse; up to 10 or 12 years of age it seems that they could develop some manner of good breeding or virtue; from then on they become like brute beasts; in short, I say that never did God create such notoriously depraved and bestial people, who have no trace of goodness or cleanliness.

Two hundred and fifty years went by, and the distinguished French naturalist Georges Leclerc Comte de Buffon wrote: "Although nimbler than the European, the New World savage is less strong of body, much less sensitive, more timid and cowardly; he has no vivacity, no activity of soul; that which his body possesses is not so much an exercise or a voluntary movement as the need for action caused by necessity. Take away his hunger and thirst, and you will have destroyed at the same time the active principle of all his movements. He stupidly remains at rest or lies down for days on end."

Contemporary with if not somewhat earlier than that of Tomás Ortiz, Amerigo Vespucci's account almost diametrically opposes the friar's description: "The women, although they go naked, have no defect in their bodies, which are graceful and clean, nor are they coarse, as some may suppose. . . . One thing we have thought miraculous: that not one of them has sagging breasts." Of the men he says that never did Castilians see anyone swim so well. And that had they worn clothing, they would have been as white as the Europeans. So clean were they that "when they evacuate their bowels (may I be excused for saying so) they make every effort to do so without being seen." Death was like a lullaby: they put the dead person in a hammock, hung the hammock from the trees, and danced about the corpse for a whole day. For the journey, they placed food and drink beside the deceased. . . . Thomas More was so impressed by Vespucci's moral portrait of the Americans that he used the images in his *Utopia*, where he envisioned a better world than the one he saw in Europe. At last, he thought, a place has been discovered in the world where peace and equity prevail!

The botanist Linnaeus is Buffon's contemporary and writes to his fellow countryman Peter Loefling when he learns that the latter has obtained his dream of going to Venezuela: "All that wonderful America will be described by you for the first time: the centuries have reserved that destiny for you and your generation. But I would love to be with you for just one day in that most marvelous of paradises! I congratulate you as much as I pity myself. My dear Loefling: think of me when you come into your kingdom, send me a sprig of some strange plant so that I may share in your happiness."

These two extremes—the dithyramb and the diatribe—have distorted America's image through endless commentaries: at times it is Hell; at times it is Heaven. Man is not as bestial as Friar Ortiz presents him, nor is he as perfect as More would have him. Nor as degenerate as Buffon supposed, nor as fortunate an inhabitant of paradise on earth as Linnaeus was thinking. But a century goes by, and once more dithyramb and diatribe arise, perhpas not altogether as an American privilege, but as a chronic disease of universal criticism. When Vespucci said: "In America I believe I am approaching paradise," Thomas More added: "And England is hell." In the Old World, there have always been those who see in themselves the unfading glory of a superior race—the white man—or the infernal Kafkaesque labyrinth where every good thing decays.

In the case of America, the Age of Reason and Enlightenment sees the rebirth of an image that the most stubborn contenders of the sixteenth century painted in the darkest colors. There is a return of the century-old doubts concerning the goodness of the earth and the rationality of man in the New World. A discussion arises as to whether the European who is going to settle there is or is not en route to his own degeneration. Debates in the Paris Academy of Science recall the polemic between Friar Las Casas—in love with Americans and America—and Sepúlveda, his detractor.

Buffon, a Victim of Rhetoric

When he describes American man, Buffon gives us the impression that he made his observations directly, firsthand. Far from it. The noble scholar never crossed the Atlantic. The texts from which he drew his information not only were insufficient; he accommodated them to his preconceived ideas. Some of the features that he describes may coincide with authentic fact, but if he had had the opportunity to visit America, he would either have written the opposite or have avoided generalization. He might then have returned with Humboldt's enthusiasm or Azara's scientific knowledge. It is certainly puzzling that a naturalist whose work was the most competently exact in France—*The System of the Planets, Moral Arithmetic, Introduction to the History of Minerals*—would leave aside the strict adherence to experience and expose himself to the risks of a rhetorical adventure. His fascination with style was too much for him to resist. He thundered at Newton, Montesquieu, or Rousseau with a consciousness of form that makes him appear like nothing more than a professor of grammar. He would write a page eighteen times if necessary, till it was perfect and indelibly fixed in his memory. He is not so strict about revising his concepts. Peculiarities of the Romantic period: Buffon, confident that he was a pontiff of *belles-lettres,* found it natural that Rousseau, on his first visit, should get down on his knees and kiss the floor.

Giving free rein to his fancy, Buffon imagined the New World a swampy, immature place. Nature there was still unorganized, animals were stunted, wild beasts were not so ferocious as those of Africa, while horses, donkeys, sheep, goats, dogs . . . even men taken there from Spain became smaller, degenerated. "Everything there languishes, spoils, suffocates. Land and air, filled as they are with humid, unhealthy vapors, cannot eliminate their impurities. They cannot benefit from the influence of our life-giving star. In vain does the sun fling its most intense rays on that cold mass, which is incapable of responding to its radiance and produces humid creatures, plants, reptiles, insects. And all that it can ever breed will be cold men, weak animals."[1]

Buffon could not imagine the breeding place that America would become after a certain period of adaptation. Chilean horses are today among the tallest, strongest, and handsomest in the world; and we may well doubt if Napoleon had horses like those of Simón Bolívar, which endured the marches from the Venezuelan plains to Potosí in Bolivia, defying the greatest challenge that an abrupt mountain ridge can present to a campaigning army: burning valleys, icy peaks, abysmal chasms, dizzying crags, trails of bare rock. . . . The mules of Montana, in the United States, employed by the men in charge of defending the national forests, may indeed have no counterparts in any other continent: they are superb animals, more than two meters high. Sheep, cows, and bulls from the most select breeds of Normandy, Scotland, or England, if they are taken to Argentina or Uruguay, produce others that surpass the original pedigree. Spanish fighting bulls that are sent to Colombia for breeding have produced beasts as ferocious as any in the Iberian pastures.

To adapt European species to America, nature has had to be reorganized . . . just as it would have to be in the Old World or anywhere else on earth, when creatures are moved from one environment to another. Much of this process has taken place after the time of Buffon's writings, but adaptation was to be expected. All the more so, one would expect, by a naturalist. In any case, nature herself replied to the French scientist, and, even admitting the rationale Buffon made within his primitive scheme of things, that is, even accepting that the size of plants and animals might be a basis for classifying a region of the world as fit or unfit for humanity, is there by chance any bird in Europe as large as the Argentine ostrich or the Andean condor? Or a tree the size of California's giant fir, the sequoia? Or anything like the Argentinian ombu or the Venezuelan saman? Do eucalyptus grow taller in Australia than they do in California, Colombia, or Ecuador? The Champagne vineyards nearly perished once, attacked by a fatal disease. They were saved by stronger stock plants brought over from New Mexico.

Buffon was impressed by the absence of ferocious beasts and enormous elephants in South America's natural history. The argument, in fact, places Europe below Africa in his own hierarchy of environments. And if he spared North America in some parts of his study after the news came regarding the discovery of mammoth bones in that hemisphere, he did not live long enough to know that they have also been discovered in South America. After all, nature was an open field for Buffon's imagination to play in; and, in some cases, he finally contradicted himself or rectified his statements to recognize that not all South America was sterile, swampy land where nothing could be transplanted:

> Nature has more beauty than art, and in an animate being, the freedom of movement enhances its natural qualities. We may see this in those horses which have multiplied in Spanish American countries, where they live in total freedom: their gait, their speed, their ability to jump are not commanded or measured; proud of their independence, they flee man's presence, despise his needs, look for and find by themselves the grasses that are best for them; errant, galloping free over limitless pastures, they absorb all the freshness of an unfading spring; having no fixed home, no other shelter than the serene sky, they breathe a cleaner air than they would in the vaulted palaces where we shut them in, measuring the space that they should occupy. These wild horses are much strong, lighter, more spirited than most domestic horses; they have what nature has to give: vigor and nobility. The others possess only what art can bestow: tameness and training.

Buffon and Linnaeus

Buffon is writing his observations at a time when other naturalists and scholarly explorers from Sweden, France, Spain, Germany, Holland, Great Britain, Italy, and Austria are finding in America the rich flora that will henceforth revolutionize medicine and open new fields for industry. Some studious Americans had been ahead of them or were participating with them in this new discovery of America. Many of them were of pure Indian extraction and made use of tribal traditions in their scientific work.

Linnaeus, like Buffon, never crossed the Atlantic, but with loving care he collected news—well or badly written—that the explorers sent. He kept up a correspondence with them, encouraged their studies, published their findings. He knew José Celestino Mutis and was acquainted with his Botanical Expedition in the New Kingdom of Granada—and with those who worked with him, studying the region's flora and fauna: whites, Creoles, men of mixed blood, Indians, some from the New Kingdom, others hailing from Quito, Havana, Venezuela. Their drawings of plants were comparable in their perfection to those of the best English draftsmen.

We should compare Buffon's work at the Paris Botanical Gardens and the efforts that Mutis was making in Santa Fe de Bogotá. In Santa Fe, it was rugged, uphill work. Paris had the advantages of the great European laboratories. Eliza Mujica gives the following description of the New Granada mission's contribution to the Madrid Garden: "Perhaps I do not exaggerate if I affirm that the 6,690 drawings (the original number was probably 7,000) that we find today at the Madrid Botanical Garden represent, apart from their scientific value, the collection of greatest artistic beauty produced so far [1973] in Spanish America. To support this statement, we can cite Humboldt, who called one of the painters, Francisco Javier Matis, the best flower painter in the world."

The Paris Botanical Garden was carrying out extraordinary work. Like many botanical gardens in Europe, it had been converted into a vast laboratory of New World natural history, at the time when Linnaeus exercised a universally acknowledged authority on the subject all the way from Uppsala.

Madrid's Botanical Garden was famous because it had the greatest access to everything that came from America. Its tradition included the famous Hernández, who had studied and drawn Mexican flora at the time of Philip II. In an ironic reversal of prestige, a few years after Buffon's death, the Madrid Botanical Garden came to be directed by Francisco Antonio Zea, an American from New Granada who had belonged to the Mutis botanical mission.

Buffon has been compared to Goethe as a naturalist: the same ingredient of genius, the same flair for synthesis in search of unity, the same richness of rhythm and style, in spite of the differences.

In Goethe, the oscillation of phrase has been compared to Bach; in Buffon, the lines develop with a continuous movement that reflects the harmony of his ideas.[2] A major difference between Buffon and Goethe regarding America lies in Goethe's warm empathy for and Buffon's initial rejection of it. Goethe formed his opinions on America from his conversations with Humboldt. He was interested in the development of the British colonies as well as in learning about Cuba, Mexico, New Granada, Venezuela. He was interested in the problem of interoceanic communication. The canal had to be opened, he said, but the United States was not going to allow any other power to open it: the enterprise would have to be theirs. Goethe placed his hopes for a better life in the New World. In his poem "De Zahme Xenien," he said:

America, thou art more fortunate
than our old continent;
thou hast no crumbling castles,
no basalts;
thou art undisturbed
in the present time
by useless memories
or fruitless fighting.

Be happy, enjoy thy moment!
and if thy children would make verses,
may good destiny protect them
from ghostly tales and chivalry!

It was not so with Buffon. He despised Linnaeus's painstaking determination to classify every single species, to follow the process of nature into its most secret recesses, to scrutinize under the microscope the development of life, searching for its original cause. For Linnaeus, the evolution of the world could be contained in the miniature of a stamen. From these two contradictory positions two schools of thought emerge, two ways of focusing that will characterize the scientific study of America. Buffon's literature—

probably with no such intention—opened the way for those who have insisted ever since in the anti-American diatribe. Linnaeus, on the other hand, aroused a generous interest throughout Europe in the second discovery. Those who worked with him in the classification of European flora developed a correspondence with their American colleagues. Stimulated by the enthusiasm that reigned in Uppsala, the horizon broadened for those who were working in New Granada, Mexico, Brazil, Río de la Plata, Venezuela, Cuba, Guiana . . . and Alaska and Canada.

The study of minute things, an enterprise that irks Buffon as much as it pleases Linnaeus, brings about an eloquent episode in the making of one of the most fertile friendships that occur between the scientists of Santa Fe de Bogotá and those of Uppsala. . . . José Celestino Mutis arrived in Cartagena in the hope of continuing the work that the Swedish naturalist Loefling's death had interrupted. The first things that drew his attention were the ants. As soon as he had enough facts, he wrote Linnaeus a letter whose richness of detail is worthy of the great entomologist Jean Fabre. He told about the habits, the mating rituals, the collective work done in the highly organized anthills. For Linnaeus, a better gift was unimaginable. Shortly after that, Mutis received his nomination for membership to the Swedish Academy, symbolic precursor to a Nobel Prize. Later, Mutis continued his study on ants in Ibagué, a city in the interior.[3] But with this "ant bridge" moving between Caribbean Cartagena and Scandinavian Uppsala in the distant Baltic, the American and European scientific academies were linked forever.

The most significant part of this ant story has nothing to do with insects; it is that it marks the beginning of a fascination with the natural history of the New World that fired the Spanish scientist's curiosity in every direction. In America, he learned things that as a student or professor in Cádiz he had never imagined. His curiosity waxed to glowing enthusiasm, and, after insisting for twenty years, he was able to convince the Madrid government to fund the Botanical Expedition. When Humboldt arrived in Bogotá, he found a group of young men collecting plants and minerals, studying antidotes for snake poison, making a specific study on Peruvian bark (whose application in medicine was immediate), measuring the height of mountains, revising maps and pointing out geographical errors, putting together the most complete herbarium known, and making drawings of plants and flowers. The institute had been set up in a village—Mariquita—deep in the Magdalena Valley, and Linnaeus received reports from there. The reward for this task was not a small one: European books began to present samples of American flora named in Latin after these obscure young students of American nature.

Pauw, the Disparager

The Abbé Corneille de Pauw—now forgotten, but an outstanding celebrity in his own day—was a skillful writer. With unfailing precision, he plucked all the disparaging words out of Buffon's work on America and expounded on them to form a general theory about the degeneration of living things in the New World. The word "new" acquired its most pejorative sense. Pauw's book appeared in Berlin, in 1768–69, in French. It was signed "M. de P***." The title was *Recherches Philosophiques sur les Américains, ou Mémoires pour Servir à L'Histoire de l'Espèce Humaine*. In the introductory discourse, he said: "No event is more memorable among men than the discovery of America. Going back from our present day to the most ancient of times, there is nothing that can compare with this. And indeed it is a great and terrible spectacle to see that half of our globe is so extremely deprived of Nature's bounty, that everything there is so degenerate and monstruous."

Montaigne's dithyrambic image of the Noble Savage was contrasted with another—of a savage beast incapable of being trained to normal, civil behavior. In America's soil, still fresh, marshy, nothing good could be born. European animals lost their size as well as their vitality and virtues. The famous city of Cuzco—the new Rome of the first chroniclers—was nothing more than a pile of windowless houses: only one great wall was still standing. In

America, man and nature were impotent: nothing could breed there except spiders, scorpions, snakes. . . .

Pauw had chosen a literary genre that, then as now, held a tremendous fascination: the exotic geography. He had already written books on China, Egypt, and the ancient Germanic peoples. He cleverly blended true facts with generous quantities of what his imagination lavishly supplied. Voltaire used to say that Pauw had a great advantage over other writers because he did not need to stick to the truth and there was nothing to restrain his fancy. The Jesuits frowned on him, saying that, before writing what he did, he should have informed himself better. (They were referring to his articles about the company's missions in the East.) But the Jesuits themselves failed to realize that one of Pauw's ways of catering to public opinion was to be anti-Jesuit. He befriended the editors of the *Encyclopedia* as a "specialist" in American affairs. Although the *Encyclopedia* was already finished, a supplement was being prepared, and this was his opportunity.

If the original *Encyclopedia* is to be considered a paragon of the Age of Enlightenment, of the Age of Reason, we are shocked—as I remarked before—by ignorance that is manifest in the treatment of the word "America" in the first edition: forty-three lines, when any French province occupies pages and pages. These forty-three lines contain everything—discovery, baptism, the manner in which the European empires had distributed the continent among themselves, the islands and their products: the gold ingots, the children of America, the grain . . . and the currency . . . silver . . . pearls from Margarita, emeralds from Bogotá, sugar, tobacco, indigo, ginger . . . and Tolú balm, copal gum, ipecac. . . . A pocket edition of a whole world, but lacking in diatribe. Upon revision of the eighteen enormous volumes of the total work, the editors themselves discover how incomplete it is and decide to embark on the *Supplement*. They see that America is chronicled in hundreds of articles—on plants, rivers, mountains, animals, cities. . . . A new general, article has to be made, and Pauw gets the assignment! He is the specialist. Diderot makes an incredibly superficial choice. Pauw, who had made himself a "citizen" of France, was a very popular figure. Because of Diderot's choice, the Enlightenment grows dim in those pages of the *Supplement,* and Pauw's contributions seem to retreat into the sixteenth century instead of characterizing the Age of Reason.

These are among the closing words of the *Supplement*'s new, extensive article—twenty pages!: "Even today, in the entire American world there is not a single nation which is free or thinks about philosophy and literature, and we must not mention the Indians in the missions, for everything tends to demonstrate that slaves are formed there rather than free men."[4]

Between the date of his book's first appearance and the time he wrote the article for the *Supplement,* Pauw could have obtained new information from the latest European explorers and compared it with his theories. But his stubbornness made him see in whatever he read only that which confirmed what he had stated in his book. He gave credit to the conclusions of Las Casas's adversaries in the sixteenth century and to their theories on American inferiority. He resembled a resurrected defender of the empire the *encomenderos* had claimed over the natives, arguing that they were beasts born for slavery. Pauw believed that Las Casas, in his defense of the Indians, was simply humbugging. Why had he invented the legend that the Spaniards had destroyed millions of Indians? Because he wanted to establish a semi-military order with himself as Grand Master "and make the Americans pay a fabulous tribute to himself in silver. In order to persuade the Court of his project's usefulness—when it was useful only to himself—he raised to astronomical figures the number of victimized Indians."

The Peruvians, he said, had no word in their language for metaphysical beings or for the moral qualities that distinguished man from beast. Everything that had been said in their favor was a farrago of exaggerations. Some theologians in the sixteenth century had agreed that the Americans were not men, but what moved them to say this was not the fact that they went naked or had no beards; it was their cannibalism. Pauw cites a contemporary author, Lullus, who said: "The Indians of the West have only the appearance of rational beings; they scarcely know how to speak, have not the least notion of shame, honesty or honor; they devour each other. . . . The Spaniards have become quite perverse, wicked and atrocious because of the example they received and also because of the climate." The subject of anthropophagy, the idea that if they were called cannibals, they would be destined, by definition, to eat their fellowmen, provided the clue to American savagery—everywhere in America and for all time. For example: The Atac-Apas (who lived at an immense distance from the Orinoco) had eaten up a Frenchman by the name of Charleville in 1719 in Louisiana, just as the Encabellados in the Orinoco made delectable banquets at which they served the flesh of their prisoners. "Conclusively, this barbarian custom is common to these nations, as they could not have imitated each other's habits or been corrupted by each other's example."

Not even the Enlightenment could modify such conditions. The sad state in which the universities in the South American colonies languished made one think "that the teachers' ignorance caused that of the students." And the truth, he goes on to say, is that the professors at Cambridge University in New England have produced nothing of any literary value. . . .[5]

Archaisms in the Encyclopedia

If there was anything old and worn out in Europe, it was those ideas that, paradoxically, the *Encyclopedia* minted and Buffon promoted—for example, the return to Friar Tomás Ortiz's diatribes, or the Laws of the Indies themselves, which, in order to defend the Indians, were based on the assumption that these were weak and miserable and needed to be protected by the king's fatherly care.

But the words of Buffon and Pauw acquire extraordinary authority, coming as they do from the most respectable platforms erected in the glowing days of the Enlightenment. The *Encyclopedia*'s prestige marked a new starting point in the history of knowledge. If one looked back from there, it was to be engulfed in the ages of darkness. If one looked ahead, reason shone. So deep was the significance of this work, so far-reaching the effects it produced, that even now, in Europe or in Latin America itself, outstanding thinkers insist many times on an American degeneration, on the sterility of American soil, the incapacity of its people, the physical and moral impoverishment of Europeans who have taken up residence on the other side of the Atlantic. From Buffon to Pauw, up to Gobineau and Hitler or any of the creators of neoimperialism, the world is divided between first- and second-class human beings. Europeans are in the first class. America (and, by extension, the "third" world) is second class.[6] The European who remained in the Old World is the depository of science, philosophy, art, grace. But if he descends from those who had the courage to move to America, he is a drifter, he barely manages to imitate the West, he lacks maturity. A North American in charge of governing the United States, even if he has as much European blood in his veins as Churchill, De Gaulle, or the president of Germany, will always be—to European eyes—an inexperienced, immature, elementary person. An Argentine is simply a barbarian. Color only serves to lower a person's position. If the American white is already second class, a bit of color will bring him down to third.

Paradoxically enough, the lazy, cowardly Americans depicted by the philosophers of the Age of Reason—those creatures whose faintheartedness contrasted with the Europeans' virile arrogance—were at that very moment, and in the four years that followed, producing a serial collapse of four Western empires: the English, the Spanish, the French, and the Portuguese. The most famous European warrior, Napoleon, when the wave of the French Revolution had passed, waged his battles through a world no larger than the one covered at that time by Bolívar's armies. And there is a philosophical contrast: in America, a whole continent is liberated by the whites, the Indians, and the blacks fighting for their emancipation—while, in Europe, Napoleon's glory turns to ashes, palled in the twilight of his imperial glories.

About the Europeans that came to America during the Conquest, Pauw says: "The least vigorous among them was able to defeat the Americans in a combat without any effort." For one thing, the victory belonged to gunpowder, steel, horses, and dogs, when it was not due to the kind of diplomatic treachery that ensnared the Aztecs or the Incas. (From the times of the early Greeks all the way to those of Chamberlain and beyond, many societies have been brought down in Europe in just the same manner.) Still, the struggle against the Araucano Indians in Chile cost the Spaniards two centuries of battling, and they never really defeated them. Less time was wasted on the Flemish wars. The Europeans, arriving where, according to Pauw, everything grew smaller, actually would grow, expand better themselves! Francisco Pizarro, born a hog raiser in Trujillo, Spain, would have died a hog raiser had he not gone to Peru to emerge as a giant among barbarians. Sebastian de Belalcázar, a man who tended donkeys in Estremadura, became a founder of cities: Quito, Pasto, Popayán, Cali, Bogotá. Cortés would have remained what he was in Salamanca—the bold conqueror of women—had he not left Spain; he went to Mexico, and we all know what he was able to accomplish. In this manner, the common men, the anonymous people, grew to unimagined proportions during the Spanish Conquest. Just as the Portuguese, Englishmen, Germans, or Hollanders grew in other regions. And they grew with the passage of generations. Bolívar, son of Basques who had settled in Venezuela, is unsurpassed in the Spanish or French Basque provinces. And the sum total of the population—when America had become a continent of natives, Europeans and Africans, mixed and combined in infinite proportions—produces an unprecedented universal event: the beginning of a modern democratic style that finally extends to every continent.

The literature of denigration awakened—outraged—American sensibilities. In the American, the spirit of doubt was being formulated at the very moment in which the duel for independence was beginning. Would a degenerate creature be able to defeat England, Spain, France, and Portugal, who were the greatest of the great in those centuries? Europe was used to measuring the greatness of nations by the fruits of their wars. But there was something else here. Supposing that the colonies won? Would the

Americans be able to install modern states? Republics were a novelty. France had imported the republic from the United States and was unable to keep it going. Could the descendants of Aztecs, Mayas, Incas, Chibchas, Araucanos, and Guaranís accomplish such a feat? Humboldt himself, after having observed the emancipation of the English colonies and being agreeably surprised at the kind of men who were creating the Spanish American Enlightenment, nevertheless said once, to a young Venezuelan who visited him in Paris: "I see that the only solution for Spanish America is independence, but what I don't see is the leader who would be able to bring it about. . . . Probably he hasn't been born yet." The inexperienced and still-unknown Venezuelan had nothing to say in response. . . . But he was Simón Bolívar.

The Controversy

The real response to Buffon and Pauw was already being seen in events. The rise of the United States and its spectacular growth demonstrated the bankruptcy of their philosophy from the first day. Jefferson was able to say in Paris to a group of friends at a small social gathering, without raising his voice, and subtly underlining the remark with a malicious smile: "It is really extraordinary that, in three volumes in twelve point—very small print—it should be nearly impossible to find in Pauw a single truth."

The opportunity to contradict in a public debate had not presented itself so far. The exiled Jesuits were the first to speak. One, a Mexican, who was a refugee in Italy—Francisco Javier Clavijero—set the example by writing the *Storia Antica di Messico*. For those Europeans who had forgotten it, the old Mexican grandeur was reborn with him. After him came a Chilean, also in exile, and he brought to light the extraordinary qualities of the Araucanos. The books became popular reading and were followed by many more in a similar vein. From the two Americas: Franklin, Thomas Paine, Miranda, Fray Servando Teresa de Mier, Francisco Antonio

Zea, José Mejía—all spoke in the salons, in the assemblies, wrote in the gazettes, published books.

Judgment Is Passed on Europe

On the other side of the coin: the European empires are to be brought to trial. For one, two, three centuries, Spain, Portugal, England, Holland, and France had been extending their empires over various continents, and the time had come to judge their actions. Critics sprang up in the two hemispheres. The independence wrested by the British colonists showed up the errors committed by the British Empire. Which were pale beside those in Spain in the south, as denounced by Jorge Juan and Antonio de Ulloa in *Memorias Secretas*. This book, a document commissioned by the Spanish crown, was published unexpectedly in London and became the main document backing charges against the state's administrative errors, the abuses committed by the authorities, the clergy's corruption, the scandalous life in the convents, the exploitations committed by priests. . . . Together with the Northern protest against laws that required the transportation of every item of merchandise in English vessels, forbade certain industries, established absurd taxes that culminated in the famous three pennies per pound of tea, laws that were to spark off the revolution: there were the corresponding Creole and Indian uprisings in Peru, Paraguay, New Granada, and Mexico, and the first revolutionary movement in Buenos Aires—all due to similar causes.

The various American revolutions produced political changes in Europe and caused repercussions in its economic foundations. If the article on America that the *Supplement* published may be considered merely the opinion of one irresponsible writer, the judgment passed on the European empires in three continents is universal. It is expressed in the wars of emancipation that form one of the most extensive chapters in history and in essays that had greater resonance than Pauw's book. . . . Almost immediately after Pauw, another abbot, also anti-Jesuit and a friend of the Encyclopedists, Guillaume Thomas François de Raynal, publishes a book: *Histoire Philosophique et Politique des Établissements et du Commerce des Européens dans les Deux Indes.* Between 1770 and 1810, thirty legal editions were made—and more than forty pirated ones. Raynal became wealthy, and his name the center of attention in political and literary salons in Paris. America became a compulsory topic for conversation.

Raynal's origins are somewhat shady. He left the church of Saint Suplice, accused of dishonest administration and of simony. This did not prevent him from being published in magazines and received in literary circles, where his anti-Jesuitism was viewed with enthusiasm. He befriended Diderot. In some points, Raynal echoed Pauw—he described a weak, helpless American and a degenerate fauna in a half-formed world; but his dialectical fury was directed against the European empires with such passionate zeal that the American revolutionaries resorted to him in their discourses. Bolívar, in his *Letter from Jamaica,* said: "The Mexicans say together with Raynal: the time has come—finally!—to pay the Spaniards torment for torment, to drown the accursed race of exterminators in its own blood or in the sea."

Raynal defends the American Revolution in tirades like the one in this dialogue, which serves to give a sample of his accusations:

"They are rebels. . . ."

"Rebels. That is true. Why? Because they do not wish to be your slaves."

"But they are our subjects. . . ."

"No. The authority of a nation over another is not founded on conquest, which is no more binding than theft; or on general consent, for the grandparents cannot bind their descendants, or on proposed and accepted compromises that nevertheless exclude the granting of liberty, for liberty cannot be exchanged for anything else, since it has a price that cannot be compared to anything."

"The land that they occupy is ours. . . ."

"Ours? Can it be called that from the fact that we occupied it by force?"

"They are ungrateful. We have become their benefactors after having been their defenders. In their behalf we have become indebted. . . ."

"You can say that again, but more *to* them than *for* them. Have they not paid more than their due, giving us everything they produce and paying for our own products at the exorbitant prices that we fix? Have they not fought for us in our armies?"

"What they want is to be independent from us."

"Are you not independent from them?"

"They will never be able to make it without us."

"If that is so, why worry? Necessity will attract them to you."

"We are the mother country."

"What! Always using sacred words to veil ambition and selfish motives."

"If all their claims are accepted, they will soon be happier than we are."

"And why not?"[7]

Raynal is considered one of the forerunners of the French Revolution. He did not hesitate to take upon himself responsibilities that others avoided. His reply to Diderot is famous, when the latter said to him: "Who is going to answer for things?" Raynal shot back: "I will! I will! I will!" His book is a collective work. It was too vast in scope to be developed by a single person. Twenty collaborated. Diderot alone dedicated two years to the writing of some chapters that appeared as the work of Raynal. Besides this, the abbot asked for, and obtained, foreign aid. For the Spanish American section, his contributor was no less than Count Aranda, Charles III's foreign minister. Upon this collective effort, Raynal bestowed his own style and wrote grandiloquent discourses, moral advice on world reformation.

A work of this kind, involving the participation of so many important personalities, was an unprecedented assay in the criticism of empires. Raynal's book is superior to the *Encyclopedia* in its presentation of the American case. It reaches more hands, circulates, keeps to one political subject. So much importance was given to it, and so much impact was it having upon French opinion, that Louis XVI had it burned by the executioner in a public square, on the pretext that it attacked religion. Frederick of Prussia wrote to Voltaire: "About your friend Raynal, I can tell you that I have seen him, and from the way he talked to me about the power, the resources, and the wealth of the globe I thought I was engaged in an interview with the Divine Providence."

The abundant statistics that the book contained were complemented—in anticipation of our time—by engravings. Everything spoke to the eye—as befitted a century known as the "Enlightenment." The four original books depicted the perfidy and abuse of the four empires—English, Spanish, Portuguese, French—in illustrations that showed how persons of other races were cheated or taken advantage of and shown no gratitude. Frontispiece of the first book: a Portuguese captain shows an Oriental a pile of cannonballs and guns and says: "Here is the King's currency with which he will pay you for your tributes." Second book: miserable scene in which the Spaniards seize Moctezuma's treasures. Third: an Englishman sells his black concubine, who turns her face away to hide her tears. Fourth: some Frenchmen are shipwrecked on Canadian shores, where the Indians save their lives and welcome them generously. In later editions, illustrations are multiplied, especially those of American scenes: William Penn buying the land from the Indians, etc., etc. Always, the black, yellow, and copper man swindled by the Europeans. We see the natives' superior moral stature compared with that of the European, for all its baseness.

In Portugal, that which shocks Raynal is the degradation to which the Oriental colonies have sunk. There, it is the European settler who becomes degenerate. India—the state of Lusitanian glories and opulence, of the poems that sing of the audacity of navigators and of the heroic actions of conquerors—becomes a scene of ruin and infamy. A good viceroy is succeeded by a despotic governor. Soldiers are a turbulent and undisciplined horde. Magistrates sell themselves to the highest bidder. Administration is unjust, based on greed. Oppression such as this, capable of annihilating the most virtuous nation—can it regenerate one that is indolent by nature?

Raynal was more scandalized by the degeneracy of the Dutch than Pauw was by that of the Amerindians. Holland had been an extraordinary nation, capable of making the sea retreat so as to increase the size of her lands. What followed after that process? Slave-hearted men, unworthy of their government. Such impure hands could not preserve the sacred fire of liberty. The old virtues were dead! Corrupt customs and magistrates discredited the republican system proclaimed by the nation. To the vices of despotism another worse one is added: an inability to repress evil. . . .

Judgment on English imperialism: "One must admit that the corruption to which the English abandoned themselves as soon as they began to be powerful, the oppression that followed, the abuses that are multiplied day after day, the total neglect of principles, everything, in sum, makes an outrageous contrast with England's past conduct and the actual constitution of its government in Europe."

America totalizes everything. No one is spared the censure:

Ferocious Europeans: first you doubted whether the inhabitants that you had discovered were or were not animals that could be sacrificed without remorse, being black, while you were white. . . . Spanish monarchs: show yourselves worthy of a destiny that led you to people the most luminous parts of the world in two hemispheres! By fulfilling this august and sacred task, you will repair the crimes of your predecessors and of your subjects. They depopulated the world that they had discovered and killed millions of men; what is worse, they put them in chains, and still worse, those who escaped the sword they reduced to idiocy. Those who died suffered but an instant; the unhappy ones who were left alive must have envied the dead a hundred times. Posterity shall not forgive you till the day when, out of the fields that you covered with innocent blood, a new generation of men shall rise, happy and free.

Out of all this, only one doubt still stands: was the discovery of America useful to Europe? Did she not lose her greatest virtues when she took possession of these empires which brought the decadence of vice upon her? Was not the European stronger and happier before he plunged into the American conquest? Raynal's answers to these and other similar questions are pessimistic. But he loved debates and their resonance. When he became a member of the Lyon academy, he held a contest offering a cash reward for the best essay in reply to this question: Was it or was it not useful? Thus, the controversy that Pauw opens with his diatribes ends with Raynal passing judgment on Europe.

Final Consequences

Today we may discuss the controversy about the New World with the perspective, experiences, proofs, refutations, and prejudices that are the product of more than a century. A verdict on Europe implied a doubt about Western civilization; and the first author of that doubt was Rousseau. In his discourse on sciences and the arts, he declares how souls are corrupted in Europe even as Europeans advance toward achieving perfection in the products of human intelligence; and once more, he compares this failure to the loftiness of spirit that Montaigne found in the Guaraní Indians. If the great ones of his day, says Rousseau in the essay on differences between men, if Montesquieu, Buffon, Diderot, Duclos, D'Alembert, Condillac, were to travel to the other hemisphere to visit Mexico, Peru, Chile, Magellan's lands, "without forgetting the Patagonians, both genuine and false," and Tucumán and Paraguay—if possible—and Brazil, the Caribbean, Florida, and upon returning, if they were to write, as only they know how, they would witness a new world blossoming forth from their pens, and we would learn to know our own world better. . . .

Rousseau's Romantic doubt about the value of letters was confirmed by the liberation movements that originated in America. Washington's armies were made up largely of illiterate men. The internal mechanism that moves man to seek freedom does not require the three r's in order to function properly. That was true then just as it is now. Julian Huxley once asked Mahatma Gandhi for a thought regarding human rights. Gandhi replied: "From my mother,

who was illiterate but wise, I learned that the rights worth merit-
ing and preserving are those that come from fulfilling one's obligations. Thus, the right to life will not come to us until we have
done our duty as citizens of the world." When Benito Juárez coined
his famous phrase, "Respect for the rights of others is peace," he
did not find those words in any textbook. He took them from what
he had heard as a child in the Zapotecan tongue, the only language he spoke before he was twelve: "La hráppa tizháa tangá que
benée tan gáana láa lláagna," which means "To respect what belongs to others is sacred."[8] The Negroes of Haiti, who had no other
schooling apart from the red-hot iron that branded them and the
whip and the stocks, defeated Napoleon's troops in order to be
free, to put an end to slavery and to found an independent nation.
Auguste Comte included the name of Toussaint L'Ouverture among
the 365 great men of the world that made up his calendar. But
eventually, what came from Europe did more harm than good to
the emancipated blacks. Beguiled by tin and tinsel, they indulged
in extravagant trappings, in copies and caricatures of the white man's
traditional ceremonies: emperors, uniforms, feathers, wire, all the
things that, if one stops to think, had better use—and have had
better use—in carnivals than in nations. Alejo Carpentier, in *El Siglo
de las Luces* (literally, "the century of lights"), uses fiction to describe how the guillotine was introduced in Haiti, and tells how
amusing toys imitating the clever French invention for severing
heads were sold in the marketplaces. . . .

In the uprising of the Spanish colonies, people from every seed-
plot on earth participated. Bolívar began his campaign coming out
of Cartagena with dark-skinned troops to reconquer Caracas's
freedom, and this was the true starting point of his dazzling revolutionary career. From Venezuela, he left to liberate Bogotá with
his plainsmen—part Indian, part mulatto, part Creole—and defeated the armies of the king of Spain. He crowned his victories in
Ayacucho, attacking with an army of Indians—Indians of the same
flesh and blood as the first liberator, Túpac Amaru. These Indians
had never read a book: they recorded their own history on pieces
of colored string, where they made knots to mark their chronolo-

gies. In Argentina—today, imposingly white—a good part of the troops that San Martín took with him on his campaign to Chile was made up of unlettered black soldiers.

In Portuguese and Spanish America, once the republics were established, racial discrimination has had more to do with differences between rich and poor than with a political norm. The constitutions, at least, find it inadmissible. Today, in the United Nations Charter, in the UNESCO programs, in political speeches or pope's encyclicals, the equalization of all men, without distinction as to race, is proclaimed as a principle of universal justice and human rights. This attitude, this position, was born in America. In America, slaves were freed. In nineteenth-century Europe, much was said against slavery, but there were no black slaves then in the Old World. The only Africans that Europeans saw were those that the English hunted in Senegal or the Ivory Coast to sell in New Orleans, Havana, Buenos Aires, Rio, or Cartagena.

The blacks of Cartagena were ahead of others as to independence. They proclaimed it from their stockades and held on to it for a century, till the king of Spain had to yield and acknowledge it.[9] The Peruvian Indians, led by Túpac Amaru, were also far ahead of their time, as were the twenty thousand Indians and Creoles in El Socorro, New Granada, who only surrendered because of false promises made by the white Europeans who deceived them. The white leaders came later. They were white Americans, fighters who would have been unable to vanquish the imperial troops had the people of America not been brought together before. Black were the Haitian insurgents. . . . A full-blooded Indian created the Mexican republic: Juárez. . . . That's what became of Buffon's theories, of Pauw's rhetoric. . . . Raynal and Diderot were able to see farther ahead. The empires whose decadence they exposed were swept into an abyss only they had predicted.

Papini, or Reality Deceived

Nothing, however, has been able to erase certain deep-seated aberrations from the European mind, which harbors ineradicable imperial remnants. Almost a century had elapsed since America had proven her capacity in so tangible a way when the theories of white superiority reemerged with renewed impetus. Hegel set down the Americans' inferiority as fact. According to him, they were morally and physically weak.[10] The racial theories of Count Joseph Gobineau and Adolf Hitler had ample sources of inspiration. When Hitler was crushed beneath the ruins of the Reichstag—dying, among other things, because multicolored America had opened the path of liberation—there could have been a change in the postulates of racist Western viewpoints, whose apostles were the heirs—unwittingly, perhaps—of the mediocre and little-known Pauw. But, no. When Giovanni Papini repeated Pauw's words, it was two years after Hitler's death. Papini had been an admirer of Mussolini because Mussolini had determined to conquer Abyssinia, an idea that Papini himself had earlier suggested. Papini was of the opinion that Italy needed to have colonies, just like the other European countries, to provide land for a population that otherwise would have to emigrate from Italian soil. But this was not the origin of his diatribe against Latin America. What he saw in the Western Hemisphere was an experience that had resulted in failure. If Europe had contributed so much of her blood to the formation of the modern American, why, in four centuries, had there not arisen over there a Beethoven or a Michelangelo or a Dante? Had their race degenerated? Rebellious, anarchistic, genial, polemic, contradictory—he was constantly trying to produce a world commotion with his pamphlets; and, in 1947, he decided to aim his fire at America's inferiority.

Angry replies rained on him. But if we give it deeper thought, we may conclude that the historical enterprises in the New World have been the work of large groups of people. There is a strange grandeur in their collective accomplishments that surpasses the exaltation of heroes. Curiously, at the time of the Conquest, no biography was written of Cortés or of Pizarro or of Balboa. Histories of the Conquest and of the discovery were published instead. Even the leaders of independence were sons of the common people, lone inventors of their philosophy—which they took from the obscure social mass. Theirs was a discovery rather than an original creation. In Europe, circumstances predispose the emergence of philosophers, geniuses. The enterprises that have determined profound historical changes in America have been a sort of democratization of human creativity. To make a whole continent independent, to produce a democratic change in institutions, to abolish slavery, to establish for all races the same civic level, to affirm individual liberty—these have been the basic themes of American evolutions and revolutions—her significant contribution to universal philosophy; it was a movement of multitudes. No American leader attains the stature of an emperor. The sedimentation process has not yet suffered that accumulation of centuries that, with time, will produce a genius. Papini mentions European musicians or thinkers, and fails to find their counterparts in America, but he overlooks the fact that a movement like that of independence may well be more important than a book left for posterity. In this case, if we consider a movement a Romantic work, it may well be the most remarkable endeavor of that period. The idea of subjugating Abyssinia—even inspired though it may have been by the type of subordination still in practice in the European states—was an idea only a historical retardate could conceive, a regression to ideas tenable only before the time of Abbé Raynal.

But even in the field of personalities, we can now check Papini's statements. The Nobel Prize provides for a certain amount of recognition of this sort.

The Nobel Prize is, in fact, a sort of exploratory measure to see what the world is producing in the way of scientists, writers, and peacemakers. A hundred or more times the distinction has been awarded to Americans. In its beginning, the prizewinners were chiefly concentrated in Europe, but as time went on a shift to North America began to occur. Now, the Nobel Prize is discovering Latin America, especially in the field of literature.

Paradoxically, it was among Latin Americans that the notion that America was inferior found many supporters no less loquacious than Pauw or Papini. The idea of a sick hemisphere that breeds decrepit men has not lacked New World promoters. To them, a European of better quality had remained in Europe; the runts had embarked on the conquest of the New World. The mature, capable, intelligent person was white skinned. Any other color made a person immature, inept, degenerate. Perhaps these diatribes have sprung up as a natural defense against the exaggerations of those who insist on the dithyramb. Defects cannot be corrected without a fierce reaction against conformism and complacency. Sarcasm may be more useful than narcissism. What intentions might lie at the bottom of all this is quite another subject. Perhaps Papini's way of loving America was to thrash it into consciousness.

8

·

The Spanish
Revolution of the
Eighteenth Century

Not Everything Was the French Revolution

The eighteenth was the century not of the French Revolution alone, but of many. They took place before and after the Bastille, in Europe and in America. The Spanish, the English and that of the English colonies in America—all took place prior to July 14, 1789. The Spanish revolution, one of the earliest, begins with the century: in the year 1700. It was, we must admit, a frustrated revolution. But not a lost cause. Its effects extend to our own day and will continue to bear on Spanish life. We must not seek its origins in French literature. Seventeen hundred is a year in which neither the Enlightenment nor Voltaire nor Rousseau nor the *Encyclopedia* existed. The authors of the Enlightenment had not even been born. The protest came from France—from the French throne. Louis XIV had proclaimed a sovereign attitude with regard to Rome, notifying the pope that to his own royal will—and not to the pontiff's—pertained the right to rule on many matters in which the Church was trying to interfere. And when his grandson, Philip

V, became king of Spain, Louis XIV cherished the idea of a tutelage that would extend his scheme to reduce Rome's aspirations beyond the Pyrenees as well. Except that, to Louis XIV's surprise, Bourbon Spain went farther than he, with his limping old man's will, had intended. The grandfather was backing away, moving counterclockwise. The grandson was coming forward with the freshness of youth. And the sources from which Philip drew his inspiration, the ones that encouraged his ministers, were very Spanish. The French influence to which history books refer has to be taken with a grain of salt.

The process begins with Charles II's last will and testament. It has been remarked that this most unique monarch was neither stupid nor degenerate. He was mentally simply not there. We must give him credit for a flash of perspicacity when he said: "I am nothing!" And added: "God alone can give kingdoms, because they belong to him alone." Were this so, he was divinely inspired the day he installed Philip of Anjou as his heir to the throne. Noteworthy change: the Austrian monarchy thus crumbled, the Bourbons took over. Without wishing or foreseeing it—he would never have understood it either—Charles left the entrance free for the *Encyclopedia* to come through with its gratuities.

The war of succession is something more serious than a struggle between two houses in search of power. Carlism—with its battling priests and its ecclesiastical connections and pretensions—led to a reduction of the traditional Church privileges. Great universal surprise. The Bourbons in Spain were going to start by going beyond all expectations, precisely because their enemies were supported by the Roman Church. The pope's imprudence in taking sides made him, finally, a participant in his protégés' defeat.

True to the first principle of enlightened monarchies, the new government teams set about to control the backwardness of the Spanish administration by emphasizing the progress making headway in the Old World. Everything had to be remade: finance, universities, commerce, engineering, industry . . . and the empire! The Spanish Empire—vast as no other—was more than decrepit. America was living testimony to the Austrian monarchs' ineptitude. Long before Abbé Raynal sounded the alarm for the universal failure of empires in their colonies, Spain had made a dramatic examination of conscience, as may be seen by the inspectors' reports. The culminating point of that examination is *Memorias Secretas* by Juan and Ulloa, used in part by the French abbot to found his accusation. Another book, *Nuevo Sistema de Gobierno Económico de América,* published eight years before Raynal's, shows that a radical criticism of the regime in the Spanish colonies was being made when nothing like it was taking place in the British arena.

This does not mean that there was no interchange of French and Spanish ideas and experiences. No sooner had Bourbon rule been inaugurated than America's doors were opening to welcome French travelers: Louis Feuillée (1702), Le Sieur Bachelier (1700), Amédeé Frezier (1713). It was La Condamine, in his famous voyage of 1735, who brought Juan and Ulloa to America, together with a group of French scholars. Everything that they recorded showed the incredible abundance of riches that the New World possessed, all of it going to waste, and the limitless disorder and neglect of the Spaniards. The trip caused an unexpected shock among the dynamic men of the Enlightenment, who were already critical of their own European situation. Americans, coming in contact with those travelers, awakened from three centuries of dreaming—or of nightmare—and their awakening gave birth to independence. The moment came when the common people themselves—Indians, blacks, Creoles, mestizos—expressed their new views in a way that the social or political literature of the day was only to register later. An uprising such as that of the Túpac Amaru in Peru or of the Comuneros of New Granada is worth many of Abbé Raynal's books.

A Revolution More Popular Than Bourgeois

The Spanish revolution of the eighteenth century draws its origin from the most ancient popular traditions. The people of Aragon had already written Rousseau's *Social Contract* in the laws that set down the privileges established for their province. Centuries before, the Comuneros of Castile had put such a statute before Charles V. And it had crossed the Atlantic, ingrained in the spirit of the most daring adventurers, when America was first explored. It was still alive when Spanish administration in the colonies came to a crisis. It is curious to remark how, in 1810, when Miguel José Sanz explains the Americans' right to rebel against a violation of the social contract, in a long essay published by *El Semanario de Caracas,* he does not quote Rousseau or base his arguments on French philosophy. He looks back at the Spanish past that everyone knows and understands: "Worthy of men's memory is the formula with which the Aragonese swore in their kings: 'We,' they said, 'and each one of us, who is worth as much as you, and that together are more powerful than you, swear obedience to you if you keep our laws and maintain our privileges; if not, we do not.' "[1] If in 1810, in Caracas, the Spanish Comuneros were so well remembered, what would not happen in Spain? The formula of the Aragonese Comuneros is the simplest, most consummate expression of the social contract and of the rights of democracy. Much has been said about "Frenchified" men, such as the counts Aranda and Campomanes, but when they introduce their own revolutionary principles, the first thing that they create—or re-create—is the institution of representatives and deputies for the commons. And it is interesting to note that they, or rather the commonality of Madrid, names the Peruvian Don Pablo de Olavide as its deputy.

The Comuneros, or the Spanish Version of the Social Contract

The Comunero uprising of the sixteenth century was another frustrated revolution, but it was not altogether a lost cause, especially inasmuch as it concerned America. Although Padilla was sacrificed in Spain, the example sparked off many events during the exploration of the New World. Balboa in Darien, preparing to undertake the journey to discover the Pacific, convoked his fellow members of the commonality. It was an assembly of adventurers from the island of Hispaniola, meeting in the vast solitudes of

Darien. Rejecting the authority of Bachelor of Law Enciso, they acclaimed Balboa as captain of the commons. And history began to unfold . . . Hernán Cortés did the same thing later in Veracruz. An election by the commons enabled him to disregard the authority of the royal governor in Cuba; and thereby begins the history of Mexico, daughter of Comuneros. . . . Sometime later, deep in the jungle, far away from Santa Marta, the commons meet on their way to conquer what was going to be the New Kingdom of Granada; and, ignoring Governor Fernández de Lugo, acclaim Gonzalo Jiménez de Quesada. . . . In this way, the idea of the sovereign people is woven into the beginnings of Spanish American life. The most pathetic case occurs in Paraguay. The adventurous settlers were putting heart and soul into the development of the town of Asunción, when, unexpectedly, a governor arrived who had been appointed by the king. He was Álvar Núñez Cabeza de Vaca, a man who certainly had a long past of shipwrecks and suffering. But *who* among the commons had authorized the choice of this man, a complete stranger to the colony's endeavors? The newcomer was locked up in a rustic prison, and the commons met to deliberate. . . . The sentence was significant. Right then and there, they built a ship and sent the governor back to Spain. Thus, two noteworthy events were accomplished: the vessel crossed the Atlantic and docked in Spain; the name chosen for it by its builders was the perfect symbol: *El Comunero*.

The populist Spain that expressed herself so eloquently on two continents rises to such a wonderful philosophical level in the eighteenth century that one could almost say she was permeated by divine grace. What did men like Aranda, Campomanes, Floridablanca . . . or Don Pablo de Olavide have to learn from France if they could draw their lessons from what José Luis Vives had written two centuries before? "No man is there that possesses anything that he may call his. Everything that nature—or rather God—produces—plants, roots, crops, fruit, herds of cattle, fish, furs, wool, wood, metals, dogs, horses, oxen—is placed by him in that spacious house which is the world, without enclosure of gate or moat, so that every one of the things that he has engendered may be common to all . . ." Never again, not with Marx or Lenin, was a nobler formula given—or a more poetic one—for the principle of common rights.[2]

Speaking of anticipations, the earliest events in America's history founded on Comunero ideas regarding "common rights" are clearly more than chance occurrences springing from desperate situations during the Conquest period. Thirty-nine years before Rousseau's *Social Contract* appeared in France, a people's uprising flashed in Paraguay. The two leaders who made it possible were not exactly Paraguayans. They were from New Granada, born in Panama: José de Antequera and Fernando Mompox. Antequera declared: "The people may lawfully oppose themselves to a prince who does not proceed *ad aequa et bone*. Not all the prince's mandates should be carried out. As the rights belong to the people themselves, they have created and delegated the municipal councils to speak in the name of the people . . ."

Antequera was arrested for his boldness and taken to Lima to be tried and punished. But Mompox became Antequera's philosophical charge, traveled to Asunción and once more stirred up the people. Mompox talked about "the power of the common people in any republic, city, town or village, teaching that it was more powerful than the King himself. And that in the hands of the common people was the right to admit the law or government that they desired, because, even if it were given by the prince, if the common people did not want it, they could in all justice resist and no longer obey."

Father Lozano, historian of the great moments of Paraguayan history, writes:

> On the 28th of August, St. Augustine's day, under pretext of honoring the illustrious Doctor's memory, the men of the municipal council proposed to go to the Cathedral with the royal standard, in order to pray for public peace. The commonality, seeing treason or at least something ambiguous in this act, blocked the town hall exit, and, in order to assure the corporation's permanence there, destroyed the staircase that led to the main floor

of the municipal building, thus imprisoning the council members. Shortly after that, the commons' militia entered the city with shouts of "Death to the bad government!" The justice went out on the balcony to speak to them, exhorting them to withdraw quietly to their homes, but a voice interrupted him: "Mr. Purveyor, what does *Vox populi, vox dei* mean? You may answer whatever you please: but know that these are the commons."

All this happened fifty-three years before the rebellion of the English colonies in North America. The example of that insurrection incidentally could have encouraged Túpac Amaru's Peruvians or the New Granada Comuneros in El Socorro. History weaves itself from many threads, and those who fight for justice and liberty use to their advantage whatever doctrines happen to appear. The rejoicing produced in many by Rousseau's *Social Contract* came from their seeing that someone else was thinking in the present moment what they had suspected years back. In keeping with the Spanish American revolutionary tradition, the appointed day to arise and take up arms came—finally!—and the battle cry was emancipation. A few days before the cry is lifted in Bogotá, the Comuneros of El Socorro confront the Spanish mayor, who is at the head of a well-equipped army. The townspeople have only stones and courage. The mayor's people have bullets and fear. The mayor takes up a stronghold in the Capuchin friars' monastery. The commons write to the viceroy: "The people howled with rage at the sight of bullets and death coming from a house that, not many years ago, had been built with the sweat of their brow, not to provide shelter to a pack of caribs, but to render worship to the Divinity." The people's fury compelled the besieged authorities to give themselves up, and there ensued the following episode: "The Mayor, the Deputy and the Ensign were locked up in the rooms of the Town Hall. Upon discussing what was to be done with them, for the *Comuneros* did not want to shed any blood, they decided to send all three to the Caribbean ports and from there to ship them to Philadelphia 'to take lessons in humanity.' "[3]

The Macanaz Trial

In Spain, the crown and the Church clash. The king struggles for his independence, trying to shake off the yoke of Rome. Phillip V picks up the traditional heritage, which is revolutionary. Earlier, another monarch who had borne his name—Philip II—had advocated the rights of the crown (two centuries before Philip V) with words that made the new Bourbon king's pronouncement sound timid in comparison. But this time Pope Clement XI's imprudence throws more wood into the fire. Under pressure of Austrian bayonets, the pope sides with the Carlistas, recognizes the Austrian pretender as heir to the throne, and exposes the Church to the consequences of a humiliating defeat. Philip V suppresses the Nunciature court in Madrid, and the papal ambassador has to leave the country. The king claims the right to appoint the officials for the Inquisition so as to transform that court into a government agency. Behind these maneuvers there is a man in whom the king has total confidence: Rafael Melchor de Macanaz. Philip commissions him to draw up a secret memorandum that is to serve as basis for a definition of the crown's position on a new agreement, or covenant, to serve as a starting point for reestablishing relations with the Holy See. In Macanaz's project, there are such eloquent clauses as this: The Church shall spend in Spain, and only in Spain, the sums collected in Spain. A hard blow for papal finances.

Macanaz's life explains his political principles. He began his public career with the reconstruction of Játiva. The old city had been left in ruins after one of the fiercest battles against the Carlistas. Philip's victorious armies commissioned Macanaz to reconstruct it. Tireless, enterprising, eager for progress and furiously opposed to the Carlistas, he carried out the work in a manner worthy of the most outstanding forerunner of enlightened despotism: he broke the chains of mortmain, made expropriations, imposed contributions from clergymen involved in the war against King Philip. He did everything he had set out to do and changed Játiva's name: he called the city San Felipe.

The nuncio, who had had enough by that time, bore a personal grudge against Macanaz anyway, for Macanaz had blocked his way when he had tried to obtain a very lucrative canonship in the Cathedral of Toledo. Even though the work on the concordat entrusted by the king to Macanaz had been secret, the nuncio discovered it, and, through him, the information made its way to the Inquisition. If Macanaz managed to escape, it was only through miraculous means. Disguised, he crossed the border; when he arrived in Paris, he received all the honors of a political refugee. At first, King Philip continued to distinguish him with his favor. The paper war raged furiously. Under pressure of the nuncio, who was also living in Paris, the Inquisition condemned Macanaz's propositions as scandalous, presumptuous, erroneous, sacrilegious, insulting to the Sacred Council of the Holy See, schismatic and heretical. . . . The nuncio had the accusation nailed to all the church doors in Paris, Versailles, and Neuilly. Philip took up his minister's defense and ordered the Inquisition to revoke the edict and the nuncio to renounce his title as general inquisitor. Unfortunately for Macanaz, the king's rigor wilted when, having lost his first wife, he married Elizabeth Farnese. But if the coming of Elizabeth eclipsed Macanaz's star, it was not forever. After some years, old and weary, Macanaz was able to return to his homeland. There he died. But the king's cause found new defenders under Charles III. Not everything was lost. A Peruvian was going to take up the flag.[4]

Don Pablo de Olavide's Moment

Like Jovellanos, Floridablanca, Campomanes, or Aranda, a certain man from Lima, Pablo de Olavide, was destined to be one of the authors of the great Spanish revolutionary adventure. He left America for the Peninsula thanks to an earthquake. On October 28, 1746, Lima was left in ruins. The viceroy selected a small group of men—the best he had—to undertake the reconstruction. At the head was Louis Godin, a Frenchman who had worked with La

Condamine. After his scientific work in Quito, he was teaching mathematics at San Marcos University. Among those who accompanied the commission was a brilliant young man from the Corte de Cuentas: Pablo de Olavide, twenty-two years old. When the earthquake's debris was removed, silver bowls were found—and jewels and chests full of gold coins that no longer belonged to anyone. Whole families had perished. From such treasures was created the main fund for reconstruction. Not only were entire blocks rebuilt; enough money remained to build a church and a theater. But doubts arose regarding the honesty of those who were in charge of the monies, and it was easy to spread rumors. These were, you will recall, the corrupt times that had elicited the accusations of Jorge Juan and Antonio de Ulloa. Malcontents fixed their eyes on young Olavide, who was becoming wealthier as the work of building progressed. The first trial came.

Diderot, in his biography of the Peruvian, says that the trial in Lima originated from the fact that Olavide had built a theater and had liberal ideas. "The clergy disapproved of the building, and it was spoken of as if it were a crime. *Hinc prima mali labis* . . . It was easy for Father Ravago, a Jesuit priest, and for his colleagues to present Don Pablo as a man of no religion, a godless knave who preferred to build a church and a theater to building two churches. Conduct typical of a scoundrel fit for the worst punishment! For that reason was Don Pablo called to Madrid to account for his conduct." In his biography, Diderot used facts provided to him by a friend of Don Pablo, Manuel Gijón, also Peruvian.

In order to have a better idea of the trial, we must follow another version, documented in the best and most recent book on the subject: *Pablo de Olavide ou l'Afrancesado,* by Marcelin Defourneaux. It happened that the young man, apart from what he had done officially, had taken advantage of the fact that his father's house was destroyed by the quake, and that presumably the whole family had perished under the ruins, to refuse acknowledgment of the debts contracted by the "deceased." He sold the family merchandise, and started to put the capital to work. The news got to Spain; the creditors went to the law. The facts were notorious and the official position of the accused made the charges against him all the more serious. The court in Lima decided at a certain point in the investigation to transfer the matter to Madrid, so Don Pablo went to Madrid. The sentence was fatal. Only a royal providence could modify it, and God knows how Don Pablo went about obtaining it; all the same of course his property was confiscated and he was banished from Lima. . . . Olavide's newest biographer was able to discover a second part to this story: Olavide's father had not died in the earthquake. Surreptitiously, he had escaped to Spain, where he established a new home.

Don Pablo, himself now free, began a new life with twice the ambition and spirit. He married a very rich widow—Isabel de los Ríos—and it was easy to buy himself the title of Knight of Saint James in order to better his social standing. Now a distinguished *señor* who was on familiar terms with the nobility, he traveled to Italy and France to refresh and enrich his culture. During the eight days that he spent in Ferney, he was Voltaire's guest. Voltaire found this new American quite amazing: "Ah, if Spain had forty men like Olavide." In Paris, Olavide opened a literary salon. The great ones of the *Encyclopedia* visited him, and were surprised at the revolutionary principles that, if they judged by Olavide, were ripening in the New World. And the wealthy knight from Lima began to put together a library that was soon the best-stocked in Spain.

When Olavide returned to Spain—a man of most ingenious resources—he managed to cross the border *with his whole library*! He carried with him the Pope's dispensation that permitted him to read all that he had. The boxes were not examined. His new Madrid salon brought together the cream of Charles III's Enlightenment: Campomanes, Floridablanca, Jovellanos, Aranda. The Spanish *Encyclopedia*! If the story of the theater in Lima had been only an invented one—if, in fact, the city had been reconstructed by someone else—the story of the Madrid stage was something else. Olavide himself translated Racine, Regnard, Lemierre, Du Bellay, Voltaire. . . . He had them performed, and the duchess of Huesca, a great enthusiast at Olavide's literary gatherings, played the leading roles.

Gracia, Olavide's half sister or niece, was a second hostess. Lively and cultivated, she translated Mme. Graffigny's *Pauline*. Mme. Graffigny and Voltaire were compulsory presences in Olavide's literary circle because of their Peruvianism. *Alzire,* Voltaire's Peruvian work, was translated by Olavide; and Mme. Graffigny's *Lettres Péruviennes* circulated all over Europe, as did her novel *La Péruvienne*.

Olavide was also a poet and a musician, and he translated comedies that were presented in his own personal theater: *Ninette à la Cour* by Duni, *Le Peintre Amoureux de Son Modèle* by Grétry. But his real theater was another: the political drama of the Spanish reform. Poets and essayists frequented his house, and so did the ministers of the Enlightenment, who were making revolutionary plans. Would they be pliant followers of the French example? Or would they keep to the democratic tradition of the Spanish commons? Campomanes had just published his *Tratado de la Regalía de Amortización,* declaring that the state had the right to limit ecclesiastical profits on mortmains. Confessors were persuading the dying to will their estates to religious communities. Olavide's radical position on this and other issues fixed Europe's attention on Spain. Defourneaux, in his biography of Olavide, relates the following: "Casanova—who in 1768 met Campomanes and 'the famous Olavide' at a dinner in the Venetian Embassy (where the Abbot Beliardi and the French commercial attaché were also present)—praises both men when he writes: 'I was delighted to meet Campomanes and Olavide, intellectuals of a type that is rarely found in Spain. Without being exactly what we may call erudites, they are above religious prejudices, because they not only are not afraid to ridicule them in public but work openly to destroy them.' "

Social Reform

Olavide inserts himself in the government as a consequence of what came to be known as the Esquilache uprising. The immediate causes of this famous riot make no sense unless one relates them to earlier ones that led its intellectual authors to rebel. The people demanded the expulsion of a foreign minister—the Italian Squillace—because he had forbidden the use of long capes and wide-brimmed hats, which vagrants and suspicious persons wore in order to hide their countenances and carry arms. The explosion of protests was so clamorous that Charles III had no other alternative than to sacrifice his minister. But since the problem of cloaked vagrants was at the root of Squillace's ordinance, the matter had to be treated in depth, by attacking vagrancy itself. Aranda and Campomanes transformed the former royal residence at San Fernando—two leagues from Madrid—into an institution where tramps were given shelter and useful work. The idea must have been suggested and studied at Olavide's literary salon; he was chosen to direct the project. Everything was carried out with the incredible speed typical of Olavide's enterprises. His sparkling imagination, his devotion, his resourcefulness surpassed every expectation. It was fabulous to see this American setting up looms, creating a needle factory, organizing all kinds of workshops. Until then, Spain had been importing needles. Now the needles from San Fernando not only supplied local demand but were exported to America. Punishments, always an indispensable feature of such institutions, were gradually replaced by all sorts of incentives to encourage the workers. The house had a capacity of three hundred. This was extended to a thousand. Olavide also founded a hospital for women stricken with the "French disease." He changed the primitive and rudimentary methods that were then used in Spain for the treatment of that illness, hired specialists who had modern, scientific training. Thus, the theoretical movement of an enlightened revolution was becoming a practical policy, animated by the Peruvian's ingenuity.

Basically, these developments fell somewhere between the bourgeois revolution, which was beginning to be consolidated in France, and that older movement whose roots went much deeper, down to the workers' guilds, where the traditional Spanish spirit still flourished. Reforms had to be made, yes, but with representatives from the commons, in the Spanish manner. When the moment of decision came, Campomanes and Aranda themselves found that if they reestablished the system of deputies and attorneys to represent the commons, they would be building a bridge to link the popular democracy to the Enlightenment's reforms. Once agreement was reached, who was to represent the commons? The decision belonged to themselves only. The votes were divided between the Duke of Frías and Pablo de Olavide, nearly equally between them. At the beginning, the votes favored Frías, who did not accept. Olavide was elected. Now he would be the arbitrator, at the most critical moment of Charles III's reign. With sleepless enthusiasm, he devoted himself to making a study of the supply system for the towns and the capital city.

University Reform

Politics were becoming more and more complicated. Charles III exiled the general inquisitor for publishing an apostolic brief without the king's prior authorization. He expelled the Jesuits from Spain and the colonies. Their university buildings were left vacant. For some time already, they had been criticized for their plans of study, denounced as inefficient and backward. It was time to make immediate changes that would issue in a new era. Olavide was a part of all this, acting directly or giving advice. He had brought books from France in which such problems were discussed. In Spain, Benito Feijóo y Montenegro had exposed similar criticisms, and in America they were not new either, for such celebrities as Mutis and the viceroy Archbishop Caballero y Góngora of New Granada had brought them over. In Mexico, Lima, Havana, Chuquisaca, Santiago de Chile, and Córdoba in Argentina, the same problems were being discussed. Olavide was well aware of it all. New plans of study had begun to be elaborated everywhere as soon as the Jesuits had left. And in Spain, who was the person to do this? Olavide.

Actually, Olavide's plan for Seville—which was to serve as a model for Salamanca and Valladolid—was even more radical than reforms envisioned by the Creoles and Spaniards in America. He believed that the university had to be a government institution. Only this way would it avoid domination by the Thomists, Jansenists, or Suarists. His idea was to secularize higher education, orienting it as a public service.

Let us admit that, in the present condition of Spanish letters, palliatives are insufficient. It is not with a poultice but with cauteries that one attacks gangrene. It would be useless to suppress certain subjects and substitute others for them; to do away with the system of alternability (of the different schools); to suppress a body and replace it with the university; to give new form to examinations; to extirpate certain abuses committed in awarding grades. These remedies would prevent some inconveniences, but they would not put an end to the partisan spirit and the Scholastic spirit, the division between the various schools, the predomination of some bodies over others, the perversion of reasoning, the futility of the subjects and all the vices that infest schools and which cannot be exterminated if a reform does not uproot them completely, changing the form and the methods of study and creating what we could call new universities and schools, based on principles opposed to those that prevail today [quoted in Defourneaux, *Pablo de Olavide*].

What would be the method? Planning sessions revealed it. It had been first indicated in approaches like the one described more than a hundred years before in the *Discourse on Method*, still banned by the Spanish reaction. This great revolution, Olavide says, is the work of just one man, Descartes, who simply abandoned Aristotelian Scholasticism, substituting for it a geometric method.

Olavide did not want a university for the poor or for the clergy. "If a plowman or the craftsman goes to the the university," he said, "he will only upset the economic balance. Sons are more useful to society if they follow their parents' professions." And, referring to clergymen, "If the university is to be a public establishment, instituted by the government to form men destined to serve the state, it is not founded for priests, who should rather withdraw in holy solitude, where they prepare for meditation." As Defourneaux observes, the underlying reason prompting him to leave out the clergy was a somewhat different one: he wished to free the university from persons whose formation would be an obstacle for a reform that intended actually to wipe out the Scholastic system.

Land Reform

If university reform was of vital importance, so was land reform. Campomanes promotes its study in a survey he addresses to the provincial intendant, where the words "land reform" make their appearance for the very first time. The circumstances were typically Spanish. The privileged caste of older sons and the Church had monopolized the land, creating a situation by that time anachronistic, but in Spain and her colonies problematic in quite a real way. On that problem, who could give a better opinion than Olavide? He had just taken charge of the most ambitious agrarian project in Spain, one that aroused admiration in the rest of Europe: the colonization of Sierra Morena. This, in fact, was Olavide's personal creation. There, in open strife against the big landowners, he broke up properties as vast as they were uncultivated; distributed plots of fifty *fanegadas* (about eighty acres) each; made villages; introduced new crops; created the city of Carolina (in honor of Charles III); opened roads, schools, workshops. Foreign visitors were filled with enthusiasm. Even today, his model is worth studying.

The report on land reform that Olavide addressed to Campomanes is considered one of the best he ever received. It does not have the literary brilliance of Jovellanos, but it is a product of personal experience. We may still read his words today and find in them an admirable lesson: "My intention is to propose laws that, producing the desired effect in themselves and without violence . . . will place the land in many hands which will apply themselves to making it produce, with the stimulus that personal interest creates, establishing settlers in such a way that they will become fond of the land, supplying it with means of bettering and enriching it, developing cattle-raising, the cultivation of trees and every type of agriculture."

The Inquisition Calls a Halt

But even a reformer like Olavide—one who defied clergymen, *latifundistas,* and powerful groups of every description—was embarking on hazardous enterprises even if he seemed to have the king himself on his side. Craftily, cautiously, with perseverance and no little perversity, the Inquisition began to spin its web. Through the shadowy labyrinths of the Holy Office, one by one, eighty witnesses came and went, and were wrung dry of whatever might help to trap the American. He spent two years in prison, strictly isolated. The sentence was known beforehand, and his friends, no matter how powerful, kept quiet out of fear. No trial could produce a greater shock at that moment. Olavide was the king's right arm and was covering the crown with glory. The Inquisition nearly summoned the courage necessary to turn him over to the secular arm of the law and have him roasted in a bonfire. That fate he narrowly escaped; he was nevertheless humiliated, green candle in hand, having to wear the penitential garment of disgrace. He was declared heretic, infamous, a decayed member of the Faith. Listening to the torrent of vituperations, Olavide collapsed in a dead faint. The marvelous dreams of a naive reformer fell to the ground with him, at the very moment in which they had seemed to become a part of the new Spanish—and American—reality.

The man whose career was smashed by the Inquisition had been about to become a reformer for the whole empire. The American territory, always present in his visions, had not been far from the scope of his projects. It was more than a matter of sending to America needles fashioned in Spain or adapting Peruvian trees to the Spanish climate; he had also planned to send a large quantity of German immigrants, as he had done for Sierra Morena—that audacious plan was the real cause of his misfortune. Olavide thought that if he transplanted Germans to mix with the population in Sierra Morena—which, in fact, he did; it became one-third Germans and two-thirds Spaniards—he could give greater impetus to the productivity of a population that had remained isolated and was consequently unfamiliar with European work systems. He believed that the same thing had to be done in America. When Miranda, then twenty-eight years old, visited the Sierra Morena colony, he was admirably impressed, proud that a fellow American should be able to carry out such a remarkable enterprise. "Ten years ago," he writes in his diary, "there was nothing here but weeds and brambles. There was not an acre of wheat. . . . Olavide is an extraordinary man. . . . He has cleared the land, made it into cultivated fields, opened roads and built towns . . . and these deserts of Sierra Morena, former refuge of bandits, have been transformed into the most pleasant spot on the way from Cádiz to Madrid. He has established factories and manufactures. The ceramics alone provide an entire commerce, and the products are as good as those of Seville. The woolens and the needles are equally good. It is hard to find something as orderly or with a better economic base than this colony." The years passed. Olavide had taken refuge in France; and when Miranda, in London, began to set up his revolutionary organization for the independence of America, his eyes turned to "old Olavide" and he began to exchange letters with him.

The sentence of the Inquisition had condemned Olavide to perpetual exile, twenty leagues away from Madrid, Lima, or Sierra Morena; and eight years of confinement in a monastery under the guardianship of a director of conscience who—every day—was to teach him the doctrine and norms of the Catholic Church, and make him go to Confession, hear Mass, say the Rosary, keep fast on Fridays and read the works of Friar Luis de Granada. . . . Those who think they invented brainwashing have done nothing new.

The scandal was universal. From Voltaire's house to Catherine of Russia's palace, passing though the salons of the Encyclopedists, all Europe flared with indignant protest. Olavide became the symbol of the struggle in Spain between the Dark Ages and the Enlightenment. Meanwhile, with Benedictine patience, Olavide was preparing his escape. First he managed to change prisons a few times, and finally he was allowed to go on a health cure—which he very much needed—to a spa quite close to the border. These were humanitarian measures that could not be denied to one who still counted on the king's gratitude, and whose friends, even if they kept quiet, were not by their silence less evident. When Olavide escaped to France, there was a sigh of relief throughout enlightened Europe.

Among those who celebrated Olavide the most was Diderot. One may see this in the biography he wrote in his praise. Olavide's fame extended across the whole European continent. There are vivid testimonies of the appreciation the Germans had for him.[5]

The Encyclopedia *Under the Main Altar*

The story of the walling up of the *Encyclopedia* is a filmlike episode that serves to illustrate relations between Diderot and Pablo de Olavide. We owe the discovery to Jean de Booy,[6] and it begins with the finding of a letter in The Hague written by Hemsterhuis—the "Dutch Socrates"—to Princess Galitsin, the wife of Catherine of Russia's ambassador to the Netherlands. Prince Galitsin had traveled to Paris to see about buying Diderot's library for Catherine, and Diderot, when he was on his way to visit the empress, had been his guest in The Hague. This business and those friendships explain the letter to the princess.

Hemsterhuis had made acquaintance with a Peruvian, Miguel Gijón, Olavide's closest friend and collaborator in Spain. It was through him that he learned what had happened to Olavide's splendid library, or to that part, quite a considerable one, that had been able to slip out of the Inquisition's clutches. It had been covered with sheets of lead, packed in wooden chests, and buried. This way it was ready to escape the barbarians until the greatness of the Age of Reason was reestablished. At such a moment, it would be there once more to serve whoever wished to learn from it and to renew the philosophy of liberty. And what was more, said the Dutch

Socrates to the princess, he had learned from Gijón that, also under lead and wood, immured under the main altar of a Spanish church, Olavide had hidden a complete edition of the *Encyclopedia:* seventeen volumes of text and four of engravings.

Booy accompanies these facts with a text from Diderot, as it appeared under the word *"Encyclopédie"*:

> The most glorious moment for a work of this nature would be that which would follow immediately upon a great revolution which had suspended the progress of the sciences, interrupted the work of the arts, and submerged in darkness a part of our hemisphere. Who could ever measure the debt of gratitude of the generation following those turbulent times for those who had foreseen the catastrophe and deposited the knowledge of the past centuries in a safe place! It would be then (and I say it without vanity, for our *Encyclopedia* will never attain the perfection that merits such honors), it will be then that, together with this great work, there would be mention of the monarch under whom it was compiled, of the minister to whom it was dedicated, of the great ones who favored its execution, of the authors who consecrated themselves to writing it, of the scholars who lent their contributions.

In which Spanish church might today's archaeologists find the walled-in *Encyclopedia?* Probably in the church of Carolina, built by Olavide himself. It would be a wonderful thing to explore and verify just how a Peruvian—author of the best accomplishments of the eighteenth-century Spanish revolution—gave a most moving demonstration of loyalty to Diderot and of devotion to those who, along with him, participated in creating the loftiest product of the Age of Reason.

The Courts of Cádiz

In effect, the Spanish reaction did arrive, and it tried to erase from the nation's memory everything that had been noble and splendid about the Enlightened Monarchy. Several years passed before the revolutionary impetus was renewed in the Courts of Cádiz. The Napoleonic invasion is symbolized in all our minds by one image: Goya's *Shootings of the Third of May*. The monarchy had lost all its greatness. In Bayonne, Napoleon turned the hapless kings into rag puppets and spoke about independence to the envoys from the American colonies. But in Madrid the people repulsed the invader with heroic valor. America joined in the clamor of wounded dignity. In La Paz, Buenos Aires, Quito, Caracas, Santa Fe, Mexico, Havana—indignation was shared and solidarity demonstrations organized. Napoleon, who had declared himself in favor of American independence,[7] was surprised to find out that, yes, the Americans did want independence: but they wanted *total* independence. No question of falling under Napoleon's shadow. The minister he sent to Buenos Aires to discuss the matter was not well received and ended up in jail.

The free Courts of Cádiz were the first assemblies in the world to have appointed representatives from the two hemispheres. In the notice of the meeting, it was clear that the inhabitants of the New World had the right to be represented. The Portuguese monarchs had understood that America was a land of freedom—they were more shrewd and cunning than those of Spain—and sought refuge in Rio de Janeiro to escape the claws of the Napoleonic eagle. For humiliated Europe, the New World was a reserved haven. Napoleon, Lisbon, Cádiz, all turn their eyes to America; and America speaks, first in Bayonne, then in Cádiz. And naturally at Don Pablo's royal court . . . in Rio de Janeiro.

When the Courts of Cádiz were installed, who was their Mirabeau? Who was the orator whom the people applauded with frenzy? Who spoke in the most lucid way about long-ignored liberties sought for centuries and now about to be obtained, thanks to a revolutionary awakening? It was a man from Quito, José Mejía Lequerica. By pure coincidence, he was representing New Granada in Cádiz. The day before, no one had known anything about him; but he became the central figure from the moment that the meetings began, and his name is still remembered in Spain. In the center of Madrid there is a street, Mejía Lequerica, where one of the largest centers of Hispanic culture is located. Who was Mejía Lequerica?

He was born in Quito. He father was a lawyer from the Royal Court of Appeals—José Mejía del Valle—and his mother a distinguished lady, Joaquina Lequerica . . . who was not exactly his wife. The boy was able to make his way through school because of his vivacious nature and astonishing talent. At twenty-one, he won a contest that made him professor of Latin; two years later, he won a more substantial reward: the hand of Doña Manuela Santa Cruz y Espejo. This young lady's fortune was not remarkable in terms of money, but she had something better: her brother was the famous Eugenio Espejo, forerunner of Ecuadorian independence, and she had his library. At twenty-five, Mejía Lequerica won (despite opposition) a professorship in philosophy at the San Luis seminary school. The key position. His predecessor had already initiated the young students in the theories of Copernicus, Kepler, Galileo. With Miguel Antonio Rodríguez, in fact, the earth in Quito had begun to turn about the sun. Following in his footsteps, Mejía Lequerica applied the Cartesian method. It was what Don Pablo de Olavide had done in Spain years before. The Dominican friars declared their disapproval of such heresies and kept the audacious professor from studying theology, arguing that he could not do so because he was married. No vow of chastity, no theology . . . His professorship was taken away from him. Five years later, he was refused the right to be received as a lawyer. An old ordinance was dug up, which stated that illegitimate sons could not become lawyers. What follows in Mejía Lequerica's life is understandable—in view of these setbacks. Quito was hell for him. He had to try his fortune in Spain. When he arrived in Madrid, Spain was falling to pieces. He joined the people in the May insurrection. When they were defeated, he was forced to flee. It took him forty-five days to go from Madrid to Cádiz, on foot, dressed as a coal man. . . . But he arrived finally: the meeting of the Courts was being prepared. . . . Philip L. Astuto, the most recent authority on Mejía Lequerica, whom we have followed in these pages, tells us: "The word 'Courts' acquired a magic force. The people believed that the ancient institution could restore representative government in Spain, that it would be the panacea for all the evils that Spain had been suffering for centuries. . . . In his speeches and writings, Mejía Lequerica tried to establish the basis for a new society founded on a new instrument of government. His implicit faith in the constitutional government, coupled with his intense desire to educate and protect the Americans, remains as a tribute to this archetype of the Enlightenment."

Mejía Lequerica entered the Courts by a sheer miracle. The delegation from the other side of the Atlantic did not arrive on time, and had to be replaced by an American who happened to be in Cádiz at that moment. Mejía Lequerica was named a substitute for the representative from New Granada. The miserable coal man who had arrived from Madrid revealed himself as the rebellious and persecuted professor from the University of Quito. From the beginning, Mejía becomes the leader of the Americans. The people idolize him.[8] The American representation, he could see, did not correspond to the basic equality that should have been the foundation for a democratic assembly. If the Peninsula had seventy-five representatives, why thirty for all of America? Equality was being discussed for the first time, and there the first step was, Mejía warned, a false one. America would become independent if the Peninsulars insisted on maintaining such a disproportion. Something like this had already happened in North America. . . . All over the New World a new generation was stirring, self-confident, well informed about its rights. This was the meaning of the uprisings in La Paz, Quito, Caracas, Santa Fe, Mexico, not to mention the large number of towns and minor cities that had already seen or echoed such movements. There was still time to formulate a just plan to prevent fatal dismemberment.[9]

The splendid thing about Mejía Lequerica's speeches was the sensation they produced in Cádiz, a city closely connected with American affairs. His words expressed no ideals that were not shared by the Spaniards of this city. What he possessed was the eloquence to proclaim them. His valiant affirmations reflected the universal spirit of revolution; and, since they came from America, they showed how the revolutionary deposit, the first and oldest in the modern world, was being formed in the other hemisphere. From Santa Fe de Bogotá, messages charged with significance were sent to him. Extremely eloquent were the "Reflections of an Impartial American to the Deputy from the New Kingdom of Granada," written by Ignacio de Herrera, or the report from the Santa Fe Municipal Council to the Central Assembly of Spain, written by Camilo Torres and known as *Memorial de Agravios (Memorial of Offenses)*. There were other documents, similar to these, expressing the same concerns.

After the debates on equal representation were over, Mejía continued to imprint American philosophy on everything that was discussed in Cádiz. He made the most assertive defense of freedom of speech and of the press and of racial equality, and he was the most eloquent denouncer of the Inquisition, so much so that he persuaded the Courts to abolish it.[10] When the great assembly was about to close, Mejía Lequerica died unexpectedly. Don Joaquín Olmeda, another Ecuadorian, paid him the last tribute.

The echo of his speeches remained as the best testimony of that revolution, already a century old. The Spanish Enlightenment extends from Macanaz to Cádiz, passing through the era of Pablo de Olavide, Campomanes, and Jovellanos. It does not matter that so many episodes have been followed by a violent reaction, a fanatic absolutism. The internal fire has not been extinguished.

If the names of Olavide or Mejía Lequerica stand out as the most important, their salience should not imply that theirs are the only names to recall. In those same Cádiz Courts, the thirty Americans carried more weight than is usually imagined; and it is an eloquent fact that among those Americans participated some of native blood—like the Inca Yupanqui, who "in the midst of his historical oppressors expressed the complaints and desires of his Indian brothers."[11] Of the thirty-seven presidents of the Courts, twenty-seven were Spanish and ten were Americans.

It was the first time that the question of slavery was brought before an official assembly. The canon Antonio Larrazábal, from Guatemala, one of the presidents of the Courts, asked that the six hundred blacks of that governorship be declared free, and José Miguel Guridi of Tlaxcala counted among his greatest triumphs in the Courts his passage of a new law banning the purchase and sale of black slaves and proclaiming the liberty of their newly born.

So if there was a color that tinted the Spanish revolution of the eighteenth century, it was that of America, of those Americans who in Cádiz proposed at the same time reforms for Spain and independence for the New World.

Under pressure from the American deputies, the Courts banned the abuses that were inflicted on the Indians, ordered their protectors to comply with their sacred duty of defending the aborigines' personal liberty and the priests in America to read from the pulpit, for three consecutive days, the corresponding decree. A pronouncement was made in favor of what thirty years earlier the commons of El Socorro had demanded: "That the natives and inhabitants of America may plant and cultivate all that nature and their skill provide for them in those climates, and in the same way manufacture and crafts in all their extension be promoted. That the Americans, Indians, or Spaniards, and the children of both groups, have the same option as the European Spaniards for every kind of employment and office, whether at court or in any other place of the realm, be they clergymen, statesmen, or military." The regency had ordered that the tribute that the Indians in Mexico had to pay be abolished. When the decree was read in the Courts, it was disposed that "the grace hereby expressed be extended to the Indians and the castes of the other American provinces." It was as if the colonial world had begun with a heave to move in another direction.

9

•

The Italian
Risorgimento

Poland, Italy . . .

The ideas of independence, while flourishing in America, produced contradictory results in Europe. Because of these ideas, England, Spain, France, and Portugal lost their colonies and because of them, the Poles and Italians rose up to fight for their own emancipation. Poland and Italy were two typical examples of nations occupied by their neighbors. Their dream of liberation was centuries old, fused into the essence of their history.

From time to time, Poland has been the victim of predatory actions by Russia, Prussia, or Austria, whose thirsts for expansion made them uncomfortable neighbors. Today's Russian intervention in Poland is but a continuation of what occurred under the czars. The overwhelmingly greater power of these neighboring empires compounds Poland's feelings for unity with a passionate spirit of independence, which is evident despite the successive partitions Poland has endured.

Italy's case is more complex. The way for invaders was prepared internally by the country's historical fragmentation and the Church's presence as sovereign power. Paradoxically, the Vatican ruled not by uniting the Italian peoples but by dividing, just as Machiavelli had advised. The Papal States developed into a vast territory that, at the time of the Cateau-Cambrésis peace treaty, in 1559, spread from the Adriatic to the Tyrrhenian seas, cutting the peninsula in half. The political fragmentation of Italy was impressive. There were two kingdoms—one was Naples, the other Sicily (Sicily was already under Spanish domination, as Naples eventually would be). There were also some republics—Genoa, Venice, Lucca, San Merino, but independence in these republics had always been fragile. And, finally, there were duchies: Savoy, Milan, Florence, Ferrara, Parma, Modena . . . When Machiavelli saw Aragon and Castile unite under the Catholic monarchs, he hailed Ferdinand's feat as a work of genius and made him the model for his *Prince*. The great paradox in Machiavelli's life is in its idealism. Everything in his theory sprang from an effort to unite Italy and obtain her independence from foreign powers.

This divided Italy became so vulnerable that, in 1799, France occupied Tuscany and Corsica and administered Piedmont, while Austria ruled Venice. The famous kingdom of Naples depended on the ever-changing fortunes of France and Spain. From 1806 to 1814, Naples's throne, which had once belonged to the Spanish Bourbons, was successively occupied by Joseph Bonaparte and Joachim Murat. . . . The war between France and Austria turned Italy into one of their many battlefields. Having defeated the Austrians, France annexed Savoy, Nice, and Tenda. Garibaldi, we know, could never resign himself to the fact that the French held Nice. Pius VI was forced to sign the armistice imposed on him by circumstances, with the French in possession, as they were, of Ferrara, Bologna, Ravenna, Imola, and Florence.

"Independence," the liberating word of modern times, American in its origin, took on real significance under such circumstances, in Italy as in Poland. The initial source of inspiration was the revolution of the English colonies; then came those of Spain and Portugal . . . not to mention Haiti. To learn the lesson of independence it was necessary to go to America, to *be* there, taking part in the liberation movements from the first day. The revolution captivated romantic Encyclopedists, adventurers from every nation. We can imagine its sweep: legions of Frenchmen and Englishmen join the struggle in the United States or in Venezuela. Jesuits and Freemasons (God makes them, the devil flocks them together) work all over Europe for the American ideals. But those who absorb the essence of the new philosophy most deeply are the Poles. Two of the greatest generals who will make history in two worlds are Kasimir Pulaski and Thaddeus Kosciuszko. They begin their careers with the United States War of Independence; and when they return home, it is to unleash the torrent of their fabulous experiences across the Atlantic.

The oath that Kosciuszko takes in the marketplace in Krakow on March 24, 1794, marks one of the glowing hours of Poland's noblest history. The veteran of American wars comes back to devote himself to the struggle against the Russian and Prussian empires, whose yoke has been more oppressive and humiliating for the Poles than the English domination had been for the North Americans. The general offers to consecrate his life to the fight for his country's freedom, integrity, and independence. Great Polish painters have recorded the greatest moments of those days in monumental canvases that dominate the national art museums: Kosciuszko's oath, painted by Stachowicz; Kosciuszko in Raclawice, by Jan Matejko . . .

So in 1794, for the first time, all the social classes in the country meet in Krakow, not excluding the peasants, whose only weapons are their scythes. The American Revolution began the same way. In the United States, farmer Minutemen made up the vanguard. When the British army set out to quell the rebellion, a silversmith, seeing the lantern that the man in charge of giving the alarm was swinging from an old church belfry, galloped away to arouse the insurgents. They ambushed the enemy troops, stopped them with stones. In Lexington, the authorities ordered the people assembled on the town square—the Minutemen—to disperse. The populace disregarded the order. And "the shot heard round the world" was fired. On March 24, 1794, it is heard in Krakow . . . Warsaw is liberated by a popular movement led by a shoemaker: Kilinski. American history was repeating itself in Poland. Long before France created a revolutionary constitution, Poland had hers, on May 3, 1791. It was the second in the world. In it, the Philadelphian inspiration was clearly visible.

The Italian movements that finally obtained union and independence name Giuseppe Mazzini as their first apostle. The secret society that he founded in 1831, Young Italy, was destined to unite the revolutionaries in the same way that the Masonic lodges in the United States had brought the patriots together there. George Washington had been Venerable Master of the Alexandria Lodge, and twenty-nine of his generals were Freemasons, as was Lafayette, as were Bolívar, San Martín, and O'Higgins in the south. The Young Italy Federation proposed to unify the initiated and to consecrate their thoughts and actions to the great enterprise of establishing Italy as a nation of free and equal citizens, a nation united, independent, and sovereign. Such a program had much more to do with the American Revolution than with the one in France. The American Revolution implied, first, emancipation from foreign invaders. Mazzini draws a distinction between the revolution he is planning and the French Revolution: "Liberty, far from being oppressed by the revolution, is born out of the revolution itself."[1] As Thomas Paine and Miranda had already pointed out, the French Revolution had fallen into the hands of terror and masked injustice, becoming a mockery of legal authority and popular will. Contradictions and confusion dragged down the republic in France and made way for the consulate, the empire, the restoration of the Bourbons. Differently inspired, the republics in America managed to endure and had united of their own free will as independent states. Mazzini's battle cry found an immediate echo across the whole of Liguria, and in Livorno, Tuscany, the Marches, Umbria, Piedmont. . . . It was like the bell that had pealed in Philadelphia.

In the end, Mazzini directed his program from England, for it was possible to pull the threads from there, as an exile: to do it from Italy would have been more than foolhardy, simply useless.

Soon there were Young Italy lodges all over the world, and especially in America. They sprang up in New York and Boston, in Rio de Janeiro, Montevideo, Buenos Aires. In New York, a newspaper, *The Italian*, was published—the same as in Rio. The merchant marine served as the conduit.

Once the Austrians were driven out of Italy, once liberation was complete and a constitution was adopted, the problem was how to go about uniting the country. The two solutions that Mazzini had in mind were the constitutions of Switzerland and the United States. He decided on the Swiss; the North American federation had never been faced with the problems of bringing together kingdoms, republics, and duchies with long historic traditions. In Italy, a weak federal government would prove ineffective. Mazzini had to consider age-old political habits and had to mobilize Italians scattered throughout the world. He was twenty years ahead of Karl Marx when he proposed an International League in 1847.

Garibaldi, a South American

Giuseppe Garibaldi, bearded and red-shirted, romantic and reckless, theatrical and fabulous, embodies the spirit of the Italian rebellion without Mazzini's mysteries, without Count Cavour's calculating reserve. His is the kind of revolution that the common people can feel as their own, the kind that survives. It is unleashed and genial passion. Half madman, half poet, novelist even, absurd, fighting against logic, he becomes the most popular man, not in Italy, but in the world. The Risorgimento takes on his embattled, adventuresome air. He is South American all over. When an Argentine or an Uruguayan visits Italy, he is surprised to discover that every town or city, large or small, has a square with the statue of a gaucho, straight out of the pampa, complete with poncho, scarf, loose gaucho trousers: Garibaldi. He is everywhere, looking as if he had stepped out of the pages of *Martín Fierro* or *Don Segundo Sombra* to be cast in bronze by the Italians. On the Gianicolo, overlooking Rome, there are two equestrian statues: one is Garibaldi, who returned from America with the gold-hilted sword that the Italians had sent him, the other, Anita Garibaldi, the Brazilian girl who was to remain with him till death overtook her in the pine grove of Ravenna.

The young Garibaldi who had only a fleeting contact with Mazzini's revolution in 1834, left Genoa in defeat, disguised as a peasant, and fled to Marseilles. "A few days later," he wrote, "I read my name in a newspaper for the first time. It was the death penalty which had been decreed for me, and *Il Popolo Sovrano* published the news." Garibaldi's imagination saw only one land, a very distant one, opening before him, inviting him to continue from there to prepare a hardier revolution with greater foresight: the land was America, South America. (His brother was already in North America.) Garibaldi arrived in Rio de Janeiro and immediately set up his Young Italy lodge.[2] The port teemed with Italians. They, and the captains of the Italian ships, and all the sailors, believed in the Risorgimento. So did the South Americans. That same year, while Garibaldi was organizing his Young Italy in Rio, an Argentine, Esteban Echeverría, who had been following Mazzini's revolutionary work in Europe, arrived in Buenos Aires to found a secret society, La Asociación de Mayo, a Creole version of Young Italy. In 1840, Echeverría arrived in Montevideo, fleeing from Rosas's dictatorship; and so did Garibaldi, after four years of campaigning in Brazil. The two were fighting for the same cause, an Italian and South American cause, whose threefold theme was universal: liberty, independence, republic.

In the south of Brazil, a republican war of liberation had been declared against the Portuguese emperor, Dom Pedro (Pedro was then eleven years old). The Italians were involved in every existing insurrection. Young Italy, a clandestine cell in the land of its birth, blossomed under the tropical sun; what in Italy was still a theory was in South America a reality. The Bolognese Tito Livio Zanbeccari had become the soul of the separatist movement in Rio Grande do Sul. In Rio de Janeiro, young Garibaldi was working in a grocery store and dreaming of revolution, when he learned that the hero Zanbeccari was in prison. He wrote at once to Bento Gonzalvez, who was head of the republican government of Rio Grande do Sul, asking him for letters of marque and reprisal before he left for Montevideo. He had written Mazzini, asking for the same, but had received no answer. With Gonzalvez's edict, he set sail for Montevideo as captain of the vessel *Mazzini*. As he was leaving Rio de Janeiro, he chanced on a schooner and attacked it. It was the *Lucia*, a larger ship commanded by an Austrian and bearing a cargo of coffee destined for Russia. The *Mazzini* sank, but not before Garibaldi loaded all his cargo—his war materials—onto the other ship. That done, he changed the name: it became the *Farropilha* (the "Ragamuffin").

Everything else was not going to be that simple. The adventure alternated joys and misfortunes—as befitted the American *guerrillero*. Along the way, he learned how to lead a gaucho's life,[3] but before long he was engaged in a hapless combat with two other vessels. One of his companions died, and Garibaldi was wounded. He went on, nevertheless, with his *Farropilha* . . . only to fall unwittingly into the hands of Rosas, the Argentine tyrant. Wounded, Garibaldi let an Argentine schooner take him to Gualeguay, where he naively told about his last adventure, a story that, as soon as it reached the provincial governor's ears, was sufficient cause to have him imprisoned immediately. The months that followed would remain impressed on his memory as the worst in his life. He tried to escape, was recaptured and tortured; and, when he finally managed to flee to Montevideo, he knew in his very flesh how things were done in South America. One thing was absolutely certain: he would join Bento Gonzalvez's war against the child emperor of Brazil.

The South American Guerrilla

The most important lesson that Garibaldi was to learn in Brazil was how to be a guerrilla. Mazzini, from his retirement in London, wrote: "The guerrilla is the natural resource of an insurgent people who must conquer their freedom by fighting against disciplined armies. Such was the method chosen by the Dutch against

Philip II, by the American colonists against England, by Spaniards and Greeks in more recent times." Mazzini could have referred with greater exactness to the South American guerrillas who fought the Spanish forces from 1810 to 1824. The South American revolution was a fresher memory than that of George Washington's in 1775, and it was more typical. The struggle against Spain, in all her colonies, used guerrilla tactics as the most effective weapon, all the way to Ayacucho. Lord Byron was so convinced that the American strategy was the best, that when he joined in the war for Greek independence, he named his ship *Bolívar*. The Spanish gazettes in those days sometimes devoted more pages to the insurrection in Greece than to events in South America. It was their way of collecting information at home, in Europe, about two things—independence and guerrilla warfare—that were ruining the Spanish empire on the American continent.

Guerrilla tactics have been employed in every age; now they are the classic way of fighting among Spanish peoples in both hemispheres. In any dictionary—English, French, Italian—the word appears with its Spanish origin. Etymologically, guerrilla soldiers are Spanish; and history confirms language. To make "small war" when big war is impossible is something that adapts itself to the circumstances of inequality that characterize the common people whether in the Peninsula or in America. Between a warrior, a *guerrero*, and a *guerrillero* (between *guerra* and *guerrilla*) there is all the difference between two armies able to encounter each other in open combat and the ambushed attack of the unarmed peasant against an armed force. For the *guerrillero*, armament begins with the stone, the stick, the machete. The woods are his trenches, his castle, his wall. The guerrilla army has no body. The regular forces, the battalions that are trained in barracks, find themselves before an elusive sort of magic whose shadows escape the hand, the eye, for guerrilla strikes provide no target. Disconnected units, lost devils who have no camp or fortress, merging into the labyrinthine hiding places of an angry wilderness, *guerrilleros* escape the cunning of the most deadly artillerymen.

We have seen already, in the commoner guerrilla troops of Castile, how the quixotic revolt of the common people against the state is a distinguishing characteristic of Iberian peoples. Charles V defeated Padilla, murdered him, and yet the shadow of this courageous fighter came back to life in other places: in Holland, to strike against Philip II; in America, to endure for centuries. The blacks in the stockade of San Basilio, near Cartagena de Indias, learned this system of warfare and were able to preserve their independence for a century.

The purest, most glorious moment in the history of guerrilla struggles for freedom and independence takes place in the war for emancipation of the Spanish colonies. The insurrection begins with unarmed troops (in Mexico they are led by two rebel priests, Miguel Hidalgo and Jose Morelos). The weapons are stones, sticks, and machetes; the cavalry rides bareback, wielding lances with macana wood shafts and iron heads; the artillerymen learn to shoot a cannon when they manage to capture one from the enemy. Without armor and, naturally, without uniform, they are Davids against Goliaths, defeating European armies more by frightening them away than by direct encounter.

Garibaldi in Brazil

For six years, Garibaldi fought in the Brazilian war, as a southern republican. The shirtless army was rising up against a European empire of Braganza lineage, which had an army of Austrian soldiers trained in modern warfare. While the rest of South America had passed from colonial rule to republics after a bloody fourteen-year struggle for independence, Brazil had established itself as an independent empire without shooting a single cartridge. The southern movement was only a foretaste of the republic that would come years later. For the moment, the combat had to go on, over lagoons, mountains, and farmlands, with brief sea skirmishes and fleeting victories. The army that Garibaldi would join was fundamentally guerrilla. In his memoirs, he says: "I served the people's cause in America as sincerely as I have fought against despotism everywhere. Having a preference for the republic as a system that most deeply reflects my convictions, I was averse to the opposite system."

In Montevideo, he found a good number of friends, Italian and adventuresome like himself. He left for Brazil with one of them, Rossetti, for he had to take his place in the fighting. "With great pleasure I made my first journey on horseback," he wrote. The atmosphere was gauchoesque. Bento Gonzalvez, the president—the best horseman in Rio Grande (which boasts the most famous in the world)—carried the archives of the republic in leather chests, in wagons that followed the armies. During the campaign, all of them, beginning with the president, ate the same roast, hunting wild cattle for meat along the way. The center of operations was going to be Laguna de los Patos. In the spacious farmhouses of large estates abandoned by runaway imperialists, the republicans found good lodgings, food, tools, hides, and hammocks. Garibaldi was to become a sort of river admiral, with a fleet consisting of two barges. On the sea side, near the lagoon, lay the imperial flotilla and its armies.

The first battle surprised Garibaldi in the barracks that he had set up in an enormous barn, formerly used to store the native tea, maté. Most of the small band was out in the woods, engaged in various farm chores. Only fourteen men were in the barn when 150 imperial soldiers swooped down on them. The battle, nevertheless, lasted many hours. The republicans compensated for their small number by pretending to be numerous (they could not be seen behind the barn walls). Garibaldi added to the impression of having a much larger force by rallying imaginary troops with shouts of "War! War! Fire! Fire! Down with the savage tyrants! Down with the patricians!" The emperor's army withdrew in defeat, leaving behind a few dead and sustaining many wounded. Of the fourteen republicans, eight were wounded. The news of such fantastic exploits swept through Italy, France, Europe, as a serial story that kept thousands breathless with excitement. Garibaldi, the adventurer, acquired fabulous stature in the popular imagination as a sort of Buffalo Bill of the South American jungle.

With what the enemy left behind after the barn battle and with what he could find on the estate, Garibaldi doubled his fleet; this he did by building an improvised shipyard and two vessels. But he had to find a way of hauling the ships out to sea—since the mouth of the lagoon was occupied by the imperial forces. Garibaldi saw the blockade not as an insurmountable obstacle but rather as a challenge. He decided to take the ships on wagons over the jungle, as the president had done with the archives of the republic. . . . Eight enormous wheels were made, with four axletrees, solid enough to support the bodies of the two trailers to haul the ships. Two hundred oxen were ready to work in relays. Ten yoke of oxen pulled each trailer. For fifty-four miles! The people of Taramanday could not get over their astonishment at the sight of such cargo appearing through the jungle. The two ships seemed to float past, although they were eight hundred meters from shore. Early one morning, they set out to defy the imperial flotilla, sails unfurled. By three in the afternoon they were foundering in the mouth of the Areringua. Quirks of the wind . . . All the Italians except Garibaldi were drowned. A barrel of brandy that they found saved the shipwrecked survivors from freezing to death.

The survivors decided to chance it and approach Santa Catalina by land. Fortune smiled on the republicans. The four-hundred-man garrison that defended the city abandoned its position. Garibaldi seized the city and three small warships. Once in command of the schooner *Itaparica*, he was an admiral with seven cannons. In fact, Santa Catalina turned out to be republican, and Garibaldi's arrival was celebrated with cheers, music, barbecues, and drinking.

This first part of the campaign had the most amazing conclusion imaginable. One day, as he was strolling on the outskirts of Santa Catalina, Garibaldi noticed the silhouette of a woman on the opposite bank of the river. The next day, he crossed the river to see her. One look and the two understood one another; he abducted her. From then on in Garibaldi's story, Anita, if not by his side, was leading the way. In a naval battle, she would be first to open fire with cannon. When the time came to burn the ships, it was she running ahead to save the ammunition. Once, Garibaldi disappeared during battle, and Anita searched until she found him lying among the dead. She brought him back to life, put him on his horse. Nurse, orator, horsewoman, in a campaign that lasted several years, she gave him children between one battle and another, shared with him victory, defeat, hunger and poverty. It was a serial story that drove the Italians at home mad with delight. Some of the highlights of this saga became immortalized in romance and song.

In the end, Garibaldi felt the need to leave his solitude and make contact with his countrymen. He yearned to know something about Italy. Perhaps to return, and there, on his native soil, to repeat what was making him a myth in his own time. Don Beno, the governor, ever grateful, gave him nine hundred head of cattle from Pedras Corral. Garibaldi and Anita herded them toward Montevideo, leaving carcasses along the way. When they arrived, Garibaldi entered the city with three hides, a wife, several children, and the tales of his extraordinary adventures.

On his Brazilian experience, these words from his memoirs remain; they serve as an instructional message to Italians: "In our camp, meat was scarce, and the infantry especially was famished. Our thirst was still more unbearable; we found no water in the places we occupied. But those people were used to a life of privation and their only complaint was that they were not fighting. Fellow citizens! The day when you are as united (and I see it very distant) and as frugal as the children of this American continent, the foreigner shall not trample your soil, shall not insult the sacredness of your marriage chamber, and Italy once more shall take her place among the first nations of the world."

Montevideo Is the University

Garibaldi's Montevideo is all action, Technicolor and panoramic screen. Rosas, the Argentine dictator, is at the peak of his bloody career. For six years, he has ruled the country like a wild gaucho, and he will stay in the saddle for nine more. His brutal shock troops—the *mazorca*—anticipate the purges of Italian Fascism by a century. The victims of Rosas's atrocities take refuge in the Uruguayan capital and from there let the world know what is happening in Buenos Aires. Echeverría invents the pun *más horca* (more gallows) for *mazorca*.

The fiction of the times becomes a kind of record. José Mármol is in Montevideo, and his novel *Amalia* becomes a romantic panorama of that period of Argentina's history. Esteban Echeverría, now also in Montevideo, had been the founder of *Young Argentina* in Buenos Aires—after Mazzini's model. He had been initiated together with another great Argentine of Italian origin: Juan Bautista Alberdi, voracious reader of Victor Hugo and Lord Byron, and author of the Argentine constitutional *Bases*. In Montevideo, at that time, Echeverría writes the best and most dramatic account of Rosas's crimes: *The Slaughterhouse*. This short novel is unequaled in its stark realism as a testimony on Creole violence. But Echeverría was to die without ever fulfilling his dream of writing a play on Policarpa Salavarrieta, the Colombian heroine of Bolívar's wars, the Anita Garibaldi of his day. Policarpa's picture was a popular print on the kerchiefs that both men and women wore around their necks or on head scarves. Echeverría did not write the drama, but another Argentine refugee, Bartolomé Mitre, who would later be president of his country, wrote and staged it.

Montevideo was full of Frenchmen and Italians. Together with the Argentines and Uruguayans, these Europeans made a universal clamor against despotism. Montevideo's theater was the freest in the world. Echeverría, who had been witness to the battles and representations of *Hernani* in Paris, returned all aglow with enthusiasm for Victor Hugo, and for Dumas and Ducange. The Argentine émigrés translated these works with amazing speed, and performed them with a freedom that Paris would have envied. People of two worlds crowded the theaters to hear the monologues and dialogues of *Ruy Blas, Lucrèce Borgia, Le Roi S'amuse, Marion de Lorme.* . . . For Garibaldi, this corner of America was the best place to understand the conflicts of his own nation, interpreted here in terms of universal theater, in the passions and epics of South

Americans or of his own countrymen who lived on the shores of Río de la Plata. Echeverría, who had bought Manzoni's *I Promessi Sposi* from Paris the same year it was published, and left Mazzini in prison in Savona, was now engaged in a literary battle against a Neapolitan, De Angelis, who, being in the service of Rosa, tried to destroy the opposition with his sarcastic writings, accusing them of being Romantics. Echeverría replied: "My God! A poor worm, used to wallowing in decay, wants to spit at the sun!" European ideas took on an American dimension when they reached Buenos Aires or Montevideo. In the midst of this turbulent and theatrical agitation, Garibaldi was part of the battle and part of the show. As for Anita, she could see the American woman's role exemplified in dramas like *Policarpa* or *Amalia*, and in the French theater, which in Montevideo became American theater. We can almost say that Victor Hugo was more of a Victor Hugo in America than in France. And Anita was also aware of the reverse of this picture, the wrong-side-out heroine embodied in the wife of the Argentine dictator, Encarnación Ezcurra, the diabolic puppeteeress of *Mazorca*.

Garibaldi had the Uruguayan navy challenge Rosas's navy, and created an Italian Legion, as the French had done, to defend the city from the Argentine siege; he fought on land or sea, in the Italian or in the American style. The serial story of his daring feats continued to spice the pages of French and Italian newspapers. The Italian Legion became famous for its deeds . . . and for its uniform! The red shirt was born in Montevideo. A store found itself overstocked with red material intended for export to butchers in Buenos Aires. With the siege, it was impossible to send it, so the store supplied the legion with material for its shirts. The flag was black, with an erupting Vesuvius in the center. The colors looked marvelous on the streets, carried by the red-shirted legionaries as they sang their songs. . . . As Indro Montanelli and Marco Nozza say: "At the cry of 'Garibaldi's leaving!' all the balconies and rooftops that overlooked the port were filled with spectators as if they were theatre boxes. In these sorties there was something spectacular that, for the poor inhabitants of Montevideo, compensated for the scarcity that the siege imposed on the city. In the port, in plain sight of the public, Garibaldi would attack an Argentine schooner and return with a cargo of sugar or flour."

It all continued until the time came to go back to Italy. Mazzini insisted on it. Letters came from Genoa, Turin, Milan. . . . One morning, Anita opened the door to find an unknown visitor with a package from Italy for Garibaldi. Together, they opened it. Inside they found a sword with a hilt of gold! It was a gift from the Italian people, sent on Mazzini's initiative. No one had been allowed to contribute more than one lira. The people themselves were calling him home.

It is Anita who first embarks for Italy, not Garibaldi. She is the one who will prepare his arrival.

The Gaucho Among the Emperors

Let us make an imaginary tableau. Let us place around a table in a most splendid royal palace—what china, what silver, what lamps!—two emperors, one pope, several kings, a count . . . and a gaucho who takes off his poncho and turns out to be wearing a red shirt. The emperors are Francis Joseph of Austria and Napoleon III of France; the kings are Charles Albert of Savoy and Victor Emmanuel of Sardinia; the pope is Pope Pius IX; the count is Camillo Benso Cavour, also of Sardinia . . . the gaucho, everyone knows. All except one are of noble origin or princely upbringing; they are either haughty or majestic. The sovereigns arrive in Milan or Turin, wherever, and the cities don flags to welcome them. There are military parades, soirées at the opera, dazzling uniforms. Garibaldi visits those cities, and it is sheer madness. The populace pours into the streets, overflows the squares, sings its Marseillaises.

Everyone has his eyes on a revolution and a dream of Utopia: the making of Italy into a single state. Mazzini and Garibaldi dream of Italy as a republic, want to take the patchwork quilt that from time immemorial has been the peninsula and to make a single tricolored flag out of it. Such a union was achieved in Spain, and could be achieved in France, Austria, or Germany with relatively few difficulties. Not so in Italy. To make the case worse, the pope, a man with his own states, a king armed in two ways, holds sway over the land. And as for the Austrian and French emperors—even the Spanish—they are accustomed to wage wars in Italian territory and change kings and dukes there whenever they wish.

The nineteenth century is more complex than the Enlightenment. Everything that the eighteenth century stirred up, the nineteenth turns to revolution, destruction of empires, birth of republics. Four empires lose their colonies in America; and, there also, the Church sees her prestige erode as she shares in Spain's crumbling authority. Now the Noble Savages, eulogized to the point of delirium by the Romantics, make their disconcerting appearance in Italy. The gaucho that we have brought to the table can be frightening. Italy wavers between the anarchy that everyone encourages and the hopes of a few idealists. In the higher spheres, men change their opinions faster than their shirts, bridges are built that give way if an army passes, compromises are reached and evaporate. Confusion is universal.

When the most famous Argentine writer of that time, and of an entire century, Domingo Faustino Sarmiento, arrived in Rome, Pius IX had just ascended to the pontifical throne and seemed about to revolutionize the Church. He was considered a liberal, capable of making friendly contacts with the Freemasons. For the celebration of the new pontificate, the city went wild with joy. Nothing like this had been seen before. The preceding pope had left jails crammed with political prisoners, rotting away in dungeons for dozens of years. Pius IX opened them, and the procession of living skeletons, their eyes still unable to bear the sunlight, made the exultant crowd weep with emotion.

This Pope Pius had been in Uruguay, Argentina, and Chile some years before. He was the first pontiff to arrive at the Holy See after having crossed the Atlantic. He was familiar with those republics, where he had seen the rising popularity of liberal ideas. In the Montevideo lodge there is the tradition that Monsignor Mastai (this was Pius IX's name) had attended some meetings and had been initiated in the Masonic mysteries. Monsignor Mastai was accompanying Monsignor Muzi, the pope's legate, in a effort to come to an understanding with Chile. In Buenos Aires, Rivadavia received the Muzi mission in the most ungracious way.[4] In Chile, their luck was still worse. "The only serious trouble came, not from the Masonic lodges, but from the theater, which was presenting plays against the papacy, like *Aristodemo*, imported from Buenos Aires. Or shadow pantomimes that insulted the pope's representative. When the first one appeared—it was Bishop Rodríguez—Sallusti tells us that the rabble yelled: 'Get out! Get out of here!' The second one, Muzi's figure, was met with cries of 'Go back to your jungle!' But as soon as Rousseau's and Voltaire's silhouettes were seen, there was loud cheering amid shouts of 'Come on! . . . Come on! Enlighten every nation!' The members of the pope's mission wished to visit Paraguay, and Dr. Francia notified them that they could go in but never again go out. This was normal policy with regard to foreigners."

When Sarmiento, who was then living in Africa, went to visit Pius IX, he was still dazzled by the surprising turn that Vatican policy was taking under the pontiff's leadership: "He has the loftiest of all claims to the veneration of Christian people, having taken away from the governments the sanction of religion, for liberty is essentially the purest realization of Christian charity and leaves each man the exercise of free will on which the whole dogma is founded, having banned the bloody and violent public executions against which Christian mildness had protested in vain for nearly twenty centuries." The papal audience opens, and the pope asks Sarmiento: "Where were you born?" In San Juan de Cuyo. Pius IX is familiar with San Juan, in the north of Mendoza. He had been around there on horseback. . . . And he asks: "What has become of Rivadavia?"

Among emperors and kings and counts, et cetera, the only one who knows anything about gauchos is Pius IX. . . . But when the revolution grows strong in Italy and he sees Garibaldi fresh from the Montevideo lodges, Pius IX feels that his early liberalism is falling apart. Years later, when he ponders seriously what might be done for America, he bestows his blessing on Maximilian and Charlotte so that they may put their throne on Mexican soil and reconquer a nation that the cancer of republicanism is corroding.

Napoleon III entered the great theater of his life as a conspirator, revolutionary, adventurer, liberal; but at the same time he sided with the Church and forced the republic to capitulate in Rome while he was president of France. Charles Albert raised the Garibaldians' hopes as Pius IX had done. When Anita's ship was leaving for Montevideo, the port rang with cries of "Long live the pope! Long live Charles Albert! Long live Mazzini!" When Garibaldi interviewed Albert, one visit was enough for him to reach a conclusion very much like the verbal portrait made by Costa de Beauregard (transcribed in Montanelli and Nozza's biography of Garibaldi): "The look in his eyes contradicted his words, his words retracted his smile, his smile covered his thoughts. In every decision he saw inconveniences; he was afraid of success; the scruples of responsibility tormented him: In other words, he possessed a soul half a hero's and half a woman's."

Garibaldi advanced as well as he could through this maze of contradictions. When he knew the pope to be liberal, he cried, "Long live the pope!" When Victor Emmanuel was in favor of independence, "Long live Victor Emmanuel!" In Europe, he was as republican as he had been in America, for the republic was in his heart, but independence came first. Charles Albert, Cavour, Victor Emmanuel knew that Garibaldi was essential to their political plans, but it frightened them to see him so much the gaucho, with his poncho and the red shirt. If they gave him troops, it was without uniform. The first campaign, in Lombardy, ended in disaster. Garibaldi was undisturbed: "The royal war is over," he said. "Now the people's war begins!" His words caught fire.

When the time came to fight in Rome, the pope saw the red-shirted gaucho coming and fled all the way to Gaeta. The city fell to the insurgent troops. Garibaldi entered Parliament and presided. He was a savage. He asked for the floor and said: "There is only one thing to do here. Proclaim the republic immediately!"

The gaucho rode over the elementary rules. He ignored the order of the day. In three days, Parliament proclaimed the republic.

Pius IX appealed to the whole Catholic world—Spain, France, and Naples were what remained of it—asking for help to reconquer Rome. Napoleon was not yet emperor, but he was president of France; and his troops arrived in the Holy City to make war on the republic. Garibaldi did not yield. Madly, absurdly, genially, he defended his territory inch by inch. One day, a pregnant woman came to the barracks. Anita, the Brazilian. She had come to fight beside him. To shoot cannon, if necessary. When the republic surrendered, Garibaldi did not. On the esplanade of San Giovanni in Laterano he assembled all those who would listen and said these words, which Churchill would have envied: "Whoever would continue the war against the foreigner, follow me. I do not offer any payment of shelter or provision: I offer hunger, thirst, forced marches, battles, death. . . ." Four thousand went with him. (With but one thousand he had taken Sicily.)

Anita rode beside him like a legionary. In fact it was madness, and the four thousand began to dwindle away. By the time Garibaldi arrived at the pine grove of Ravenna, facing the Adriatic Sea, the pregnant Anita was in agony. She died. He had barely time to bury her in the sand and flee before his pursuers could capture him. . . .

Time passed, but the ideas had not died. Cavour took the cause of independence into his own hands. First of all, he had to attract Napoleon III and involve him in the war against Austria. For this enterprise there was already a circumstance in his favor. Napoleon had lost his heart to a very beautiful Italian woman, the countess of Castiglione . . . who was Cavour's cousin. Napoleon joined in the war, and in his declarations made incredible promises: "Let us unite in a single endeavor: this country's liberation. If you prove yourselves worthy of the ideal of independence that you seek, it will be yours." Shortly after that, Garibaldi was back on the scene as general of the Italian army.

What each of them thought of America just then was soon made evident. Napoleon, and especially his wife, the cold and beautiful Eugénie de Montijo, a Catholic fanatic who yearned for the reconquest of the Spanish colonies, or at least for their submission, agreed to bring Francis Joseph's brother to the throne of an "empire" concocted in Paris—Mexico. But a coalition of England, France, and Spain declared war on Mexico. Just before embarking, Maximilian and Charlotte went to Rome. Pope Pius IX blessed them warmly, wished the two of them a vigorous and lasting empire. . . .

America Is Always in the Background

Conspicuous by either action or omission, America's presence was always felt. When one reads Cavour's studies for the Italian constitution, the example of the United States is clearly in the background. He must decide what to incorporate and what to omit from the American text. Always distant from the total Italian republic envisioned by Garibaldi, Cavour suggested instead a confederation ruled by Piedmont. Garibaldi did not lose the idealism that he had brought from America; Cavour worked with elements taken from the tradition of Italian realms and with European ideas. "He continued to believe," say Montanelli and Nozza, "that Italy had to be created by means of diplomacy, without war or South American leaders." Curiously enough, Cavour, one of the greatest statesmen of his time in Europe, was mistaken in this and in his plans for the great Italy, while Garibaldi, gaucholike and wild as he was, proved to be right. After Garibaldi's expedition to Sicily— the most quixotic of all his enterprises—Cavour had to say: "It is the most poetic exploit of the century." He had touched Europe to the core. With their red shirts on, the Garibaldians seemed to have marched into Palermo from the streets of Montevideo. And, in fact, among the thousands there was a Brazilian: Menotti, Anita's son. . . .

Mazzini was more American in spirit than Cavour. When he wrote to Charles Albert, asking him to take command in the struggle for Italian independence, he cited the example of two ideal heroes, two fighters for American emancipation: George Washington and the Pole, Kosciuszko. And when he saw that it was the right time to go to war, he turned his eyes to Montevideo and sent Garibaldi the gold-hilted sword.

When Francis Joseph sent the Austrian ultimatum that determined the beginning of the war, people thought about Cavour and said: "Either he fights or he goes to America." When Garibaldi was left out of the Italian conflict, Lincoln—whom Mazzini worshipped—offered to place him in command of a fleet against the proslavery rebels of the South. In America, Garibaldi continued to be the hero and a vital part of that continent. Although Garibaldi did not accept Lincoln's offer, he traveled once more to the Western Hemisphere. He went to look at the other side of his America. He visited the Pacific coast, and in his meanderings met Bolívar's version of Anita Garibaldi: Manuelita Sáenz. Aged and forgotten, she had ended up in Paita, a little town on the Peruvian coast, where she sold candles, tobacco and sugar. . . .

In those days, there came to be two White Houses. One was in Washington. The other, Garibaldi's, was on an island of rocks and goats: La Caprera. On this island, Garibaldi built his house with his own hands. It was not built in the manner of the Italian "contadinos": it was South American, built in remembrance of Anita. Here, her son, Menotti, who eventually studied at the military academy in Nice, would grow up. The Italian colony in Montevideo would probably have been surprised to know that there was another White House: the one in Washington. For them, the truly American one was the home of Giuseppe and Menotti Garibaldi.

10

•

The Frustrated Reconquest

Toward International Justice

———

The self-determination of peoples, today an international postulate, had—and still has—the most surprising consequences. Although the United Nations Charter is now formally recognized, the great powers do not always respect it. Free determination and its natural corollary, nonintervention, constitute the last phase of the principle of independence born in America, and they represent the Western Hemisphere's greatest contribution to public law in modern time. But independence is obtained by one nation to the disadvantage of another, and in the end those who pay are the empires, accustomed to the benefits afforded by a colonial regime.

France, in her enthusiastic revolutionary literature, echoes the principles of American independence, incorporates them into public law, grants French citizenship to the notables from Philadelphia, and to Paine, to Miranda; she celebrates their emancipation in an hour of wild rejoicing . . . but almost immediately the Napoleonic reaction sets in. The emperor sends his armies—even his sister—to subdue the blacks in Haiti; or he imposes on Spain and Italy rulers he selects from his family clan. The Negroes of Haiti had to teach the French leader that their own rights were also worthy of respect. The Spanish common people introduced the word "independent" into their political vocabulary, for their own benefit, on the Goyaesque occasion of the Third of May uprising, and underlined it with noteworthy heroism.

It was not easy, nor has it become any easier, to modify century-old bad habits. When Europe smirked her formal acknowledgment of the colonies' independence—acknowledging the alien ones rather more readily than her own—she hastily began to organize the framework for neocolonialism. Second-class states were established de facto, and in the nineteenth century a new style of domination came into being. The new American states were born poor, and their republican initiation, built on the ruins of the wars that had given them their independence, led to anarchy. Not a window was left whole. (Europe is also familiar with such things. France is not unaware of the cost of disorders, destruction, ruins, and riots that occur each time a republic is proclaimed within her borders.) The poverty and disorder of the American nations made them easy prey for their European creditors.

Victorious independence not only paves the way for new government reforms; it is an attempt to establish an initial public principle of justice. But for an armed power, it is difficult to be just if what it has before it is a small defenseless state. At that moment, law pushes away from justice—rejects it. An empire may perhaps go so far as to favor the weak state with fatherlike protection, with assistance that comes close to being charity. Whoever feels powerful tends to exercise his power on international waifs. To insist instead on the idea of justice is an attempt to bring into being international rights that have not existed in centuries. Today, the third world is trying to do this.

A new empire is more impetuous than an old one. Soviet Russia, new in the trade, does not accept the self-determination of neighboring states and rejects the idea of justice at the roots of the original American philosophy of independence. The march on

Prague, the invasion of Poland and Hungary, repeat in our time the North American aggressions history has known: "the big stick," the U.S. Marine Corps invasions in the Caribbean. Seeing themselves blessed with an armed force, they are unable to resist the imperial temptation. They are far from being initiated in a process destined to introduce the idea of justice into the law. They are great underdeveloped nations in what concerns justice. They proclaim the right to strike down, in counterpoint to the right to protect, legitimate rights. Those who fight against racial discrimination in the United States or assume an attitude like that of Solzhenitsyn in his defiance of Soviet despotism—will they be able to inspire, in either case, an internal revolution likely to reflect itself in international policies? Perhaps they will. For the moment, it is all nothing more than a hope.

The case of Latin America is unique, and so is the case of Europe in recent times. The United States and the Soviet Union have placed all their emphasis on the words "united," "union." It is the key to their enormous power. If Latin America were able to unite, or the states that border on the Soviet Union would do so, it might be possible it think of a balance of masses that, through physical law, would accomplish that which moral law has failed to do. This, of course, is wishful thinking. There will be no federation; and, if the great powers subscribe on paper to nonintervention, theirs is only a developing philosophy. In the past, when one spoke of the "king's justice," the law was nothing more than the king's royal whim. "The divine right of kings to govern wrong." Law was on the wrong side of human rights.

The Nineteenth-Century European Big Stick

In the nineteenth century, millions of Europeans left for America to engage in commerce that would yield profits of 100 to 1. (Today, 1 percent is thought proper.) Such exaggerated profits fired the adventurers with unrestrained ambition. Since the object of their journey was inordinate gain, they did not accept passively the risks that were an inherent part of life in countries beset by civil war. They were determined to convert the payment of an uncertain debt or the burning down of a shop into productive business. They felt that they had the right to collect their debts with the cannons of the fatherland's navy. They saw themselves as their country's commercial ambassadors, and sold trifles at exploitative colonial prices. Cases abound in which Italians or Frenchmen appealed to their governments and obtained the battleships. It was necessary to invent continental doctrines—Monroe or Drago—to prevent the blockade of ports in Venezuela or Colombia.[1]

The most important case was that of Mexico. Spain, England, and France blocked Veracruz, disembarked troops . . . and imposed the "emperor of Mexico," Maximilian. The pretext was a number of imaginary debts. The end of the story is Maximilian's execution, which very opportunely made clear the right of nations to choose their own rulers and forms of government and to enjoy the benefits that current law grants to a debtor who is in difficult straits.

England, France, and Spain Serve a Group of Adventurers

In Mexico, in the middle of the nineteenth century, the Church owned one-third of the arable land and continued extending its vast properties through donations and wills. The liberal government decided to correct the situation and passed the Lerdo Law, which forbade the Church to make new acquisitions. The Church rebelled, elected the royalist Miguel Miramón as its leader, and war broke out. Franciscans and Dominicans refused to abandon their estates. In the churches, chalices were melted down to buy arms. The country split under two presidents: In the capital was Miramón, recognized by the foreign powers. Outside the capital was Benito Juárez, recognized by the nation. Finally, the people won. Miramón escaped and later served Emperor Maximilian.

Miramón had needed a much greater amount of money than the churches had been able to collect. He took 600,000 pesos from the British embassy. A Swiss banker, Jecker, lent him a million pesos; fifteen million in bonds, they agreed, were payable with the customs revenue. When Miramón was defeated, the British and French embassies demanded that Juárez pay these sums to France—for the Swiss banker had become a French citizen on the eve of the day before.

Juárez had received the republic in ruins. With empty treasuries, starting from zero, he found himself "between society and civilization on one side asking him for peace, order and guarantees, and the foreign creditors on the other demanding almost the totality of the public income." The only solution was a moratorium. Chancellor Zamacona said: "The government understands that the debtor, when he is honest and has the firm intention of fulfilling his engagements, can assume a dignified attitude if he presents himself before his creditor to declare his temporary inability." The payments of the debt would be suspended for two years. Juárez recognized Miramón's debts as legal. He did not want an armed Europe coming down on him.

The "creditors' " reaction was brutal. Before the government had time to announce the moratorium to each embassy, protests, threats, ultimatums rained on him. The French even refused to receive the Mexican prime minister. At least, demanded the ambassadors—they who were such experts in public law—the president should annul *ipso facto* a law that had been approved by Parliament! There had to be some advantage in ruling over a republic of ignoble savages. . . . Sir Charles Lenox Wyke, the English ambassador addressed the chancellor in the following manner: 'A printed paper, as strange in its whole appearance as it is in the nature of its contents, has been proclaimed today in those parts of the city where traffic is heaviest and has been reprinted, as I now see, in the pages of this afternoon's *El Siglo*. . . . According to the words of this document, it would appear that Congress has decided to make a free donation of other individuals' property, not belonging to the government or to the Republic, totally suspending payment to the bond holders in London for two years. . . . I cannot believe that a self-respecting government can sanction such a great violation of the most sacred obligations toward other nations." Four days later: "I have no other choice but to protest solemnly against that decree . . . and advise Your Excellency that, unless the aforementioned decree is not revoked within forty-eight hours beginning at this moment, I shall suspend every official relation with the Mexican government, as maintaining them would be incompatible with the dignity of the nation I am honored to represent. . . ." Forty-eight hours later, Sir Charles Wyke declared that relations were broken.

Count Alphonse de Saligny, in the name of France, reported: "It is now thirty-six hours since in the main streets of the capital, and with the signature of the President of the Republic, a document, strange in its form as in its significance . . . Pertaining to a law . . . in which, by its first article, without taking into account the other dispositions which are totally inadmissible, the payment of the foreign conventions is ordered to be suspended for two years . . . I have not hesitated to consider this document apocryphal and fallacious. . . . I would have believed myself to be offending your government if I believed it capable of disposing in this manner of others' legitimate property, despising its most sacred promises, or of taking part in such a bold and senseless attempt against the rights and dignity of France." Four days later, he addressed himself to the chancellor in his capacity as "Envoy Extraordinary and Minister Plenipotentiary of His Majesty the Emperor of the French, in charge of protecting Spanish interests in Mexico . . ." Let us explain the Spanish part: The ambassador of the queen of Spain, Francisco Pacheco, had passed through Veracruz (where President Juárez was), ignoring him and continuing on his way to the capital to present himself before Miramón. He had the intention of placing himself at his service, and did so. As soon as Juárez entered the capital, he sent Pacheco home. Pacheco placed "the sacred affairs of Spain" in the French ambassador's hands.

Four days later—as we were saying—the Count de Saligny declared: "If said decree is not suspended and annulled within twenty-four hours beginning at this moment, I will break all official relations with your government, as they have become incompatible with the dignity of the nation that I have the honor of representing."

The sacred interests were those of the Swiss Jecker, who had obtained French citizenship only a few months prior to that date.[2]

Neither Sir Charles Wyke nor Count Saligny were acting haphazardly. From Washington, the Mexican representative wrote immediately to his chancellor: "It may happen that, when this letter arrives, you may have learned of a serious matter concerning the claims made by France and England. They demand that the constitutional government pay the $600,000 that Miramón stole from the English . . . and that the question of Jecker's bonds be resolved favorably for that gentleman." In those days communications were slow. On July 17, the law suspending the payments was published, and on October 31, the order for blockade was signed by the queen of England, the queen of Spain, and Napoleon III. To put things in feminine terms, let us say that France also spoke through the lips of her empress, Eugénie de Montijo. The final article of the "convention" stated: "Her Majesty the Queen of Spain and His Majesty the Emperor of the French agree to adopt immediately after the signing of the present convention, the necessary measures to send to the coast of Mexico combined forces of land and sea, whose number will be established in the subsequent communications exchanged between governments, but whose total number should be sufficient for taking and occupying the various fortresses and military positions on the Mexican coastline."

The blockade and the occupation took place. Karl Marx wrote in the *New York Tribune:*

The proposed intervention in Mexico by England, France and Spain is, in my opinion, one of the most infamous enterprises that has ever been recorded in international history. Palmerston and his press organ have the exact knowledge that "Mexico has an existing government"; that the liberal party, ostensibly favored by England, is now in power; that "the ecclesiastical domination has been overthrown"; that "the Spanish intervention is the clergy's and the bandits' " only hope, and finally, that Mexican anarchy is gradually coming to an end. They know . . . that joint intervention with the sole declared purpose of rescuing Mexico from anarchy will produce . . . the contrary effect, weakening the constitutional government and strengthening the clergymen's party, supported by the French and Spanish bayonets, rekindling the embers of civil war and . . . restoring anarchy in its most perfect flourishment.

Some time later, in a Viennese newspaper, Marx insisted: "One of Palmerston's press organs, *The Morning Post*, has announced that Mexico does not constitute a state organized by a stable government, but that it is a nest of thieves. That, in consequence, it should be treated as such. The expedition has one purpose: the satisfaction of English, French, and Spanish creditors against the Mexican state."

Carlotta and Maximilian

Marx had only half the story. In his desire to make an economic interpretation of history, he thought that it was simply a question of serving English, French, and Spanish creditors. Actually, things went deeper. It was a matter of putting a European monarch in Mexico. Of turning history backward. It was preferable to leave the debts as they were and to go ahead with the emperor. Lincoln wanted to make a treaty in which the United States would assume the payment of the debts, leaving the political status of Mexico as an independent nation intact.[3] The French emperor refused to accept that offer. France and Spain were for reconquering. The discussions were over.

Spain at first thought of one of her own princes. The Mexican representative in Paris knew about it when he wrote to his chancellor:

Spain's intentions, which were a rather penetrable secret, are not a manifest reality. Spain's plan to give us a king . . is now fully confirmed. . . . Your Excellency will be convinced of this upon reading the important revelation that has just been made to me

by Mssr. Dayton and Adams, United States ambassadors in Paris
and London. . . . Mr. Dayton had come into the positive
knowledge that the government was determined to organize in
Mexico a party headed by a prince of the Spanish royal family,
not Don Juan, as had been suspected before, but Don Sebastian, the Queen's uncle. . . . Mr. Adams asked me if in Mexico
there was a party that sought to establish a monarchic government in the country, under the rule of a Spanish prince. . . .
Mr. Adams told me . . . that the United States Ambassador in
Madrid had written to inform him that Spain's plan consisted
of having her Mexican friends ask for a prince of the royal family . . . and that Spain would then condescend and send a body
of troops to support the new king.

Prince John of Bourbon published a manifest in London: "Being
heir to the Spanish throne by rights of birth, I may still hope to
become a king. . . . But for me the land of Mexico has no attraction . . . . I can leave the field free for others." He left it to Maximilian of Austria. The essential thing was to have a New Spain,
not a republic, not an independent state. It had to be an extension
of Europe.

England and Spain withdrew their troops from Mexico. Only
the French remained, controlling Veracruz and advancing toward
the interior. England had had no part in Napoleon's plan apart from
claiming the debts. As for Spain, General Prim, commander of the
forces that had been sent from Cuba, was a man of liberal ideas:
"In Mexico," he said, "there are no royalists . . . they are not even
one in a thousand; and the rest, the immense majority, will fight
the monarchy. . . . The monarchy imposed by foreign bayonets
can wound the country to death." Spain had to accept the evidence. But Napoleon III had an irreversible plan.[4]

As a candidate for emperor of Mexico, Napoleon proposed the
Archduke Maximilian. The plan was attractive. The emperor of
Austria was glad to have his brother leave him in peace and settle
down on the other side of the Atlantic. The Belgian monarchs,
Carlotta's parents, were delighted to have their daughter become

an empress. Through Belgium, Napoleon III hoped to gain England's friendship; and in the end he was successful. Queen Victoria wrote to Maximilian: "The Divine Providence has placed that empire under your rule, and with the expression of my wishes for your personal happiness and the continuation of the glories of your reign . . . ," etc. Royalist Spain had won. Empress Eugénie had been the soul of the scheme. The pope could not have been more pleased. And there were the Mexican royalists, too. They had gone from court to court, looking for a way to wipe out the republic; now they seemed to be succeeding.

The story of Miramón's debts was the last thing on the French emperor's mind. The expenses that the war and the enthroning of the monarchs entailed were going to be a hundred times greater than that. For the expedition, 270,000,000 francs; 400,000 for each trip from France to Veracruz (twice a month). All this charged to Mexico. And 1,000 francs a year for each soldier . . .

The scene of Maximilian's and Carlotta's proclamation took place at Miramar Castle, overlooking the Adriatic. They swore loyalty to a land that they had never seen. The Mexican royalists and the non-Mexicans cried: "Long live Emperor Maximilian! Long live Empress Carlotta!" While the French troops marched to the capital of Mexico—after a defeat at Puebla that made them momentarily bite the dust—Maximilian and Carlotta made farewell visits to the different courts in Europe. At the end there was the blessing. The pope in Rome would give them patent proof that everything had been the work of Divine Providence. The "Mexican emperors" arrived at Civitavecchia on a luxury steamer, and from there a carriage took them to the Eternal City. Under a rain of flowers, saluted by the arms of France and embraced by a radiant Pope Pius IX, what else could they think?

Maximilian, Napoleon III, and Pius IX had made a great show of their liberal ideas at the beginning. At the Quirinal, when the moment came to exchange speeches, a little residue of the freedom-oriented literature was evident, but . . . Before he gave the Emperors' Communion, the pope warned them that "the rights of the people were certainly great and had to be satisfied, but those of the church were even greater and more sacred." On the streets, the crowds cheered the new monarchs. The bishop of Buegla visited the imperial couple and was delighted with the grave, sweet way in which they received him, making him forget the weariness of his journey. He wrote to a friend: "Great is the sacrifice that these princes are going to make, but great also will be their reward. What an angelic couple. How charming and pleasant they both are! How engaging they are when they speak and smile! It would be hard to find other princes like these. God has deigned to judge us worthy of having them with us for long years!" For the bishop, God's name was Napoleon III.

Carlotta wrote to Empress Eugénie: "I take this opportunity to express my gratefulness to your Majesty for the interest that she takes in this unfortunate country. Your Majesty, who always favors the cause of righteousness, clearly seems to have been chosen by Providence to begin an enterprise which we could, in all justice, call holy because of the regeneration that it is destined to produce and . . . the new impulse that it should give religion in a nation where civil strife has not been able to extinguish the ardent Catholic faith of our ancestors."

Eugénie answered: "I know in advance that Your Highness will be the good fairy for all those people who are at present abandoned to despair but who . . . are ready to rally around those who are going to unite their own destiny with them. . . . This will be the reward for the Prince who abandons his Homeland and his family to bring regeneration and life."

Clerical Mexico, lords of the capital at that moment, greeted Maximilian with all the bells ringing merrily in one hundred churches. In the castle of Chapultepec or in the mansion at Cuernavaca, with its gardens of fountains and flowers, the emperors often did think that they really were fairy folk and really were going to reign with better luck than Moctezuma and Cuauhtémoc. The shadow of Juárez, roaming other distant provinces, was as unreal as a dark bird destined to flee forever. And at some moment of blind optimism they thought that they could extend their empire through Central America, all the way to Panama.

Voices That Favor Mexico

The pope, the emperor of France, the queens of England and Spain, the emperor of Austria, the kings of Belgium, set up the European empire in Mexico. They trampled those formulas of international law that were considered to be the main achievements of civilization. Not only did they refuse to recognize the most essential rights of the Mexican people, they also defied European liberal opinion. If Maximilian's empire had been consolidated, Western thought would have been turned back several centuries. Could the monarchs' defiance remain unanswered in free Europe?

Victor Hugo was at that time in exile at Guernsey, and all eyes were focused on him, especially from South America, where his name had a magic prestige. From all of Europe, and from America, messages came for the poet. Even more so at this moment, when he was the most caustic critic of "Napoleon the Small." He had the latest information on the Mexican expedition. When he heard of the battle of Puebla, he addressed his message to both Pueblans and Mexicans:

People of Puebla!

You are right if you believe that I am with you. It is not France that wages war on you; it is the Empire. I am with you. You and I are fighting the Empire; you in your homeland and I in my exile.

Fight, struggle, inspire terror, and if you think that my name can be of any use, use it to advantage, aim at that man's head with the bullet of liberty.

Resist, brave men of Mexico.

The republic is with you, waving over your heads the flag of France with its rainbow and the flag of America with its stars.

Hope. Your heroic resistance is based on the law and has the certainty of justice in its favor.

The attempt against the Mexican republic is an attempt against the French republic. One ambush is the complement of the other.

The French empire will fail in its monstrous intent, this I believe, and you will overcome. But whether you overcome or are overcome, France will continue to be your sister, the sister of your glory and your misfortune, and I, since you appeal to my name, repeat that I am with you: if you are victorious, I am your brother as citizen. If you are vanquished, I am your brother as proscript.

—Victor Hugo

When Victor Hugo's manifest reaches Juárez, Juárez feels he has won the second battle of Puebla. And he is not mistaken, because he also wins a victory in Europe, and it is an irreversible victory. Juárez papered the streets of Puebla with this authentic voice of France.

In Spain, criticism began with General Prim himself. His first gesture was to withdraw the Spanish troops under his command when he saw that what France intended was to set up the empire she fancied. That was not what had been agreed to. Prim wrote: "In Mexico there are no royalists." Those few who would be royalists "are not even one in a thousand, and the rest, the immense majority, will fight the monarchy, each one in whatever way he can, some with arms, others with silence and inertia, and the monarchy imposed by foreign bayonets can wound the country to death and the foreign prince's throne shall roll to the ground the day that European soldiers are no longer around."

It was not hard for Prim to make these prophecies. Direct contact with the Mexicans had opened his eyes. There were similar manifestations throughout Europe. But the important voices were French, and these spoke out in the National Assembly, before the emperor's ministers. Achille Jubinal opened the trial: "If we go to Mexico, trailing behind vulgar conspirators [the Mexican royalists, who were stirring up courts in Europe] with the deliberate purpose of . . . removing a free government, of overthrowing an independent power and imposing any other form of government on a nation that depends on itself alone, I would permit myself to ask the government what has become of the great principle of nonintervention which it has proclaimed elsewhere, enforcing it in such an effective way." (These words were heard at the Assembly while the emperor was still concealing his project of sending Maximilian to Mexico, and the fact was nothing more than a rumor.)

Deputy Adolphe Gueroult: "The principles of the Mexican liberal party are the same as ours, they are the principles of the French Revolution and of modern civilization. In order to maintain them, that party had made efforts which unfortunately are stained with violence, and these I do not justify, as I do not justify those of its enemies. But if we had to take part in that country's affairs, our natural ally would be the party that professes our own principles, not the party against which we are compelled to fight in France . . . and that teaches everywhere, in the manner of a dogma, the rejection of the postulates that constitute the basis of modern public law."

Deputy Jules Favre: "In Mexico there are two factions: that of the Mexicans who accept the empire, and these are protected; and that of those who protest against it, and these are stripped of their properties and shot. . . . Acts of this kind have been committed against these people's rights that establish that neutral persons should be respected, that private property should not be destroyed without reason, that the sacking of cities should not be considered as a measure to produce the healthy state of terror that will assure the success of a pretender."

Six years elapsed after the start of the imperial operation, an adventure whose price was Maximilian's life. Adolphe Thiers, the historian of the French Revolution, was at the National Assembly and made a balance sheet for the disaster. He showed how the invasion of Mexico had weakened France's position in Europe both in a moral and in a military way; and he said: "It is not true that our fellow-countrymen, victims of real injuries, have been the cause of this enterprise. It is not true that it had probabilities of success, for, according to universal opinion, it had none. It is not true that we have given up at the wrong moment, for, had we persevered, we would have had worse disasters. The events themselves have forced us to stop." Thiers alluded to some bloody scenes in Mexico. Maximilian's execution was on everybody's mind. Favre profited from the occasion to declare: "There had been an attempt to create a sort of exceptional justice for one man, and to justify, invoking I don't know what principle that was already condemned forever, a divine right that protects thrones and marks with infamy whoever violates it. Let it be understood clearly: the death of a son of France, fallen unnoticed in a strange land in the fulfillment of his duty, is more worthy of our sympathy than that of a prince defending his crown."

The president of the House of Representatives: "Monsieur Jules Favre protests not only against the House's opinion but also against that of all Europe. . . . If he continues to express such views, I will be forced to call him to order."

Deputy Eugène Palletan: "We are putting a Frenchman before an Austrian archduke!"

The Duke of Marnier: "No distinction between the victims!"

Contradictory debates like this one probably went on all over Europe. The revolutions of the eighteenth century had not been produced in vain. Mexico once more had awakened everyone to the ideas that clearly had transformed the world. In the British Parliament, Disraeli had sounded the alarm:

I cannot forget that England was the first nation to recognize Mexico's independence . . . . The motive that compels Her Majesty's counselors, and England, to go against the independence that they themselves helped to create must be extremely serious. But there is another reason that makes us regard this announcement with apprehension: If we can believe reports that are presumed authentic and that are read by the public in the best newspapers, the reasons that motivated the intervention now occurring in Mexico have changed in a short space of time. First, we were told that the purpose of the expedition was to obtain reparation for British subjects who had been victims of extortions and confiscations, and today the rumor has it that the matter is more serious: not only is that satisfaction claimed, but the alliance may also have at its goal the introduction of new principles of government in that country and the implanting of new dynasties.

For Whom the Bell Tolls

The French occupation and the arrival of Maximilian aroused Mexico's nationalistic spirit. The war between the clerical party and the liberals continued with renewed impetus. In Europe, Napoleon envisioned the establishment of a modern-style monarchy; Eugénie saw the avenging of the Spanish empire; the pope, the reimplantation of clerical power.

Maximilian entered acclaimed by the clergy, but he had a liberal monarchy in mind. He observed the reactionaries' pretensions with disgust. In the town of Dolores, he rang the bell of the independence movement's hero, Father Miguel Hidalgo; the monarch seemed full of high hopes for establishing an independent, progressive government. But he was working with the people given to him by those who had brought him to Mexico. His generals, Miguel Miramón and Leonardo Márquez, were cruel, unscrupulous men. Favre read before the National Assembly the following letter from Miramón to Márquez: "Most Excellent Sir: On this same afternoon, and under Your Excellency's strict supervision, you will order the execution of all the prisoners in the class of officials and chiefs, informing on the number of those who have undergone that fate. God and the Law. Mexico, April 1, 1859.—Miramón." As for Márquez himself, in 1861 he dictated the following: "Let it be known that, using the authority with which I have been invested, I have resolved to decree the following: Art. 1. Benito Juárez, down to the last of the individuals who obey him or recognize his government, are considered traitors to the Fatherland, as are all those who, under any pretext or in any way, give them aid, no matter how insignificant. Art. 2. All those persons to whom the preceding article applies will be put to death immediately and on the site of their arrest, with no other requirement beyond their identification."

If Maximilian had found the laws of his reform correct (he had only to see for himself the abuses of the preceding regime), Pius IX felt the word "reform" already sounded too much like Protestantism; and, like the most zealous reactionary, he wrote Maximilian a very long letter, in which, among other things, he said: "Sir! In the name of that faith and that piety which are the adornment of your august family; in the name of that Church which, in spite of our unworthiness, has constituted us Supreme Head and Shepherd; in the name of God Almighty, Who has elected you to govern that Catholic nation, with the sole purpose of healing its wounds and honoring once more its sacred religion, we beg you to leave aside every human consideration and, guided by prudence and a Christian spirit, to wipe the tears of this part of the Catholic family which concerns us so greatly, and, with this conduct, may you be worthy of the blessings of Jesus Christ, Prince of Shepherds."

He gave the instructions regarding Maximilian's course of action to a nuncio that Carlotta believed to be mad and good only for throwing out the window. The nuncio refused to consider the concordat project that the emperor presented to him, till finally Maximilian had to send it to his delegation in Rome in order to negotiate it there, because the emperor was convinced that nothing could be done with the nuncio. The truth was that the battle had to be fought in Europe. On one side, Napoleon III congratulated Maximilian for the energy that he had shown in the matter of the clergy's properties, and, on the other, Pius IX in his letter had told Maximilian what he should do: "That the Catholic religion, excluding every other dissident cult, continue to be the glory and the support of the Mexican nation . . . ; that the religious orders be reestablished and organized with arrangements according to the instructions and powers that we have given; that the Church's patrimony and the rights annexed to it be defended and protected; that no one obtain authorization to publish false or subversive maxims; that education, both public and private, be directed and supervised by the ecclesiastical authority; and, in short, that the chains which had kept the Church bound to the dependence and despotism of the civil government be broken."

Within his own sphere, the pope, in his expectations of intervention, turned out to be more ambitious than the emperors. With his firsthand knowledge of the clergy's abuses, when the archbishops of Querétaro and Tunancingo presented him with a sort of memorial of offenses, Maximilian answered with a long letter in which he put things in perspective, with such words as these: "You say that the Mexican Church has never taken part in political matters. Would to God that it were so! Unfortunately we have a great number of undeniable testimonies . . . which are sad but evident proof that the Church dignitaries have engaged in the revolutions, and that a considerable part of the clergy has exhibited a obstinate and active resistance against the legitimate powers of the state." Maximilian knew this from experience.

And it was not just Maximilian who thought like this. Carlotta was indignant at the nuncio's pretensions and wrote to Empress Eugénie that, with his blindness and stubbornness, he wanted to turn Mexico into a theocracy and give the clergy back its properties.

Everything in the Mexican empire was a comedy of errors. And everything in the republic, ruled by the Indian president Juárez, a patient affirmation of the republic's reconquest by the people. Thus Juárez kept advancing for several years until he overcame the imperial army at the narrow site to Querétaro. The European powers abandoned "their" monarch to his fate. Carlotta decided to make a desperate journey in the hope of obtaining support. Vicente Riva Palacio wrote "Adiós a Mamá Carlotta," a poem in five stanzas, which portrays the mixed feelings the romantic scene aroused:

> Gone are the palace gatherings
> that merry folk assembled;
> the friars grieve and tremble,
> the rabble roars and yells.
> The tumult from Las Cruces
> makes all the city shudder;
> Farewell, Carlotta, sweet mother,
> my tender love, farewell!

The end would be insanity for Carlotta and the firing squad for Maximilian. Carlotta speaks with Napoleon, paints the most dramatic picture, gives vent to her anguish before Eugénie, and obtains nothing. Napoleon had impaired France's position in Europe and that of his own throne when he sent forty thousand men to Mexico to support Maximilian. He had already given orders for the troops to return to France and his letter to Maximilian is brutal: from now on, he will give Mexico not one penny nor one man. Carlotta then resorts to Rome. She writes to Maximilian: "Tomorrow I leave for Miramar, passing through Milan: this should tell you that I have had no success."

Maximilian oscillated between abdicating and resisting. He had to give the French one-half of the custom revenues and the French had taken control of this sole possibility of income. The representatives of France, Spain, England, Prussia, Belgium, and Italy took a sort of sadistic pleasure in making the most scathing written criticisms of the official positions granted to persons who had robbed the treasury in a way known to everyone, and for having given Márquez and Miramón command of the army. "In Europe the memory still lives . . . of those two officials who violated the seals of the British Delegation and smashed the safes to extract several millions remitted by the liberal government for the payment of the interest on the English debt, millions which immediately disappeared. Only Márquez and Miramón are responsible for the cold-blooded murders committed in Tacuya against defenseless young men, humanitarian doctors and peaceful citizens."

Upon leaving the capital for Querétaro, Maximilian had written to Miramón: "My dear General Miramón: I recommend to you very particularly that, if you are able to capture Benito Juárez, Don Sebastian Lerdo Tejada, Don José María Iglesias, and General Don Miguel Negrette, have them court-martialed and sentenced to death."

Respect for the Rights of Others

As the siege tightened around Querétaro, Europe learned, as if for the first time, that America was a republican continent. This had not figured in the invaders' schemes. Pope, emperors, kings, queens were not only discovering America, they were being surprised by it. The sentence against Maximilian ended all hopes of reconquest, monarchy, intervention. Now it was only a question of whether Juárez would grant the pardon. It was his decision. To shoot an emperor seemed a grave step, and the whole world held its breath. Messages from every corner of the globe rained on the president, beginning with those from Mexico's friends.

Garibaldi was among the first: "When a nation frees itself from its oppressors as Mexico has done, she merits a word of praise and a salutation from her sister nations. A sprout of European despotism transferred to the New World has not been able to take root. Thanks be to God! . . . Nevertheless, being opposed to bloodshed, we beg you, spare Maximilian's life. Forgive him! The fellow citizens of General Ghilardi, shot by his orders, beseech you to pardon him. Forgive him: return him to his family, that is to say to our murderers, as an example of the generosity of the people who overcome but in the end forgive."

A curious detail: When Carlotta was in Mexico, Empress Eugénie wrote to her: "It seems that the reception given to Garibaldi in London defies all description. I have been told that Lady Mary Jon knelt down before him. As for the Duchess of Sutherland, she distinguished herself in particular by the bizarre things that she did: every night she accompanied him to his apartments as if he were a king. Lord Shaftesbury, when he took his leave of him, raised eyes full of tears and lamented, 'We will never see his like again till the Lord returns.' . . . Prince Edward of Saxe-Weimar told this to Maria de Bade, who wrote it to me."

Victor Hugo asked for the pardon in a letter to the president. In that letter, he places Juárez beside John Brown, who was the Romantics' idol in those days: "Brown, to whom we owe the death of slavery; you in whom liberty has triumphed . . . After five years of smoke, of gunpowder, of blindness, the cloud has cleared and two empires have been seen to fall to the ground. No monarchy, no armies. Nothing but the enormity of the usurpation in ruins, and in the midst of this awesome destruction, a man stands tall, Juárez, and beside this man is liberty . . . You have just defeated monarchies with democracy." But Victor Hugo was above all an enemy of the death penalty. "Let the world see this prodigy: the republic has captured its murderer, which is an emperor; at the moment in which it should annihilate him, it discovers that he is a man, grants him freedom and says: 'You are of the people, like all the others. Go!' "

Princess Salm had gone to the most dramatic extreme for the emperor's life, to no avail.[5] She decided to present herself to Juárez and beseech him. Juárez: "It grieves me, Madam, to see you kneeling at my feet. But even if all the kings and queens of Europe were in your place, I could not pardon his life. It is not I who takes it, but my people. It is the law. If I did not obey it, the people would take his life and mine as well."

The scene of Maximilian's execution is still alive in French memory. Manet painted it in a splendid canvas: between General Miramón and General Mejía, against the wall, Maximilian appears, wearing a wide-brimmed Mexican hat, calm as the firing squad loads its guns or takes aim. Fifteen years after Manet, Jean Paul Laurens painted the emperor's last moments, when the firing squad presents itself at the entrance to his prison, when the emperor takes leave of his friends. All this continued to be remembered in books, magazines, poems. . . . The Mexican consul in Paris wrote about the dazed astonishment with which sovereigns all over Europe received the final news about one to whom all were linked by family or simple friendship. The pope had to comply with Maximilian's last will: to say a Mass for him.

If Maximilian's execution was calculated, it was for the purpose, once and for all, of letting it be known that Europe's intervention in the internal affairs of Latin American republics was a thing of the past. It was also a victory for the liberal trend that had been opposed to the adventure. Émile Ollivier: "Never had the attempt against nations' rights met with such prompt and terrible punishment." Napoleon's troops returned home without glory . . . only to fall in the Franco-Prussian War, which finally ended the Napoleonic Empire in France.

In brief, Europe was forced, this time quite seriously, to recognize America's independence. And after all the strife and the adventure, the maxim that Juárez had pronounced came out shining clean, a monument to political philosophy, placed before the consideration of the Old World, as the most consummate expression of American thought: "Respect for the rights of others is peace."

11

·

Romanticism

The Revolution Looks Backward

———————

From the beginning of the eighteenth century, Europe was seeing the rise of nonconformists who rebelled against the classical models. They detested the strict traditional forms in literature as one would hate a straitjacket. Their protest was also a counterpoint to geometry and reason, which, by the end of the century, were placed on altars and worshipped. Music, opera, painting—all participated in this movement. At the beginning, the pacesetters were small, scattered groups. Poets who felt themselves engaged in a conflict against the world dramatized their situation. Escapists disgusted with everything around them searched the distant past for heroes from the days of chivalry or looked to other continents, where they imagined a better kind of life.

From the deepest recesses of popular romance, fabulous figures were rescued. The story of their quests and adventures brought to light magical powers capable of subduing the Age of Enlightenment by means of fiction, lies, illusion. Savage man and the landscapes of Asia, Africa, America became fashionable. Literature looked backward or far away. These revolutions taken from ancient times were nothing new. The humanists of the Renaissance had borrowed—from archaeological Greece and Rome—the bases for a protest that changed the face of the earth. Paradoxically, if one wished to revolutionize contemporary structures, the positive knowledge of the past promised more solidity than the uncertain adventure of a future yet to be tried. That the old days have always been better turned out to be a revolutionary formula.

The word "Romanticism" to identify the rebels of the eighteenth century recalls the old, popular insurrection whose consequences have long been deeply felt. The language of the plebeians—of the Romans—came to confront Latin, which was then the official tongue of Church and State. Creators of genius, such as Dante or Boccaccio, saved the common people's language for literature. This adventure was extended to every nation under the Latin empire. The incredible feat of turning the language of the man in the street into a literary language was accomplished over and over— in Castile, Catalonia, Provence, France, Portugal, Romania. . . . The Roman, or Romance, languages—the romantic ones—became those of the troubadours. Alphonsus the Wise wrote his *History* and the *Siete Partidas* in a Romance language. As were the *chansons de geste*—*El Cid, The Song of Roland*. Rabelais and Cervantes used the common people's language. The word "romantic," so significant in its origin, finally imposed itself as a symbol, in Germany, Sweden, Poland, and by then it had nothing to do with the protest of one tongue against another. For the common people of Spain, *hablar en buen romance* ("to talk a good romance") became synonymous with saying things clearly. It was *Ladino,* not Latin. In the French dictionary, "Romantic" is defined as a new literary genre that is not written in Latin but in the common "Roman" tongue, a genre not subject to rules. The Spanish Royal Academy dictionary defines "Romanticism" as a literary school of the first half of the nineteenth century that is extremely individualistic and disregards the rules or precepts held by the classics.

Apart from this, there is the ingredient of magic, which is opposed to reason. In the English dictionary, "romantic" refers to narratives that stray from the truth, to exaggerations that ignore it. For the French, it is anything fictitious, marvelous, or fabulous in a narrative; the chimerical exaltation of characters in fiction; the romantic bravery of knights in armor. In France, works of the imagination came to be called *romans,* as they had been called in the past. This term continues to be used, even though novels are often just another way of saying the truth, which is sometimes hard to find in history. . . .

Romanticism can thrive in every age. Moses—in command of his people, singing the glory of Jehovah in heroic song, "Thou hast sent thy breath; the sea covered them—they sank like lead in the terrible waters . . ."—is a full-bearded Romantic. A Romantic of our day was Ché Guevara, roaming the Bolivian briarlands and moors. The historians of Romanticism in Europe are uncertain as to the dates; they set down its origin in the pre-Romantic eighteenth century. In the nineteenth century, the protest takes shape. It tilts full battle with Victor Hugo. A whole century of passion and combats. It has been said that Romanticism should be considered neither a school nor a movement but an experiment in instability.

America at the Roots of Romanticism

For three centuries, the American scene was being prepared as an ideal backdrop for Romantic drama. Already in Columbus's time, or Vespucci's, and certainly in that of the conquistadors, its virgin landscape seemed paradisal. Natural histories found their favorite territory in the New World. To talk about nature and think of America was the same thing. When Chateaubriand feels the first pangs of the fire that is going to make him write the great novel of his times, he goes to America, explores its wilderness and loses himself in the contemplation of Niagara Falls. He talks with the Indians, and even owes his life to one of them, who saves him when he is about to fall into the foaming abyss of a mighty cataract.

Goethe dedicated his closest attention to Humboldt's stories of his voyages through the Orinoco and the South American mountain ranges. We picture him a second discoverer of the New World. His image remains, engaged in conversation with the Indians at the foot of the Chimborazo or examining a flower in the jungles of Guiana. The adventures of La Condamine or Bougainville are essential to Montaigne as he shapes his concept of the Noble Savage. Much of the past from which the Romantic revolution was inspired is an American past.

Gilbert Chinard and Silvio Zavala have done some lucid research to learn up to what point American ideas were present at the origin of French Romanticism. They have rescued from oblivion certain works that were highly influential in their time. Chinard rediscovered books like that of Jean Bautiste de Tertre on the French Antilles, or Morelly's *Code of Nature*. Tertre, in his description of hummingbirds or his images of Caribbean fruits and flowers, wrote, in 1654, some pages that Bernardin de Saint-Pierre or Chateaubriand would envy. Morelly did not travel, but he took from a Peruvian source the information that permitted him to write a poem and *The Code of Nature*. He was more interested in men than in landscape and, in the manner of More's *Utopia*, composed a poem on the Floating Islands that he entitled "Brasiliada." Everything in it seemed incredible; and, in order to explain it and provide it with a solid base, he wrote the *Code*. The two works are immediate antecedents to Rousseau. Chinard not only supplies the proofs, but also signals a surprising thing: the influence of these works on the political ideas of their time. The Marquis of Argenson commented, referring to the *Code*, that it was "the book of books." The French revolutionary François Babeuf, during his trial, defended himself with quotations from it. Fourier took inspiration from it for his communities. Tocqueville wrote: "All the economists' doctrines about the state's power and its unlimited rights, and many theories which have produced upheaval in France in recent times, whose birth we thought we were witnessing, are in Morelly's *Code*." The anarchistic communism that Proudhon synthesizes in "property is theft" is an echo of Morelly. Morelly is at the base of the Russian anarchist Prince Kropotkin's message to youth . . . and all this came from America: from the Inca Garcilaso, from Vespucci.

Morelly writes in 1755, but years before, in the seventeenth century, the Inca's *Royal Commentaries* had been published in France, and Morelly was familiar with them, with the additional advantage of his having made the acquaintance of American travelers. Through one of them, he learned that in that continent greatness consisted in serving others, not in humiliating the small. Savages was what the Americans would call the Europeans. And they were right: "What innocence is there that can survive bad example?" Private property in Europe had destroyed the foundations of justice. Common property brought happiness to all the Americans.

The prize offered by the Abbé Raynal for the best essay about whether the discovery of America had been beneficial to Europe or not was as popular as the latest riddle making the rounds of the salons. The question was no longer, as it had been in the days of Montaigne, a matter only of South American Indians, but included those of the entire hemisphere, with particular reference to those in the United States. Remember Chateaubriand. But there were also some minor studies, which Silvio Zavala has investigated. Madrillon wrote, in 1784: "Scattered over an immense continent, free as nature is all around them, surrounded by cliff and mountain, standing before the vast, uninhabited plains, close to the forest where everything is still wild and nothing recalls either the bondage or the tyranny of men, the North American natives seem to derive from every physical object lessons of liberty and independence."

All America is thus involved in the shaping of European Romanticism. The North's greatest importance lay in the independence of lands inhabited, not just by the English, but by settlers from France, Germany, Poland, Ireland, the Netherlands. . . . Chateaubriand comes back from America, a novelist charged with a poetic force found in nature and in the rugged life of jungle dwellers.

Today, the dawning of Romanticism is associated with three

confluent circumstances: the Industrial Revolution, the American Revolution, and the French Revolution. Actually, the impulse came from farther back, from the New World itself.

Transfiguration of the Noble Savage

Toward 1773, there was an unexpected event that made a deep impression throughout Europe. It was the crumbling of a universal empire: that of the Jesuits. The spark ignited in Paraguay in 1758. The clash between the mission priests and the Portuguese colonial empire, which was then under the iron rule of Minister Pombal, produced the expulsion of the Jesuits from Portugal, Spain, and their colonies, as well as from France, Naples, and Parma. They were condemned by the conclave of 1769, and finally suppressed in 1773. Their missions in China and Japan were closed.

On the eve of their collapse, public opinion could not have been more favorable to the Jesuits. Lodovico Muratori, the father of Italian history, had praised them highly, as had Montesquieu and Voltaire. Suddenly, white becomes black. The entire *Encyclopedia* turns against the Jesuits. Voltaire, in *Candide*, portrays them as coarse, sensual, and dishonest, with no other thought than to take advantage of the natives, who are portrayed as the noble creatures of Montaigne. It is the natives who take Candide to El Dorado, the scene of Voltaire's Utopia. Voltaire did not really believe in the Noble Savage, but no matter; not only does he describe him in El Dorado, he takes him to the theater. *Alzire* is the famous play in which he presents the Inca in all his glory for the European spectator, and with such forcefulness that Verdi feels compelled to write an opera for the story, and Mme. Graffigny writes—with even greater repercussions—her *Lettres Péruviennes*, from which Goldoni takes the plot for *La Peruviana*. The Noble Savage has ceased to be a defiant anarchist: he is the wise American, the *Amauta* who conveys his nation's history by the rope knotting system of the *quipu*. Mme. Graffigny has an edifying correspondence with Raimondo di Sangro, which gives origin to the "Lettera Apologetica" of that distinguished academy member, published the same year as Rousseau's essay on the superiority of oral to written language. Raúl Barranechea, who has done the most exhaustive research on this work, writes: " 'La Lettera' exposes all the historical and dialectical reasons . . . to prove the excellence of the *quipu* as a means of transmitting thoughts. It makes a dissertation on the signs that substitute for spoken language, and cites Plato to affirm that reading is harmful to memory. The *quipu*, with its different kinds of knots—triangular, square—its rolls, the objects fastened to it, the tassels that hang down, can express all the various shadings of a word."

The interest in the Noble Savage leads to an interest in American civilization. The day was to come when one of the most illustrious historians in the United States, William H. Prescott, would publish his monumental works on the Aztec and Inca civilizations to complement those first attempts to defend their culture. But at that time the Jesuits themselves took the initiative. This enabled them to contradict and discredit the Spanish crown. Bologna was the place where they met to discuss Indian grandeur. Father Francisco Clavijero wrote his extensive history of the ancient Aztecs. Likewise, other illustrious companions of Clavijero devoted themselves to demonstrating the Indians' peerless qualities, their bravery, their virtues, from Canada to Chile.

Another American event took place in 1780 (seven years after the dissolution of the Jesuit order): the Indian rebellions in South America. The first commons had risen up years before in Paraguay: now the revolt was being repeated in New Granada, in Peru, Ecuador, Venezuela. In Peru, it was completely Indian. Túpac Amaru had descended directly from Inca royalty. In New Granada, the insurgents were Indian, white, black. Francisco de Miranda, who was spreading the news of an impending Spanish American revolution, from England and France to Russia and Sweden, learned about these movements, and, from then on, wherever he went, this topic was discussed.

Most historians have neglected to record European and American events exactly as they have been interwoven for more than four centuries. Today, Claude Manceron, in his monumental work *Les Hommes et la Liberté*, breaks with that tradition. This collection contains a great number of American documents on the period of greatest agitation in the eighteenth century. When he comes to the month of May, 1781, he dedicates quite a long discussion to the execution of Túpac Amaru. On the twenty-first of that month, Louis XVI had Abbé Raynal's (and Diderot's) *History of the Indies* condemned. The abbot had to flee to escape royal "justice." In the salons of Paris, it was impossible to talk of anything else. It was during this time that Túpac Amaru's execution by the Spanish authorities took place in Lima. "Everything began for Túpac Amaru," Manceron tells us, "on the fourth of November 1780; and everything ended on the 18th of May, 1781. The Indian had never read Diderot and knew nothing of his existence. But his blood fell like a torrent on the margins of Raynal's book. It was the philosophical and political history of the great revolt of the South American Indians. . . . A red chapter that Europe will take centuries to decipher."

Túpac Amaru's revolt illustrates that Spanish America is ripe for revolution, but the Inca Garcilaso's *Commentaries* demonstrate the Indians' capacity to organize a government. Discussing with European statesmen the need to create an original formula for a South American government (as Montesquieu had desired), Miranda suggests a Peruvian monarchy: an Inca organization. He talks about this with William Pitt, the British prime minister. The Englishman says to Miranda: "If you attempted to introduce a French system in Colombia, I can assure you that we would prefer to have the Spanish Americans continue for a century as obedient subjects to the King of Spain's oppressive government, than see them submerged in the calamities of the abominable system of the French." Miranda explains: The government would be presided by an Inca, two *curacas* would be in charge of the execution of the laws, the armed forces would be under an *hatunapa* . . . as in the days of old Peru. Romanticism was arriving in London. Pitt nodded and commented: "Well, all this is fine, and nothing keeps me from approving."

Napoleon also discussed American problems with Miranda at a

dinner where the future duchess of Abrantes, who was present, remembered these words from the emperor: "Miranda is a Quixote; the difference is he isn't mad."

South American things were becoming increasingly popular. An exotic ballet by Rameau, *Les Indes Galantes*, mixes South Americans with characters from China and India. Jean-François Marmontel had aroused popular interest with his novel *The Incas*, where he imagines the loves of the Inca Phani Palla, and the sun festivals, which becomes a theme for ballet.

Romanticism's Masterpiece

Romanticism's masterpiece was American independence. It is worth more than a novel by Sir Walter Scott or a Beethoven symphony or Victor Hugo's *Hernani* or Verdi's *Aïda*. The theme is not the protest of a man oppressed by circumstances or the song of an old legend. It is the liberation of a continent many times larger than Europe. Millions of Europeans who have crossed the ocean during four centuries are going to be freed. Indians and blacks march toward the conquest of their human dignity. They will become— to use the language of the time—citizens. In literature, the Romantics often express themselves in speeches and proclamations: this naturally leads to action. Napoleon writes proclamations that seem to have come out of a novel, and Beethoven transposes to a "heroic" symphony the ideas that the Corsican had announced at the beginning of his career. In America, the theater was vast like no other, the experience more radical; the heroic quest one that included millions and millions of people of every color.

The English statesman George Canning once said to the Duke of Wellington: "In the world's present situation American matters are infinitely more important than those of Europe." This belief explains his profuse correspondence with Bolívar. Bolívar, in turn, commenting on one of Canning's expressions, wrote to Santander: "What is happening in America is not a problem or even an event, it is a sovereign and irrevocable decree of destiny: this world cannot be linked with anything because the two great oceans of the world surround it; yes; do not worry about the recognition of our independence or about peace: these things will come quite soon, whether or not this pleases Europe and Spain." Nine years before this, as he was leaving Paris, he said to Flora's mother, Teresa Tristán: "I want to be the Noble Savage and set up a tent in the Venezuelan woods where I can live with nature all around me."

Lord Byron took some time deciding whether he should go to war in Greece or live in Venezuela. In 1819, he wrote to his friend John Hobhouse: "I have two projects: one is to visit England in the spring; the other is to go to South America. . . . Europe's decrepitude is growing. . . . There the people are new." He was not able to organize the journey to Venezuela. He went to Greece. But the yacht on which he traveled, the same one on which he took Shelley's remains to Rome, had a symbolic name: *The Bolívar*.

Chateaubriand said in France:

> No one that I know of looks for the influence of America in Europe in the establishment of the American republics. They always insist on seeing the ancient monarchies as they were: stationary societies that neither advanced nor retreated. There was not the least notion of the revolution which in the span of forty years has taken place in man's spirit. . . . The most precious of all the treasures that America contained in her bosom was liberty; every nation is bidden to delve into that inexhaustible mine. The discovery of the representative republic in the United States is one of the greatest political events in the world.

Chateaubriand did not find in the Spanish colonies those same antecedents that had made the republic possible in the United States, and, like a true royalist, he believed that any solution began with a throne, as in Brazil. The Spanish heritage inevitably imposed a delay in evolution. But the wise thing was to accept independence, and, as chancellor, he persuaded Louis XVI to write Ferdinand VII about this. Once the letter was written, he considered that he had accomplished his most important mission, and he retired from the government. Afterward, Ferdinand VII's attitude made him understand how useless his work in favor of peace and independence in America had been: "It was the last dream of my old age: I dreamed that I was in America and I woke up in Europe."

Calling to work the legislators of the First Colombian Congress of Angostura, Bolívar quoted Volney's words in the dedication of *The Ruins of Palmira*: "To the new peoples of the Castilian Indies, to the generous leaders that guide them towards freedom: may the errors and misfortunes of the ancient world teach the new World wisdom and happiness."

Hidden and Direct Romanticism

While the European Romantics looked backward, or looked far away, while they wrote parables, it was easy to catalogue them as escapists. Actually, they were dissimulators. But if what they sought was personal independence, there would have to be someday a direct allusion, an action, as there was for Victor Hugo, whose dramas, poetry, and novels place him on the political tribune. With a keen lens, Hugo takes images, remote examples, and brings them up close for dramatic effect. Romanticism in America was different.

The American Romantic was neither exotic nor nostalgic. The Indians were his Indians, the landscape was his landscape, and the immediate consequence was the war of independence. The old guard of European thinkers—Montesquieu, Locke, and the rest—became Jefferson, Washington, Bolívar, San Martín, Hidalgo. The gaucho Artigas was a Rousseau, a master of the social contract who explained to his fellow insurgents, there in the wild Uruguayan countryside, the foundations of revolution as if these notions were born of the wild. America was the continent where ideals acquired body and soul, and, as ideas traveled back and forth over the ocean, American Romanticism inserted itself into the European revolutions. Then, once more, the ideas became French, Italian, Polish. . . .

European novels, poems, or dramatic works of the first Romantic period frequently tend toward melancholy and sadness. There is usually a suicide at the end. More often than not, tuberculosis leads the way. Vanished natural splendor is searched among ruins. As opposed to gardens that take shape under the civilized man's shears, ruins are the thing. A statue is more beautiful if it is broken, fallen amid nettles and wild acanthus, with lizards crawling over the soiled marble, than if it is put back on its pedestal. This type of Romantic aesthete emphasizes the drama of his own miseries, the poetic impact of things remembered—he looks on his bohemianism with nostalgia, and satirizes the farce of a glittering and decaying aristocracy.

When the American Revolution becomes European, and the rights of man are engraved onto the French constitution by its new conquering heroes, the bourgeoisie and the enlightened people, France is reborn. Victor Hugo composes the song and there is thundering applause. The European Romantic has changed, and if America applauds him . . . unconsciously, she is applauding her own. She feels her role has been played well.

Literature as an instrument became a mighty force—as did music, painting—rejecting the traditional norms. This is a superficial characterization, for the weight of that force lay in the deep-seated defiance beneath the words, in the masses' rebellion, in the collapse of empires and monarchies. In Victor Hugo's tirades against the death penalty. In the proclamation of liberty. In the revolt against the Church and against whatever philosophy prevented free spirits from prospering or crushed man's dignity. In the worldwide upheaval that takes place in the nineteenth century, there is nothing childish or foolish, and in it America has the role of precursor. America took the initiative, in America were fought the first battles, and it was there that the empires died. France participated in the great American war in the hope of weakening England, playing a game for power. Romantically, Lafayette and his men enlisted . . . and came back full of revolution. A revolution that was universal as the war had not been.

Romanticism changed everything in European life. The fervor, the passion, the spontaneity that had been restrained for centuries broke their barriers and a new era was opened. Man began to declare his own rights, at the risk of anarchy. When one reflects with sufficient perspective on this deep, radical change, one finds the words that define this new course: *Independence. Freedom.*

Italy, Germany, Spain

In 1733, Antonio Vivaldi presented first in Venice, then in all Italy, an opera, *Montezuma*—a fact that Alejo Carpentier, delving avidly for musical treasures, disinterred to the surprise even of the experts on that revolutionary Italian musician. For the first time, a great European composer had written a work on a strictly American subject. The date—1733—places this Romantic prelude before anything "Romantic" occurred in Germany, England, France. Why did Vivaldi choose the theme of Moctezuma?

Europe was already teeming with American heroes. From the time of Columbus, discoverers and conquerors had passed from chronicle to poetry and novel, and with them the Indian heroes and kings. Columbus, Pizarro, Balboa . . . and Atahualpa, Moctezuma, Cuauhtémoc, Caupolicán. As in the idea of the Noble Savage, once more Montaigne's influence is felt. The portraits that he had made of Atahualpa and Cuauhtémoc prepare the Indian's entrance into the world scene. Atahualpa's greatness contrasts in his essay with Pizarro's vile treason. Cuauhtémoc is a splendid figure when, put to torture at the same time as one of his courtiers, and hearing the latter implore mercy (while his own feet are being burned with blazing coals), turns to him and says: "Am I by chance in the delights of a bath?"

Montaigne soars into such peaks of enthusiasm that he belongs in what two centuries later would be called the Romantic period: "Our world has just found another world, quite as large, rich and strong as ours, but at the same time so new and young that we are teaching it the alphabet. Fifty years ago there was no knowledge there of letters, weights, measures, garments, wheat or vineyards. Men went naked and took their nourishment only from such things as nature offered them. . . . Today this world marches towards the light, while our own declines!" And he adds: "Let us fear only the contagion that can make the Old World afflict the new with decadence and ruin: we have brought there only our power: neither justice nor mercy." He takes magnificent examples of the strength and stoicism of the Americans that make the best ones of ancient times look dim by comparison.

These images had multiplied in poetry, engravings, narrative works, and Vivaldi's Moctezuma was a well-known character. Vivaldi does not discover him. He gives him new life. Twenty years later, Karl Heinrich Graun—whom Frederick the Great had called to his court when he was crown prince, and who had been conductor of the Berlin Orchestra—presents a new opera on Moctezuma. The difference from the Vivaldi piece is that the author of the libretto is Frederick himself, while the author of Vivaldi's text is quite an unknown, at least to most of us—one Girolano Giusti. Frederick wrote the libretto in French, but Italian being a better language for opera, J. P. Tagliazucci transferred it to Italian. Graun's Moctezuma has survived the passage of time; it was replayed in a German version in 1936. We must not forget in passing that Verdi also composed an opera on Moctezuma, which never attained the popularity of most of his other works. Musical influence is not what is important here; it is the theme, whether it be the American hero or the nobility of nature, although the message itself does not have the scope of Spanish, Italian, or German opera themes.[1] (The operas on Moctezuma or Spontini's *Fernand Cortez* are exceptions.) The musical presence of America is a phenomenon of modern time. Afro-Cuban and West Indian music, Brazilian melodies and rhythms, Inca airs, Negro spirituals, American dances, ballets, even instruments—wind, percussion . . . jazz—are modern and have nothing to do with the so-called Romantic period. They are not within the scope of this chapter. Nevertheless, we should record what the new revolution that shook the world and set it wildly dancing has in common with the elements of protest and free expression that characterized Romanticism.

In Spain, the American influence was greater than in the rest of Europe. Spain's Romanticism, in a certain sense however, had its cradle in London, where Spanish political exiles went and where Americans brought news of independence. In magazines, books, academies, societies, cafés—it was all like a great political club— the Americans were what gave impulse to Romantic rebellion. Passing through that section of town inhabited by sleepless folk and poets, the Londoners must have stared curiously at these Latins who talked so much, both with their tongues and their hands, and formed the strangest group of passionate idealists. Books and magazines were published in Spanish. The *Repertorio Americano* asked that the statue of Las Casas, the defender of the Indians, be erected in Panama; and Heredia—the same Cuban poet who sang to Niagara Falls in verses that Chateaubriand would envy—published his song to Cholula, the handsomest example of such colloquial lyrics:

I was sitting on Cholula's ancient pyramid.
At my feet, the vast plain lured my eyes
across its distances.
What silence! What serenity! How could it be here,
amid these fields, that barbarous oppression
should reign with such insolence!
How can this soil, sprouting such rich grain,
owe its wealth to the spilling of men's blood?

When the emigrants return to Spain and the Romantic movement begins to grow there, those who give it a shove are not all Spaniards. There are Americans among them, and a Cuban woman stands out—Gertrudis Gómez de Avellaneda—who earns a place among the highest talents of Castilian letters. In 1848, she publishes her novel *Guatimozín* [Cuauhtémoc], *Last Emperor of Mexico*.

Madame de Staël's Salon

Poles, Irishmen, Englishmen, Italians, and Frenchmen had taken part in the American wars of independence. In Paris, Humboldt, La Condamine, Miranda, Bolívar had been seen in the same salons. Heinrich von Kleist—who has been called the precursor of Kafka—arrived in Paris accompanied by a German beauty, Ulrike, with whom Byron and Chateaubriand fell in love. All three men became promoters of American subjects through vast regions of Europe. Kleist wrote two novels that had a wide audience: *The Earthquakes in Chile, or The Nun of Santiago* and *The Lovers of Santo Domingo*. They all frequented salons like that of Mme. de Staël, who inspired French Romanticism with her book of travels through Germany. She was a friend of Miranda and of other Americans. Some of these Americans returned to their homeland, others remained in Paris, London, Rome. In Paris, a Mexican, Friar Servando Teresa de Mier, and a Venezuelan, Simón Rodríguez, founded a school to teach the Castilian tongue and made the first translation to another European language of Chateaubriand's *Atala*. They had translated it as a Spanish textbook for their French students. Simón Rodríguez had been Bolívar's teacher. Friar Servando was one of the precursors of Mexican independence.[2]

Presence of the American Woman

In the Romantic period, there are two salons in Paris, dominated by two women, opposite in character, who are directly related to Latin America and whose importance in French and world history would have to be considered at the same time that we speak of the salons of learned women like Mme. de Staël. Of these two, one is born in the West Indies, in Martinique, and the other is the daughter of a Peruvian from Lima: Josephine Tascher, the West Indian, becomes empress of France; and Flora Tristán, the Peruvian, creates the international workers' union.

Josephine brought the unique sensual charm of the Caribbean to the French throne. In American terms, no one has told it in such a pleasant way as Teresa de la Parra:

I believe that, like tobacco, pineapple and sugar cane, Romanticism was an indigenous fruit that grew, sweet, spontaneous and hidden, tucked into the innermost recesses of colonial languor and tropical indolence till the end of the eighteenth century. It was more or less then that Josephine Tascher unsuspectingly, more like one would carry an ideal germ, took it with her, tangled in the frills of one of her lace caps, and this was how Napoleon caught the disease in that acute form that we all know about, and, little by little, the troops of the First Empire, seconded by Chateaubriand, propagated the epidemic everywhere. No matter what you say, no matter how much you're going to laugh at me, I assure you that Mama and Napoleon were very much alike.

Josephine's salon is the salon of the world. The empress's crown (that the pope and Napoleon place on her head) is the most complete homage that could be rendered to a West Indian come to the heart of Paris. Flora's salon on rue du Bac is another story. It is the revolutionary hearth that brings together writers, poets, statesmen, workers, craftsmen. From her Peruvian experiences, Flora has absorbed the essence of a socialism that anticipates Marxism, that penetrates into the new philosophy of proletarian insurgence. Her journey to Peru—*Las Peregrinaciones de una Paria* (*The Pilgrimages of an Outcast*)—is the announcement of a profoundly human rebellion. In the *Revue de Paris*, she publishes *The Convents of Arequipa*, first example of the American background to her socialism. Flora is the anti-Josephine when she writes:

Napoleon is the monarch who has taken his power farthest over the nations that he has dominated. His forces drag the poor out of their miserable dwellings, the rich out of their palaces, for no one can escape. But what lasting thing has he left for mankind? Which of his institutions has improved its condition? What has he done that is permanently useful? The codes that he presents as title to his personal glory are, in the opinion of the experts in these matters, very much inferior to the so-called intermediate legislation that existed before his rise to power. With his prejudices and his tyrannical instincts, he has substituted the liberal principles of republican legislation; he has turned marriage into bondage, the businessman into a suspicious person; he has attempted measures against equality; he has established the privileges of the first-born and the confiscation of property and also the non-revelation of crimes; he has withdrawn the actions of public officials from the jursidiction of the court; nearly canceled the jury. . . . Under his reign censorship extends to include everything. He treats the French as if they were children, teaching what they should think and say, making himself the lord of public opinion.

Flora came close to the English workers and had experiences that Engels never knew. In 1844, she was ahead of the radicals in declaring that property was theft, and anticipated Marx in the invention of his slogan "Workers of the world, unite!" in her newspaper, *L'Union Ouvrière*, where she cried: "Union is strength! Union, Brothers: Let us unite!" She wanted to promote everything: human, social, and political union; equality for men and women; the right to work; the right of education for men and women; wealth shared by all; the realization of equality, liberty, and justice; the organization of work; equitable compensation for work, talent, capital. . . . Marx, who was then twenty-six years old, did not follow the advice of a friend who told him to go to Flora's salon. But workers visited her, and it is a moving thing to see the list of subscribers to *L'Union Ouvrière*: typographers, washerwomen, locksmiths, refugees, students, actors, deputies. . . . Jean Baelen, in one of the most recent studies on Flora, says:

> In the history of socialism, Flora Tristán has her own place, but there is no doubt that, in an orthodox Marxist system, that place can be heretical. The attitudes of Marx and Engels at the time the *Communist Manifesto* was published, concerning heresy, are but the foreshadowing of what opposition would inspire in future Marxists: silence or anathema for any form of socialism that does not bear the official mark. For the moment, we must admit that those who wished to bury Flora's memory have won; and if today, on the occasion of a congress, the table of the Presid-

ium were ornamented with a red cloth bearing Flora Tristán's signature under the words "Proletarians of the world unite!" it would be considered a sacrilegious cry.

With such injustices, will it be possible to fight all the others? Time will tell. But Flora Tristán will remain the Romantic expression of a socialist woman, an American, and a forerunner of the author of *Das Kapital*.

12

◆

Dinner
Is Served

Discoveries of the Discovery

This book would be incomplete without mention of the gastronomic revolution the discovery of America brought to Europe. In fact, it was the European palate that propelled the discoverers. An ingenious—but erudite—Italian once said that America was the result of a search for pepper. And it was. Trade with the East was stimulated and supported by those who prepared the Western table with exotic seasonings: cinnamon, pepper, cloves, nutmeg, saffron. . . . Fleets sailed from Venice, Genoa, Pisa, and went to India, Sumatra, Java, Ceylon. One day, the Turks blocked the way. Traders had to look for another route. It was in the search that they discovered America.

Pepper was counted by the grain. Cinnamon was more expensive than gold. Sugar was weighed in the finest of scales, by scruples. Surprise—and disenchantment—was great for the discoverers of the New World when, instead of those delicacies, they found the potato, dirty as truffles, dug out of the ground; corn, the misshapen and coarse spikes of an oversized kind of wheat; the bitter chocolate that Moctezuma drank. Things were reported confirming such barbarities: that the Mexicans made bread with that corn-wheat and that there was not one fistful of flour in the whole of America to make a holy wafer with; that from that same corn, if allowed to ferment, they made their wine: a thick wine that they called "chicha" and drank in cups made from the husk of a fruit: the gourd. When potatoes and corn were brought to Europe, it was discovered that they were good for pigs. People gave them disparaging names. The potato, which was named *turma* ("testicle") in Peru because it looked like a testicle, was called a variation of "truffle" (*cartoufle*) by the Europeans. In Ireland, they said that if a pregnant woman ate potatoes at night, her child would not be born normal. In Switzerland, Daniel Langhaus said that potatoes produced scrofula. In Russia, the powerful group of the Bezpopovshchiny argued that, since the Bible did not mention potatoes or tobacco, they had to be considered a botanical incest, an incarnation of the satanic spirit. The Besançon parliament, considering that the potato was a harmful substance and that the eating of it could cause leprosy, forbade anyone to plant it within the territory of Salins, under penalty of heavy fines. All this happened in the 1600s, but, later, Diderot's *Encyclopedia* blames the potato for producing stomach gases, although he goes on to say that for the peasants, who are the ones who eat potatoes, such winds are no problem as their work is in the open air. . . .

There are places in Europe where, for four centuries, the use of corn was limited to fodder for cattle and food for chickens and, especially, hogs. Italians called it "turkish grain," which had a contemptuous sound in those days. The Covarrubias dictionary says: "Corn: A kind of panic grass that makes ears wherein grow yellow or red kernels, large as chickpeas, which, when they are ground, make bread for the lowest people."

Tobacco was held to be the filthiest thing in the world, and there are those who affirm that the tobacco war has lasted three centuries. This war has been waged by popes, king, queens, statesmen, religious sects, moralists. . . . In a 1635 ordinance on police action in Paris, one reads: "All persons are forbidden, under any pretext, to sell beer or any other alcoholic drink, to sell tobacco or to procure it for use in their homes, under pain of imprisonment and flogging [*fouet*] according to the ordinance. . . . Henceforth it is forbidden to all persons, with the exception of pharmacists with a medical order to sell tobacco." Half a century later, another ordinance forbade cadets to use "Nicot's herb" . . . "there being nothing more inducing to drunkenness or likely to cause fire." (No one was allowed to enter a stable carrying a lighted cigar.) Louis XIV gave express orders commanding all those who sold tobacco (young ladies of easy virtue had been selling it near the barracks of the royal guard) and all the idlers and tramps to confine the sale of their tobacco to the barracks. Twenty-four hours after the publication of that ordinance, they were ordered to refrain from visiting the barracks. On the first infraction, their merchandise was to be confiscated. The second infraction brought corporal punishment. . . .

King James of England said that "tobacco turns the internal parts of the body into a kitchen, infesting them with oily and sticky soot. . . . Man's sweet breath," he added (forgetting that there was a time when all that man breathed was garlic), "being a gift of God's mercy, how can he corrupt it with this foul smoke?" Today, in the Louvre, there is a hall dedicated to the display of tobacco and cigar boxes in gold, silver, ivory, or rubies, gifts from one king to another.

In the Europe of barbarian days, armies would march out to offend a neighbor with that sweet breath, that garlic breath, so highly praised by King James. Garlic was what the soldier chewed, and his breath was stronger than lances, a better shield than bucklers. But when America entered the game, a new air—if not unpolluted, at least pleasant—came into the game of war. The soldier marched into war, his knapsack stuffed with tobacco to keep him warm. The stuff had its charm; as Don Andrés Bello once said:

and the leaf is thine
that when transmuted into vagrant softness
of spiraling smoke escapes,
will solace the dull hours of idleness . . .

Speaking of charm, what would our holidays be without the American turkey? Our salads without American tomatoes and avocados? And what would a Russian Cossack dance be without vodka? Vodka is potato alcohol, nothing more, nothing less. Potatoes from Russia, potatoes from Poland, potatoes from all places where vodka is consumed were originally potatoes from Peru. It is America that makes the Cossacks dance.

And then there is chocolate. Early chroniclers told how in the marketplaces of Mexico things were paid for with cocoa beans. It was extraordinary currency that made usury impossible. Peter Martyr wrote to Pope Clement in amazement: Chocolate—*xocoatl*, as the natives say—"is not only a useful and delicious drink; it also does not permit avarice, because the beans do not keep for too long a time." He was referring to cacao beans—*cacahuatl* in Aztec. With a hundred of them one could buy a slave, and other things were priced accordingly. The rich made their chocolate with chili, rocoubomba, and honey; the poor with corn flour and other everyday ingredients. It was said to be an aphrodisiac. Moctezuma would drink it from a golden cup at the end of his banquets, then call in his wives. With the first shipload of cacao beans that arrived in Spain, chocolate immediately became popular in court and among the clergy. Ten years after it came to Spain, chocolate arrived in Italy. One of the most intricate theological discussions came up— it lasted a century: the pope was asked if drinking chocolate interrupted fasting. Pius V replied: "No, it doesn't." But doubts remained. . . .

The Infanta María Teresa married Louis XIV, and that was how chocolate got to France. "The King and chocolate were María Teresa's two weaknesses: her two great loves." Spanish nuns revealed to the cardinal archbishop of Lyon, Alphonse de Richelieu, brother of the great Richelieu, the secret of chocolate; and Richelieu recommended it as a way to moderate the vapors of the spleen and to overcome choler and bad humor. Doctor Bachot, when he presided over the ceremony of discussing a thesis on chocolate, said: "It is a noble confection and a true nourishment for the gods— better than nectar and ambrosia—and worthier of being proclaimed divine than the Emperor Claudius's mushrooms."

In Sèvres, in Limoges, or wherever good porcelain was made, the greatest artistry was put into the making of candy boxes. Chocolate shops sprang up next to jewelry shops in the great avenues of Paris, Vienna, or London. In Mme. de Sévigné's correspondence there is a lengthy exchange with her daughter on the subject of chocolate. In Paris, just as there were tearooms, there were places where chocolate was served. The elegant customers would have appreciated Andrés Bello's poem to the Torrid Zone:

In coral urns thou hast thickened the almond that in the foaming cup is overflowing . . .

American Wars in Europe

In Europe, nothing is accomplished without one or two wars. America finally won the tobacco war—and it won the potato one, the chocolate one, the corn. . . . Some of these wars lasted more than a hundred years. When they were over, and everyone could smoke a cigarette or eat a potato in peace, it was possible to enjoy some measure of the paradise that had once been thought to exist in the New World.

Sir Walter Raleigh's case was doubly serious, because his name became involved in two of the major controversies of his time: tobacco and potatoes.

At the peak of his glory, Sir Walter bewitched Queen Elizabeth with his tobacco, and once, exalting the goodness of the smoke that came from his pipe, said to her that he could even weigh it. He finished by making a bet. The queen accepted it. Raleigh had the finest scale brought in, and there he weighed a quantity of tobacco. He smoked the whole load, emptied the ashes on the scale, computed the difference . . . and there was the weight of the smoke! There were other moments: the time when his manservant saw smoke coming out of his mouth and nose; he thought Sir Walter was on fire and doused him with a bucket of water.

When the wheel of fortune turned again, and Raleigh found himself at the bottom, the *Gazette* declared: "Raleigh is generally hated for having acquired the habit of smoking from the bestial Indians, slaves of the Spaniards, filth of the world, and, as such, excluded from God's community. . . ."[1] The author of this diatribe could very well have read the description left by Friar Bartholomew de Las Casas when Columbus saw the Indians smoking for the first time: "The men take a brand in their hands and certain herbs to make their incense, which are dry herbs put into a certain leaf, also dried, like the paper rolls that boys make on Whitsunday, and, lighting one end of it, they suck at the other, or breathe that smoke through their mouths, with which they numb their flesh and almost fall into a drunken state, and it is said that by doing so they feel no weariness." More or less what Churchill delighted in in Cuba and brought home to puff at in his offices.

In France, tobacco entered through the king's road. Joseph Nicotin, who was Catherine de Médici's ambassador in Lisbon, learned that the queen was in poor health and sent her some leaves to help her get better. This was how tobacco came to be known as "queen's leaf" (later it was called "grand prior's weed," because the grand prior of France used it; or "of the Holy Cross" for the cardinal). Jean Colbert was the first to see the business aspect. Government-monopolized cigar stores in France owe their existence to him. In 1674, he declared the manufacture, sale, and distribution of tobacco a royal privilege. When it became a question of saving the French Company of the Indies from bankruptcy, the company was given that same privilege. Time went by, and now it was Honoré Mirabeau who asked the National Assembly to vote for a state monopoly, but the Assembly, which in those days was gaily flaunting new freedoms, voted for its free cultivation and manufacture . . . to which Napoleon reacted and again proclaimed the monopoly.

The Church sometimes smokes tobacco in the higher spheres, sometimes takes snuff, and sometimes condemns this American sorcery. In Russia, Peter the Great adopted tobacco in spite of ecclesiastical disapproval.

In Francesco Montani's "Lettera Sopra il Tabacco," written in 1736, we read that tobacco cures cancer. . . . Montani and his letter plunge into the literary debate that originated with Girolamo Baruffaldi's ode "La Tabaccaide," written in 1714. In his letter, Montani says:

> From Florida, this plant was brought to Lisbon and was planted in the King's gardens, where, one day, when Joseph Nicotin, ambassador to the King of France, was taking a stroll, the guardian gave him a sprig which Nicotin took home and planted, and was soon able to make multiply. Moved by I know not what empirical curiosity, he experimented on a cancer, and, having obtained positive results initially, tried it on eight or ten more— again with admirable healing effects. He then proceeded to apply the juice and the paste of this herb on all manner of ulcers, wounds, scrofulae and fistulae, and each case showed it to be infallibly specific. Nicotin's house became a most frequented place. People came from far and wide in the hope of being cured by this minister, for which reason the plant came to be called *ambassador's herb*.

This was the first victory in the tobacco war. . . . A cure for cancer!

The tobacco war is so far considered to be a five-hundred-year war. It is impossible to imagine a longer one. It is still raging. The potato war is more nobly democratic (this we must say). The potato's destiny was to make war on hunger. During the Seven Years' War and Thirty Years' War, which mark two stages in European life, hunger made her traditional entry, and this was how the potato asserted itself. Frederick the Great sent Kolberg a wagonful of potatoes, hoping to allay the famine. "Not even dogs will eat that stuff around here," they told him. He had to send (from another location where potatoes were eaten) a gendarme who would sit without saying a word and eat potatoes in full public view. In a few days, the potato became a popular food. The tools used to plant the potato? The pike and the hoe—no different than the tools of the Inca, the *taclla* and *loy*.

For some countries, the new food meant a rebirth; and if they are in existence today, it is thanks to the potato. Ireland, for instance. The very people who burned cities in America, and even stole the church bells, and cursed the pope, pillaged towns and attacked ships, brought in gold and potatoes. Drake,[2] Hawkins, Raleigh[3] were the first to introduce potatoes to the British Isles. The Irish story begins with the vandal raids of the English upon their islands. Recently, these have been compared with things that Adolf Hitler did in this century. In 1641, the massacre was devastating. The English raiders burned grain, set fire to windmills. The people began to feed on roots: that is to say, on potatoes. They lived on potatoes for two years. To them, they were manna from Heaven. And so they are still, even in our own day. To quote a 1690 chronicle: "The common people are content with very little bread but consume great quantities of potatoes, which, together with sour milk, constitute their chief nourishment; beer they drink very rarely. They all smoke—men and women—out of a single pipe, one inch long, which the whole family uses for years . . . seven or eight will smoke together, each one inhaling once or twice and passing the pipe on to the next, almost always keeping the smoke in their mouths until their turns comes again. . . . In every orchard there are a few stalks of grain . . . and the dearly beloved potatoes." It would be hard to find a better description of American life anywhere.

In Offenburg, there is a statue of Francis Drake, in his hand a potato plant complete with blossoms and tubercles. On the pedestal: "To Sir Francis Drake, who introduced potatoes in Europe. A.D. 1580." The sculptor offered his statue "in the name of the millions of peasants who bless his immortal memory." The city of Strasbourg had ordered the monument, but at the last moment did not pay for it. The artist donated it to Offenburg with just one condition: that the statue be placed with its back (its bottom) toward Strasbourg. Anyway, the inscription exaggerates nothing when it says that millions of people were thus saved from starvation during the worst famines in many centuries. In a peasant and democratic gesture, Van Gogh dedicated some of his works to the potato, in the same way that the Peruvians had honored it in their ceramics. It was the best treasure that could be extracted from Inca soil. To explain his canvas of peasants eating potatoes, Van Gogh would say: "I have tried to portray how the common people, eating their potatoes by lamplight, have worked the soil with those same hands that they take to their plate, showing that they have earned their food with honest work."

Potatoes entered Rome in a manner befitting their Spanish American name—*papa*. Philip II sent some to the pontiff (also, the *papa*)—expressing the wish that their tonic properties (they were considered to be aphrodisiac) would restore his health. The pope shared his gift with one of the cardinals. Then, as a time of famine came, the *papa* descended to the poor man's table, and from the poor man's table, men like Parmentier took it and placed it once more on royal table linens. Every time such a change in levels takes place, there has been a story to tell. Parmentier, the pharmacist at Les Invalides, was a very enthusiastic potato grower. On Saint Louis's Day, he brought the king an unexpected present: a dainty basket that contained potatoes and was trimmed with potato blossoms. Louis XVI took one of the flowers and put it in his buttonhole. Marie Antoinette took a flowery sprig and put it in her hair: the potato had come to stay. The king gave Parmentier some land in Sablon to be used for growing potatoes. And potatoes came to be eaten in France. When, during the revolution, Parmentier was proposed as member of the Assembly, one of the deputies cried: "No, don't elect him! He who invented the potato will make us all eat it!"

The story of corn is a more delicate matter, because corn is America. The gods might have made Europeans out of wheat, Asians out of rice. The American was made of corn. Corn is as old as the oldest potsherd in America's archaeological dumps. Rudimentary ears have been found that are eighty thousand years old. Five thousand two hundred years before Christ, the inhabitants of the Mexican region of Puebla were already growing this cereal, which is an essential member of godly families, whether Mayan or Aztec. From Chile to Canada, this essential grain could be had. Tortillas, mush, bread, tamales, chicha—all these things were present at the American table from the time when tables were blocks of stone or simple mats spread on the ground. In the most beautiful Mayan monuments, in the pyramids of Palenque, man and corn emerge as the representation of life, with an elegance typical of pre-Columbian sculptors, equal to the best in Egypt. And poetry (because magically beautiful poetry was made in that fascinating past) sung to the goddess Xilonen, she of the tender grain, hair adorned with quetzal feathers, wearing the gold and turquoise necklace and the embroidered dresses and red sandals . . . All this to come to the conclusion that maize is to fatten pigs with? Heaven help us!

Time was the necessary ingredient. The Italians, who had given corn the ugly name of *grano turco,* ended up making polenta as popular a dish in Italy as spaghetti. Not only Europe, but Asia, Africa, and Australia finally accepted corn, which, after rice, is now the most widely produced cereal in the world. America supplied Europe, too, with gold and silver at a certain time, but gold and silver were already known and could be found in many other parts of the world so that America's mineral wealth meant only a change in the abundance of the moment, not a change in lifestyle.

But from questions of astronomy to the food on the table, America began transforming Europe the moment European explorers set foot on American soil. And what a transformation it was—to the degree that Europe came to be, after America, quite simply another Europe.

Notes

CHAPTER 1

1. The words of Vespucci show the extent of his revelation: "In days past I wrote you of my return from those lands that we have sought and discovered with a fleet fitted out at the expense and at the orders of this Most Serene King of Portugal, and which I can lightly call the New World. . . . We learned that that land is not an island, but a continent, because it extends along far-stretching shores that do not encompass it and it is populated by innumerable inhabitants. . . . I have discovered the continent to be inhabited by many more peoples and animals than our Europe, or Asia, or even Africa, and have found the air more temperate and pleasant than in other regions known to us. . . . A part of this continent lies in the torrid zone on the other side of the equator toward the antarctic pole, whereas its beginning lies 8° above that equinoctial line."

2. Very keenly Stefan Zweig explains the impact produced by the news from the New World (In *Amerigo, a Comedy of Errors in History*) thus: "The actual event of this letter consists oddly enough not in the letter itself, but in its title—*Mundus Novus*—two words, four syllables, which revolutionize the conception of the cosmos as had nothing before. . . . These few but conclusive words make of the

Mundus Novus a memorable document. They are, in fact—some two hundred and seventy years before the official one—the first Declaration of Independence of America. Columbus, up to the hour of his death, blindly entangled in the delusion that by landing in Guanahani and Cuba he had set foot in India, has with this illusion actually decreased the size of the cosmos for his contemporaries. Only Vespucci, by destroying the hypothesis that this new country might be India and insisting on its being a new continent, provides the new dimensions which have remained valid to this day."

In contrast with these lines of Zweig, let us remember the lines written by Emerson: "Strange . . . that all America should wear the name of a thief. Amerigo Vespucci, the pickler from Seville . . . whose highest naval rank was boatswain's mate in an expedition that never sailed, managed in this lying world to supplant Columbus and baptize half of the earth with his own dishonest name." Naturally, Emerson ignored the larger point of the discovery, and in this ignorance one must search for a way to excuse what he says in such few lines.

3. This information is taken from *L'Arte dei Medici e Speziali nella Storia e nel Commercio Fiorentino,* by Raffaele Ciasca (Florence, 1927), a very rich study on that period.

CHAPTER 2

1. In chapter 11 of his *History of the Indies,* Bartholomew de Las Casas "takes his authority from Pedro de Aliaco, Cardinal, great theologian, philosopher, mathematician, astrologer, cosmographer, which greatly influenced Columbus and confirmed all of the past." He says: "I believe that among those of the past, this doctor moved Christopher Columbus the most towards his enterprise; the book . . . was so familiar to Christopher Columbus, that all of it did he note and mark on the margins, writing there many things that he read and collected from others. This very old book many times did I have in my hands, taking from it a number of things written in Latin by the Admiral."

2. If we follow the notes that Columbus wrote on the margins of his *Imago Mundi,* we can see how he makes a synthesis of the cardinal's scientific observations, as if he were trying to memorize them. D'Ailly said: "One part of the earth is less heavy than the other: that which, due to its greater height is farther away from the planet's center. The rest, except for the islands, is entirely covered by water, according to the philosophers' opinion. Earth, being the heaviest element, is in the center of the world and constitutes, in fact, the world's center of gravity. According to others, the center of gravity for earth and water is the center of the globe itself. Although the earth is modeled with mountains and valleys, which are the cause of its imperfect roundness, it may be considered round." Columbus

summarized on the margin as follows: "Water and earth together form a round body. . . . The center of gravity for earth and water is the center of the world." If we read any page of Columbus's marginalia as if it were a continuous text, his idea about the earth's structure, based on D'Ailly, begins to emerge. On India: "Among her mountains there is an incalculable number of islands, and, among these, there are islands full of pearls and precious stones. That of Trapobana contains gems and elephants. Chryse and Argire contain gold and silver. There are the Ganges, Indus and Yd rivers. India contains many kinds of aromatic spices, many precious stones and mountains of gold. It is the third part of the habitable world. It is composed of 118 nations. Her boundary extends as far as the Tropic of Capricorn. There are men two elbows high. They take three years to conceive and die on the eighth. There is white pepper. The macrobies, twelve elbows high, fight against griffons. They have the custom of killing their parents when these grow old and preparing their flesh to be eaten. The women give birth only once and breed white children who become black with age."

CHAPTER 3

1. Marx (*Contribution à la Critique de l'Économie Politique*) makes the following direct reference to *Utopia*: "In England, for example, the development of industry in the Netherlands during the sixteenth century gave the wool industry great commercial importance, and also increased the need for merchandise, especially from Holland and Italy. So that, in order to obtain enough wool to export, the tillable lands were transformed to pasturelands for sheep, the small farms died out, and this caused the violent economic revolution that Thomas More deplored."

In the introduction to Silvio Zavala's essay, *La Utopía de Tomás Moro en la Nueva España*, Genaro Estrada quotes the work of N. W. Chambers as the best contemporary study on More, and adds: "With no small surprise, but with an immediate reaction of approval, one may read there that one of the ministers of the British Cabinet owes his political career to the accidental purchase of a copy of *Utopia* in a secondhand bookstore, and that one of his colleagues commented, referring to this work, that nothing else is better calculated to nourish a radical's heart. Because *Utopia*, Professor Chambers adds, has become a textbook for socialist propaganda and made William Morris more socialistic than Karl Marx could have made him. All this testifies to its permanent force, although we must not think that More wrote it for nineteenth-century radicals or twentieth-century socialists."

2. In *Utopia*'s Polish edition, in an introduction to the chapter on mutual relations between citizens, the translator, Marcelle Bottigelli-Tisserand, remarks: "Everything in this chapter treats the ideas of contemporary socialism: dignifying

work and workers as creators of wealth, compulsory work for all, organization of culture and rest for every citizen, planned production to assure plenty and permit a decrease in working hours. In other words, that expression of Humanism which imposes an irresistible comparison with the fundamental economic law of socialism expressed by Stalin (*Economic Problems of Socialism in the USSR*, 1952): 'To assure the satisfaction of material and cultural needs, which increase constantly in every developing society with the unceasing improvement of socialist production on the basis of a superior technique.' "

3. Alain Guy, "Vives Socialista y la Utopía de Moro," *Moreana* (November 1971).

4. Because it is impossible to reproduce in its entirety Erasmus's literary portrait of More, which appears in a letter to Ulrich von Hutten, I shall copy at least a few lines: "In shape and stature More is not a tall man, but not remarkably short. . . . His complexion is fair, his face rather blond than pale, but with no approach to redness, except for a very delicate flush, which lights up the whole. His head is auburn inclining to black, or if you like it better, black inclining to auburn; . . . his eyes a blueish grey with a sort of tinting in them. . . . His countenance goes with his character, having an expression of kind and friendly cheerfulness with a little air of raillery. . . . His right shoulder seems a little higher than his left, especially when he is walking. . . . In the rest of his body there is nothing displeasing—only his hands are a little coarse, or appear so, as compared with the rest of his figure. . . . What charm there was in his glance when young, may even now be inferred from what remains; . . . for he has not yet passed much beyond his fortieth year. . . . His health is sound rather than robust." After describing with the same exactness and detail the habits, manner of dress, voice, everything that could serve to give the most complete idea of his character, he tells about his studies and work, observing: "He published his *Utopia* for the purpose of showing what things create mischief in commonwealths, having the English constitution especially in mind, which he so truly knows and understands."

5. The fact that More was on a business mission brings some commercial references and advice into *Utopia,* as when Raphael suggests that English wool be made into cloth in their own country instead of being exported as raw material to Holland. Campbell, in his book, *Erasmus, Tyndale and More,* remarks: "Raphael's suggestion, in the opinion of some critics, places More as founder of modern capitalism. In Russia, if it were still possible there to speak of patron saints, More would be considered the patron saint of communism."

The complexity of this problem is described by Alexandre Cioranescu in *L'Avenir du Passé,* where we find observations such as these: "More's role is rather that of a reactionary than that of a friend of progress. He is opposed to capitalism, which already presented visible inconveniences, but which certainly meant progress. . . . In the great historical process between agriculture and industry, he sides with the first. . . . He is revolutionary only in the measure that it is admitted that the new can be made only out of the old."

6. Arinos de Mello Franco: *O Indio Brasileiro e a Revolução Francesa. Os Origens Brasileiros de Theoría da Bondade Natural.*

7. Paul A. Ladame has made an in-depth study of European immigrants in *La Rôle des Migrations dans le Monde Libre.* One of his most remarkable conclusions is this one: "65,000,000: a very impersonal figure, which the imagination is unable to conceive in all its size. But it is necessary that we try to understand that this stands for an individual 65 million times. An individual who contributes— within an atmosphere of liberty whose value is all the greater if he has paid dearly to obtain it—his arms, his brain, his knowledge and his traditions, his energy and his emotions, his body and soul, in order to be successful in a common experience that has no precedents in the history of mankind. The Free World has been born this way, from 65,000,000 small creatures during three centuries. They have built a political, economic and social system that is still quite imperfect, being subject to man's imperfection, but which is better than anything that had been done before."

8. Marcelle Bottigelli-Tisserand, Introduction to More's *Utopia* (Paris, 1966).

9. Marcel Bataillon and André Saint-Lu, *Las Casas et la Défense des Indiens.*

10. *Somnium,* by Juan Maldonado, is summarized and presented by Marcel Bataillon and André Saint-Lu in *Moreana* 5 (1965).

11. In his publication of Silvio Zavala's essay on Quiroga and Thomas More, Genaro Estrada comments: "The intellectual affinity between Quiroga and Thomas More seems to have been elective by necessity, not only in what concerned *Utopia*'s rules transported to the Ordinances and to the practice of the organization among the Michoacan peoples, but also because this man, who made way for himself with his works and strove in his day to implant in Mexico a doctrine of apostolic spirit and social improvement, seems to have imbibed the spirit of him who paid for his opposition to Thomas Cranmer's reform and the excesses of a corrupt monarch with his own life."

12. In the notes of his essay on Thomas More's *Utopia* in New Spain, Zavala reproduces a large part of Vasco de Quiroga's work on Lucianus's *Saturnials.* In the introduction, we may see how Quiroga transferred to the American reality what he had read in More's translation: "Almost in the same way as I have found that Lucianus tells in his *Saturnials* about the subjects of those peoples who were called golden or of the golden age at the time of Saturn's reign, where it seems that in everything and for everything there was the same equality, simplicity, goodness, obedience, humility, festivities, games, pleasures, drinks, amusements,

idleness, poor and despised belongings, apparel, shoes and food, according to what fertility the land gave, offered and produced by its own grace and with nearly no toil, care or concern of theirs, it seems that there is and is seen in the New World, among the natives, a carelessness and indifference for all superfluous things, with that same contentment and very great and free liberty in their lives, and the blithe disposition with which these natives are endowed and the great calm which they have, so that it seems that they are not obliged or subject to what fortune causes to befall them, so pure, prudent and simple are they, so that nothing troubles them: instead they wonder at us and our things and the anxiety and uneasiness that is ours, as many times they have said so, wondering greatly about this."

It is possible that More was able to guess about this first transplanting of his work to America. Alfonso Reyes says: "More, in one of his letters, tells about a man who is so virtuous that he deserved to be named Bishop of Utopia. . . . Lo and behold, that the real and genuine Bishop of Utopia was here in these American lands, and we have scarcely investigated. But who says that America has been discovered?" And Zavala comments: "Not one, but two bishops: Quiroga and Zumárraga . . ."

13. Montesquieu never doubted that Plato's Republic had been realized in Paraguay, and he declared it in the articles that he wrote for the *Encyclopedia*. Voltaire says in his essay "The Jesuits in Paraguay": "The Spaniards, in their conquest, from Buenos Aires to Peru, were aided by the Jesuit missionaries as soldiers could not have been able to aid them. These missionaries had penetrated little by little into the interior of Paraguay since the seventeenth century. They took some savages when they were still children, educated them in Buenos Aires and then employed them as guides and interpreters. Their hardships and difficulties were like those of the conquerors of the New World. The courage of religion is at least as great as that of the warrior. They never retreated and, because of that, they were successful. The oxen, the cows, the lambs taken from Europe to Buenos Aires had multiplied in a prodigious way; they took a great quantity to Paraguay, had the carts loaded with tools for agriculture and architecture, planted some of the plains with every European grain and gave all this to the savages, who became domesticated like the animals which one attracts with rewards. They taught them to plant, to make bricks, to work in wood, to build houses. . . . Their children became Christians."

All this had been predicted by Montaigne, with one difference: he believed that the Guaranís had the foundation of all the virtues. "It is a pity that Lycurgus and Plato had not known them, because it seems to me that what we are seeing through experience in those nations surpasses not only all the images which poetry has given us of the golden age and all its inventions, destined to create a fiction on man's happiness, but the concept and desire of philosophy itself. They were not able to imagine such pure and simple candor as that which we now have before us."

The book by Jose Peramás, *De Administratione Guaranica Comparate ad Republicam Platonis Comentarius*, to which this note refers, was translated into Spanish by Juan Cortés del Pino in 1946.

14. It is significant that the man who transformed Vespucci's narrative into *Utopia* was an Englishman, as was Francis Bacon, the author of *New Atlantis*, published in London in 1627. A group of sailors are cast on an island by a storm, where they find a scientific society that surprises them from the first moment, when they are given hospitality in a house for foreigners. The food that they receive is in the form of pills, an anticipation of vitamins. It is a prophetic book, in the manner of science fiction. Raymond Reyer in *L'Utopie des Utopies* summarizes Bacon's novel as follows: "The president of the house shows them the island, which is called Bensalem and is Christian. Twenty years before the Ascension, Saint Bartholomew had sent a chest sealed with a beam of light. It contained the two Testaments and the Apocalipsis. This is how we know about Bensalem's most ancient history, ingeniously related by Bacon to Plato's Atlantis and to his idea of great vanished civilizations. Plato's Atlantis, explains the Director, was America. There, as in Bensalem, a great civilization flourished. Plato was mistaken when he said that Atlantis, that is to say America, had sunk beneath the sea. It had been simply a flood, sufficient nevertheless to cause a regression in the vast continent's civilization, whereas Bensalem was saved."

15. Alexandre Cioranescu, in *L'Avenir du Passé*, writes: "The discovery of the American continent transforms an idea that is vain, abstract and dangerous from the medieval point of view into a tangible reality which it was impossible to underestimate or hide."

CHAPTER 4

1. The origin of the name "America," or rather how it was invented by the canons of Saint-Dié, was revealed by the casual finding of the book *Cosmographie Introductio*, written by Humboldt when he was preparing his *Géographie du Nouveau Continent* (Paris, 1836–39). About the works of the canons in the manuscript of Saint-Dié many articles have been published in the *Bulletin de la Société Philomatique Vosgienne* of Saint-Dié. For additional information, see *Amerigo and the New World* by Germán Arciniegas (Buenos Aires, 1956).

2. The letter by Amerigo Vespucci to which we refer was published by Roberto Rodolfi, who discovered it in that year and reproduced it, together with a Spanish translation in *El Nuevo Mundo* (edited by Roberto Levillier, Buenos Aires, 1951).

3. The name "Copernicus" originated from the village of Koperniki, in Silesia. "Koperniki" comes from "Koper" (fennel). Copernicus was born in Thorn, in

1473, and died in 1543; Columbus was born in Genoa in 1451 and died in Valladolid in 1506.

4. Jan Adamczewski, in *Nicolaus Copernicus and His Times*, says: "What kept Copernicus from publishing his book for such a long time could have been the activity of the Inquisition. He may have been influenced by Horatius's advice that a work should be published nine years after it has been written. . . . But Copernicus's books remained hidden—as he himself wrote—not nine years but four times nine. The reason for such a prolonged hesitation may very well have been the fear of being condemned together with his books."

5. Goethe said: "Of all the discoveries and criteria that have been published, nothing has impressed the human mind as much as the Copernican theory. Our world was barely recognized as round and enclosed within itself, when it was forced to renounce the enormous privilege of being the center of the universe."

6. Jan Adamczewski says: "*De Revolutionibus* was published by the printing house of Jan Petreius. The Protestant theologian Andreas Osiander was in charge of the edition, and he has gone down in history as a falsifier of the work of Copernicus. It was he who added—without the author's knowledge and in contradiction with objections that he made—a prologue of his own making: *Ad Lectorem de Hypothesibus huius Operis*, where he explained that the theory which this work presented had to be considered a 'fictitious mathematical scheme.' Besides this, the prologue was not signed, and could give the impression of being written by Copernicus himself."

7. It is a curious fact that in the beginning the Protestants were much more active against Copernicus than the Catholics. Eugeniusz Rybka says: "The University of Salamanca in Spain was probably the first to present the Copernican theory. It is also true that Walenty Fontana taught *De Revolutionibus* from 1578 to 1580, but he probably limited himself to explaining the use of the planetary tables in the book for astrological purposes. In any case, there is no evident proof that the lectures given in Krakow in the sixteenth century referred to the theory of the structure of the universe according to Copernicus. . . . The peremptory objections against the theory of the earth's movements came from the Protestant theologians. . . . The Catholic Church had not yet condemned the teachings of Copernicus officially in the sixteenth century. The reason for this apparent magnanimity may be attributed to the fact that it was so ardently combatted by the Protestants. Another possible explanation is that, in spite of the letter of dedication to the Pope, the anonymous prologue treated the studies as a mere hypothesis, and besides, the author himself was a canon of the Roman Catholic Church, and his works awakened great interest in persons in the highest ecclesiastical hierarchy."

8. An antecedent to Galileo's trial is the one against Giordano Bruno, the Italian Dominican friar and poet. Bruno revealed the Copernican system in an Ash

Wednesday sermon in 1584. He declared that it was contrary to nature and reason to suppose that all the heavenly bodies, large and small, revolved around the earth, instead of accepting the contrary. "The ideas that Giordano Bruno exposed," explains Eugeniusz Rybka, "were directly against the whole system of theological concepts of his time: and what was worse, his opinions on purely religious matters were also outside the general viewpoint. Consequently, the Roman Catholic Church authorities, whose attitude towards the teachings of Copernicus had been passive up to a certain point, resolutely objected to the theses presented by Giordano Bruno. He was tricked into going to Rome, and, upon his arrival, in 1592, was taken to the Inquisition dungeons. After eight years he was burned at the stake. Thus the great Italian thinker became a martyr for having revealed the Polish astronomer's theory."

9. Bertrand Russell in *The Scientific Outlook* copies in detail the Inquisition's sentence against Galileo, as a basic document for the study of the first act in the dramatic dawn of modern science. In the *Dictionnaire Apologétique de la Foi Catholique*, published under the direction of A. d'Alès, there is an extensive presentation of Galileo's trial, seen from the Catholic point of view, with the reproduction of its essential records.

10. Throughout the *Discourse* one sees the impact that Galileo's condemnation made on Descartes. In Descartes's opinion, the Florentine had stayed behind, gone only halfway: "I believe that his work is incomplete because of the constant digressions that he makes, without stopping to explain a subject in depth, and this shows that he has not examined them in order, and that, without having considered the first causes of nature, he has looked only for the reasons that explain some particular effects, thus constructing with no solid foundation." Nevertheless, Galileo had taken the definite step, and Descartes declares in the fifth part of the *Discourse* how he had abstained from publishing the study that had led him to the same conclusions because he wished to end his days in peace and let the "experts" think whatever they wished, while he himself kept out of that wasps' nest. It was better to wait, as Copernicus had done, and have the consequences of his reflections come out when he was already dead. His studies would not be published during his lifetime, so that "neither the oppositions or the controversies to which they may be subject, nor the reputation that they might give him would result in his having to lose the time that he wanted to spend in learning."

11. The references to America in the *Discourse* appear as proofs of the diversity of human societies or of the limitations of knowledge within which men have lived. "Having learned in school that everything, no matter how strange and incredible it might seem, was encompassed within what the philosophers have said, I later saw, in my travels, that other men, whose feelings are in sharp contrast with ours, are not barbarians because of that, but, instead, a large number of them make use of their reason in the same way as we, and since all reflect like one and the same

man, with their wits, had they spent their childhood among Frenchmen and Germans and I lived among Chinese or Cannibals (peoples of the Caribbean) . . . we would each find such things ridiculous and extravagant." He concludes by accepting the plurality of societies, on whose recognition the new philosophy is to be constructed. "We have to know something about other people's ways in order to judge our own from a more reasononable viewpoint. If our will tends only towards the things that understanding shows to be possible," faraway kingdoms like China or Mexico, projected into distant worlds, should not be forgotten.

CHAPTER 5

1. The documents are published by Martín Fernández de Navarrete in his *Colección de los Viajes y Descubrimientos que Hicieron por Mar los Españoles desde Fines del Siglo XV*.

2. Paul III's bull, *Sublime Deus*—June 5, 1537—says in the pertinent part: "The enemy of humanity, who opposes all that is good in order to obtain men's destruction, seeing this with envious eyes, has invented means, hitherto unknown, to disturb the Word of God, which is the salvation of the world; he has inspired his satellites, who, in their desire to please him, have not hesitated to diffuse far and wide that the Indians of the East and South, and other peoples of which we scarcely have knowledge, must be treated like brutes, created for our service, claiming that they are unable to receive the Catholic Faith.

"We, although unworthy, exercise on earth the power of our Lord and strive by every means to bring the sheep to the fold that has been entrusted to us. We consider that the Indians are real men and that, not only are they capable of understanding the Catholic faith, but that, according to our informations, they are anxious to receive it. Wishing to provide some remedy to these evils, we define and declare by these our letters, and by any faithful translation subscribed by a notary public, sealed with the seal of any ecclesiastical dignitary, which will be given the same credit as the original, that no matter what has been said or shall be said to the contrary, those Indians, and all those which Christians shall henceforth discover, cannot be deprived of their liberty by any means, nor of their property, even though they do not belong to the faith of Jesus Christ: and they shall freely and rightfully enjoy the use of their liberty and their properties, and they shall not be slaves, and whatever be done to the contrary shall be null and void."

3. Eric Williams, to whom Jamaica in great part owes her independence, has written an impressive contribution to the study of this subject in *Capitalism and Slavery*.

In his book *From Columbus to Castro: The History of the Caribbean (1492–1969)*, he contributes such facts as these: "Liverpool's first slave ship, of 30 tons, sailed for Africa in 1709. In 1783 the port had 85 ships, of 12,294 tons, in the trade. Between 1709 and 1783, a total of 2,249 ships, of 240,657 tons, sailed from Liverpool to Africa—an annual average of 30 ships and 3,200 tons. The proportion of slave ships to the total shipping of the port was one in a hundred in 1709, one in nine in 1730, one in four in 1763, one in three in 1771. In 1752, 88 Liverpool vessels carried upwards of 24,730 slaves from Africa. Seven firms, owning 26 vessels, carried 7,030 slaves.

"Half of Liverpool's sailors were engaged in slave trade, which, by 1783, was estimated to bring the town a clear annual profit of 300,000 pounds. The slave trade transformed Liverpool from a fishing village into a great center of international commerce. The population rose from 5,000 in 1700 to 34,000 in 1773. It was a common saying in the town that its principal streets had been marked out by the chains, and the walls of the houses cemented by the blood of African slaves. The red brick Customs House, blazoned with Negro heads, bore mute but eloquent testimony to the origins of Liverpool's rise by 1783 to the position of the most famous—or infamous, depending on the point of view—towns in the world of commerce. What Liverpool was to England, Nantes was to France."

4. Vitoria's indignation is so great when he learns what the *Peruleros* are doing against the Indians, that, in another part of his letter, he says: "If I greatly desired the position of Archbishop of Toledo, which is vacant, and it were offered to me on condition that I affirm the innocence of these *Peruleros* with either my signature or my word, there is no doubt that I would never dare do so. I would rather have my tongue and my hand wither away than say or write anything so inhuman and devoid of all Christian spirit."

5. For Erasmus, and Thomas More as well, America became the place where they could use the lever of their criticism of European life. It was Erasmus who persuaded More to write the first chapter of *Utopia*, which gathered all the information that Vespucci gave on Brazil. Likewise, Erasmus, in *The Praise of Folly*, presents the character that directs the whole discourse against the ideas then prevailing in Europe as someone who had come from the Fortunate Isles, where toil, old age, and sickness were unknown. Traditionally, these islands were located beyond the Pillars of Hercules—from the time of Homer to that of Horace—and were at times thought to be the Canary Islands, but as Columbus's followers continued their explorations, they were moved farther and farther westward. Thus the legend of the Seven Cities of Cíbola in Mexico was born and titillated the mind of many a conquistador. When Erasmus writes his *Praise*, the Fortunate Isles are already considered as part of the America that is being explored. And Erasmus's name is the cornerstone for the foundation of the University of Mexico by the Erasmist Cervantes de Salazar.

6. In his essay "Des Cannibales," Montaigne refers to this decoration in his home, tells about the Guaraní way of life and takes many facts from Vespucci's letter, among others, those that refer to the natives' excellent health, their long life, and their tendency to make use of it in the manner of the Epicureans instead of subjecting it to discipline like the Stoics. Montaigne cites a few texts by Seneca and Virgil that are more in accordance with Guaraní life than with that of the Europeans.

7. Jean Plattard in *Les Cannibales de Montaigne* establishes a relation between the literature born of the Guaranís' presentation in Rouen and the literature of the Golden Age and the Fortunate Isles, making reference to Ronsard: "In 1554, Ronsard composes a poem entitled *The Fortunate Isles*. He sees civil war looming over France. The country is torn apart by dissensions. Disgusted by all this, he sees no other choice than to go away to the Fortunate Isles. . . . Of course he refrains from saying what or where they are. The ancients had given that name to islands that could be the Canaries. In any case, there is nothing in this poem that one could take for a reference to the New World. But this changes. First, at that same time, and for the same reasons, La Boétie writes a poem in Latin on the theme that Ronsard had developed in *The Fortunate Isles*. 'If France becomes uninhabitable: Let's go away! Where? To the newly discovered nations, where lands are not divided, where everyone has agreed that they should not be distributed, to this continent that seems to have emerged out of the waters and is the New World.' "

CHAPTER 6

1. There are many examples that illustrate how, in the independence of Spanish America, the theory of rebellion and the bases of popular justice went back to the Comuneros of Castile. When we study the Spanish revolution of the eighteenth century, we see how the flag of the Comuneros was returned from America to Spain.

2. This little-known episode of American history has been studied and documented by Roberto Arrázola in his book, *Palenque, Primer Pueblo Libre de América*. The republic remained free till 1690. The king's royal decree stated that persecution of the rebels should be suspended. And it added: "It being certain beyond any doubt that, without the prior infallible assurance of their general and absolute liberty, they would never submit, I order that you request the owners of these slaves to relinquish their rightful claims, considering that, in truth, they are losing nothing, as their recuperation is impossible."

See also María del Carmen Borrego Pla: *Palenques Negros en Cartagena de Indias a Fines del Siglo XVII*.

3. Durand Echavarría in *Mirage in the West: A History of the French Image of American Society to 1815* provides excellent documentation on these gazettes and, in general, on America's presence in revolutionary France. R. R. Palmer's *Age of the Democratic Revolution* has an impressive list of the books on American subjects that were published in Europe—in English, French, German, Dutch, Italian, and Spanish—between 1760 and 1790.

4. The American insurrection aroused the European conscience from the day new began to be received about Washington's perseverance in defying England through armed conflict. Washington begins his war with troops of small farmers who have no uniforms, who have no training, and who alternate their brief campaigns with farm work. And yet he was able to destroy the English military power. It is useful to recall how European revolutionists began to partake in this American conflict. Eduardo Cárdenas says in his *Nueva Historia de los Estados Unidos*: "Later, Washington would be able to count on the help of distinguished European military men such as Baron Steuben, a Prussian engineer who contributed to the troops' training; and the valiant Poles, Pulaski and Kosciusko; Baron Kalb, and the Marquis de Lafayette, a noble Frenchman with democratic ideas, who, at his own expense, clothed and equipped a great number of soldiers. But in the beginning he was alone, and it took great prowess of energy and activity to organize the volunteers so that in March 1776 he felt strong enough to threaten Boston."

The Europeans who participated in the American Revolution returned to Europe like a democratic leaven that was to produce a deep and thorough transformation in political philosophy. The best example is given by Lafayette. R. R. Palmer, in his book *The Age of the Democratic Revolution: A Political History of Europe and America*, refers to this channel through which America's image reached Europe: that of the soldiers who returned, the first being the Marquis de Lafayette. America's influence on Lafayette is well known thanks to the research made by Professor Gottschalk. According to him, when Lafayette enlisted as a volunteer in the American army, he was not inspired by any ideal of liberty formed in France. It was his American experience that gave him the love of liberty, and he returned to France filled with a powerful predilection for so-called republican sentiments.

5. Gilbert Chinard in *La Déclaration des Droits de l'Homme et du Citoyen et ses Antécédents Américains* reproduces Lafayette's project on the Bill of Rights proposed to the National Assembly on July 11, 1789, and previously submitted to Jefferson's approval, according to a manuscript that is preserved in the Library of Congress in Washington. Chinard reproduced these words from the report presented on July 27, 1789, by Champion de Clisé, archbishop of Bordeaux, in the name of the Constituent Assembly with relation to the usefulness of making a declaration as Lafayette had suggested. "Above all, we have believed, just as you have, that the Constitution should be preceded by the Declaration of the Rights of Man and of

the Citizen. . . . We had thought that this would be a permanent guarantee for us against the fear of our own lack of knowledge. . . . If later any foreign power tries to impose laws that do not stem from those same principles, this original affirmation, always present, would immediately denounce the crime or error before all the citizens. That noble idea, conceived in the other hemisphere, should by preference come down to us. We have partaken in the events that gave North America her liberty, and she shows us on what principles we should base our own; the New World, whose chains we forged in the past, now teaches us how to defend ourselves from the misfortunes that may befall us." Further on, Professor Chinard writes: "After Italy had liberated herself from the Austrian yoke, when, by order of the French government, the constitutions of the republics of Cisalpina and Liguria were printed in Paris, they were naturally taken from the constitution of the year III, which was followed to the letter. But heading this volume, which was destined for public distribution as a sort of guide for civic education of peoples, before the Declaration of the Rights of Man and of the Citizen, they reproduce in four tongues—French, English, German and Italian—a document entitled *Declaration of the Representatives of the United States of America Assembled in General Congress the 4th of July of 1776.*"

6. We must not forget the paradoxical fate of Citizen Momoro, editor and bookseller, who had the three words "Liberty, Equality, and Fraternity" engraved on all public buildings, including churches that were closed to Catholics; we can still see this everywhere in France. This passionate lover of liberty was guillotined . . . like Desmoulins, like Robespierre . . . and like Louis XVI.

7. Paine said: "Let the United States serve as asylum for Louis Capet. There . . . remote from the miseries and crimes of royalty, he may learn, from the constant aspect of public prosperity, that the true system of government consists not in kings, but in fair, equal and honorable representation. As I remember this circumstance, basing my proposition on it, I do it thinking that I am citizen of both countries. I propose it as an American who knows that France helped America, the land of my love, burst her fetters. . . . I propose it as a man who, although an adversary of kings, does not forget that they are subject to human frailty. I propose it as citizen of the French Republic, because it seems to me the best measure" (quoted by Conway, *The Life of Thomas Paine*).

CHAPTER 7

1. At the time of Las Casas, the polemic was very similar. "There was always someone," he wrote, "who would bring in the argument about the five zones, three of which, according to many, were completely uninhabitable, and not so

the other two, and this was a common opinion among the ancients who, after all, knew very little. Others perhaps, which naturally are able to have a spirit of contradiction, for which all things, good and clear though they be, are found to have inconveniences, and there is no lack of reasons with which to contradict" (quoted by Gerbi, *Disputa del Nuevo Mundo*).

2. The parallel between Buffon and Goethe is made by Roger Heim in his work *Les Grands Naturalists Français* (Paris, 1952).

3. The correspondence between Mutis and Linnaeus has been compiled by Guillermo Hernández de Alba in the two volumes of Mutis's letters published in Bogotá.

4. This affirmation (in the *Supplement*) is very typical of Pauw: "It always has to be surprising that in an entire hemisphere, before 1492, there should be no idea of the sciences, which obliges us to consider there a delay of 3,000 years."

5. At the time when Abbé Pauw wrote this, John Adams was living and had graduated from Harvard; Jefferson had graduated from William and Mary College; Madison from Princeton . . . or there was Benjamin Franklin, who only attended secondary school and, nevertheless, was received with every honor by the Paris Academy of Sciences.

6. Gobineau wrote in his *Essay on the Inequality of Human Races*: "The white race has the monopoly of beauty, intelligence and physical strength. By its union with other varieties, hybrids resulted gradually, and these may be beautiful but without strength, strong but lacking in intelligence, or intelligent but weak or ugly." Hitler said: "Everything that we see before us as human civilization, the products of art, science, technology, are almost exclusively a product of Aryan creative activity, and this permits us to conclude, not without reason, that they have been the only ones to found a superior humanity, and that, consequently, they represent the original type of what is understood by the word 'man.' The Aryan is the Prometheus of mankind. . . . History establishes with striking evidence that, whenever the Aryan has mixed his blood with inferior peoples, the result of such cross-breeding has been the ruin of the civilizing people."

7. As Diderot's participation in the works of Raynal is so direct, Jean Descola says in *Les Messagers de l'Indépendance* (Paris, 1973), after transcribing this dialogue: "Whether he inspired or corrected this prophetic dialogue, Diderot is one of the first anticolonialists, even before the word existed or the subject was discussed at all. It is necessary to liberate all colonies! So much the worse for the rum and the chocolate if we like them so much!"

8. This version was found by Salvador Cruz and published in his essay "Gran Prosa Para la Vida de Juárez."

9. Mallafe (quoted by L. A. Siles Salinas in his work, *Negritude and the Formation of the Latin American Nation*, Dakar, 1974) lists the black insurrections in America as follows: "In 1537 the slaves in Mexico rebelled; the following year they did so in Cuba; in 1546 in Hispaniola; in 1548 in Honduras; in 1550 in Santa Marta. Between 1555 and 1556 there was such an important insurrection near Panama, that the Viceroy of Peru, Marquis of Cañete, who was passing by on his way to assume the office of his governorship, was compelled to arrange an armistice with them. In 1577, the privateer Francis Drake, after taking and plundering the city of Nombre de Dios, made incursions in the environs and attacked estates, aided by the *cimarrones* (runaway slaves) of the region." Siles Salinas continues: "In 1612, in the wealthy and turbulent city of Potosí, in High Peru, there was an aborted uprising led by Alfonso Yañez, the son of a mulatto woman, who had intended to liberate the blacks (as Bernados registers). In 1656 an extended rebellion flares up in Guadalupe." On the creation of an independent republic in Palenque de Cartagena in the first half of the sixteenth century, there is an outstanding book by Roberto Arrázola, *Palenque, Primer Pueblo Libre de América*, in which he produces a remarkable quantity of documents taken from the Spanish archives to recreate the history of this tiny republic that remained free for the space of one century, having compelled the king of Spain to recognize it by royal decree.

10. In *The Philosophy of History*, Hegel says: "What has happened in the case of the New World in the modern age is that, even if a native civilization existed at the time of its discovery by the Europeans, that civilization was annihilated by their contact. The country's submissiveness determined its fate. . . . Of America and its degree of civilization, especially in Mexico and Peru, we have information, but it imports nothing more than that this culture was an entirely natural one, which must expire as soon as the Spirit approaches it. America has always shown itself to be physically and morally powerless, and still shows itself so. For the aborigines, after the landing of the Europeans in America, gradually vanished at the breath of European activity. . . . Among the animals we find the same inferiority that is seen in men. American fauna possesses lions, tigers and crocodiles which have some resemblance to the species of the Old World, but which are, from every point of view, smaller, weaker, less potent. As far as we know, even the animals that have been imported from the Old World are less nourishing there."

CHAPTER 8

1. In no. 4 of the periodical *Semanario de Caracas* (December 9, 1810), in an admirable series of articles on the recently proclaimed independence of Venezuela, Sanz wrote: "Abandoning the arguments of sophistry, and cutting through the

thick fog of deceit, we must say that the general will of the people, congregated in one form, is the true sovereign, for it is higher and more powerful than each and every one of its members in particular: it is independent, it does not recognize nor does it have a superior upon the earth, and its power cannot ever be alienated, transmitted, nor prescribed. . . . Just as through God the leaf on a tree moves, and just as through God those who execute the supreme will of the people cease to reign, when they fail to observe the covenants, and proceed against the fundamental laws of the State, the mutually binding social contract breaks."

2. More than Vives, those who exerted an influence on the formation of popular ideas regarding the social contract and the sovereignty of the people were the philosophical Francisco Suárez and his Jesuit disciples, for whom sovereignty lay in the community of citizens, and the breaking of the covenant due to the prince's failure to observe the laws authorized not only the right to insurrection, but also tyrannicide. The repercussions of these teachings are found all over America, and for the specific case of New Granada, for example, one may consult the work of the historian Rafael Gómez Hoyos, *La Revolución Granadina de 1810*, pp. 133–48.

3. The Peruvian Jesuit Juan Bautista Vizcardo, in a famous letter published in Philadelphia, and addressed to the Spanish Americans—a letter that is considered one of the basic documents that are forerunners of independence—said that for him the history of America under the Spaniards was summarized in four words: ingratitude, injustice, servitude, and desolation. He speaks of the Spaniards as adventurers who exploited America through robbery and violence. . . . And brings to mind once more the oath taken by the communities of Aragon, linking these principles of old popular Spain to the uprising of the commoners of New Granada.

4. As regards the Trial of Macanaz, an admirable book was written about this, which excels in the variety of documents consulted in the archives—its author, Carmen María Gaite. When Macanaz was able to return to Spain, he was an old man, close to death. He died in 1760, when he was more than ninety years old. The following year, the prosecutor of the Inquisition said "that although after death it is possible to inquire against the heretic, pursue his cause against his memory and his fame, condemn his status as if he were alive . . . deprive him of ecclesiastic burial and have his bones burnt, it is when there is evidence that he has died a formal heretic with a heretical conscience . . . and he has died with undecided personal accusation . . . and the suspicions, although they may be vehement with the death of the accused, are extinguished and are not sufficient proof to condemn the memory and fame of the deceased. It is therefore considered that the cause of said Macanaz be suspended and in the state in which are deposited in the Holy Office his effects and income received, may these be delivered freely to his daughter." (Carmen María Gaite, *El Proceso de Macanaz*.)

5. Estuardo Núñez published in *La Nación* of Buenos Aires (1965) an article from which I quote the following parts:

"In recent research in German libraries we have found valuable testimonies written on the myth or legend of Olavide in Germany and neighboring countries at the close of the XVIII and beginning of the XIX centuries, which the critics have not yet noticed.

"In 1799 there appeared in Copenhagen an epic poem entitled 'Olavides,' by the German poet and writer August Hennings (1746–1826); born in Pinneberg, near Hamburg, he lived in Denmark, and later studied at the University of Goettingen. His anticonservative ideas had brought upon him, like his hero, political persecutions, which were accentuated with the diffusion of the poem. It sings of the tragic lot of the Peruvian and an idyllic scene shows the happiness and prosperity which prevail in the lands colonized by him, in contrast with the 'obscure' designs of his persecutors.

"At about that same time, Johann Pezzl (1756–1823), Bavarian writer who studied in Salzburg and Vienna, wrote an account of a voyage entitled *Faustino o el siglo filosófico (Faustino or the Philosophic Century)* (Zurich, 1783), to which were consecrated several editions. It tells how Faustino finds some emigrants in Genoa, travels with them to Sierra Morena and becomes a settler and the secretary of Olavide, and lives through the difficulties of the Peruvian with the Inquisition. Shortly after the initiation of the process Faustino flees to France, taking in his spirit the admiration for his superior. Olavide—Faustino affirms—had fallen as defender of mankind and of freedom of thought and gave up his life for this noble cause. Pezzl had read some accounts of travels of the time and was deeply moved by those accounts. *Faustino* not only was a success as regards number of editions, but was also well received among the imitators, for in 1785 another, an apocryphal, *Faustin*, appeared.

"The same author, Pezzl, then wrote a sort of biography entitled *Sincerus, der Reformatur* (Frankfurt, Leipzig, Zurich, 1787), and his character has many points of contact with Olavide, his inspirator, the object of fervent admiration.

"Finally, Heinrich Zschokke (1771–1848), writer and playwright, a German Swiss, with an extensive bibliography and intense liberal activity, wrote an unfinished novel on the great Peruvian from Lima, with the title, *Olavide, der neue Belizar.* Like his predecessors, Zschokke also had liberal and revolutionary ideas, was well received at the Weimar theater by Goethe, was greatly influenced by the French illustration, and with great friendliness protected in Switzerland some Spaniards who had fled from Spain during the Napoleonic invasion. He compared Olavide with Belisarius, the unfortunate Roman general of the ancient legend, who through jealousy or adverse circumstances was dispossessed of his great power and influence and fell into the greatest ruin, a personage who is put into drama by the Spaniard Mira de Amescua in the XVII century, and by Goldoni and Marmontel, among others, in the XVIII century."

6. Jean de Booy, "À propos de l'Encyclopédie en Espagne. Diderot, Miguel Gijón et Pablo de Olavide," *Revue de Littérature Comparée* (October–December 1961).

7. As a political move, Napoleon showed himself most favorable, in Bayonne, to the independence of America, and even had one of the American delegates, who went to Bayonne to defend his attack on peninsular Spain, Francisco Antonio Zea from New Granada, designated as political head of Málaga by Joseph Bonaparte. The idea of this independence accompanied him until his death. Remembering Napoleon's last days in Saint Helena, Jean Descola says: "In the course of his long soliloquies, he would return to the idea of the independence of the Spanish colonies, which he found to be both in agreement with the evolution of all peoples and highly desirable: it would give the United States new allies and therefore new enemies to England. He predicted the emancipation of the Indies and of all the British possessions. The colonial system is finished, he affirmed." And thinking of the mixture of races in Latin America: "What was to be done so that these peoples, so different, might live in good intelligence? Napoleon had an idea. Authorize men so that they could each marry two women of different color. Thus the children of this double marriage would be raised together and, in spite of the difference in color, they would become accustomed to living together and would consider themselves equal" (Jean Descola, *Les Messagers de l'Indépendance*, Paris, 1973).

8. Ramón Solís, in his book *El Cádiz de las Cortes*, says that "Argüelles and Mejía Lequerica were the orators that were better received, for their word was easy and inspired." The Courts met initially in Isla de León, and were soon transferred to Cádiz, but the question was still open as to whether Cádiz would be a safe place, with the threat of Napoleon close by, and the idea was not strange to many to have them transferred to America. And was it not true that to be safe, the crown of Portugal had moved to Rio de Janeiro? Ramón Solís says: "The French, five days after the decision to move the Courts to Cádiz had been made, bombarded it. . . . Spirits were very low when during the session of 19 January, Mejía rises to speak. He says that in his opinion, such bombardment was political, and the judgment of congress should not change. . . . In Cádiz there was the allegiance of the people and, in extreme circumstances, it was possible to embark from there for some other safer place. Perhaps he thought of America as a final refuge." Labra y Martínez, in *Los Presidentes Americanos en las Cortes de Cádiz*, remembers that the canon Antonio Joaquín Pérez, representative of Puebla, said: "If the Courts have to be moved to Mexico, let it be with all possible security."

9. Ramón Solís, in *El Cádiz de las Cortes*, says: "American congressmen had not only a numerical but a political category in the Courts of Cádiz, and this category was reflected in that of the city. Let us add to this the many newspapers that existed in Cádiz, dedicated to the defense of American interests. Because of all

this, López Cancelada was able to say: The General Headquarters of the Revolution is in Cádiz and the General Staff in London. . . . The Americans were not modest in expressing their opinions clearly. Congressman Liperguer, alternate for Buenos Aires, in a public session during the first days of the Courts, calls the Spaniards who came over to America 'barbarians and thieves.' "

10. Ramón Solís, *El Cádiz de las Cortes*: "The people accept with extraordinary joy the abolition of the Tribunal. When the decree is read in the Cathedral, a fiery crowd is present at the event. According to Father Velez, the popular classes commented lazily in the streets of Cádiz: The Saint has died!" Labra y Martínez, in *Los Presidentes Americanos*, takes these words spoken by congressman Andrés Jáuregui, of La Habana: "From Recaredo to the Catholic Kings, did Spain need to have an Inquisition so that in her would flourish the Catholic religion? What a glorious time that was for the Church in Spain, when the Leandros, the Fulgencios, the Isidoros shone . . . and so many other illustrious and learned prelates, splendors of the Church and an honor to our country."

11. A Peruvian writer, a contemporary, the very curious and controversial Manuel Lorenzo de Vidaurre, wrote: "Independence! Independence! Have we not already obtained something? Are not our rights beginning to be recognized? Are not our spokesmen already being heard? Morales Duárez, my teacher, has he not been able to impose general equality between the Spaniards of the peninsula and the inhabitants of the Americas? A son of Peru, the same Morales Duárez, has he not received as a demonstration of this equality, the honor of being elected President of the Courts in which our happiness is being incubated? Has not Feliú spoken before the Spanish constituents as he might speak before his most intimate compatriots? If this were not sufficient, a member of the very race of the Incas, has he not permitted to be heard in the midst of the whites, in the midst of his historic oppressors, the claims and desires of his Indian brothers?"

CHAPTER 9

1. In his writing on the French Revolution of 1789 and the Italian one of 1859, Mazzini says: "As to Italy, it is even more manifest that her revolution did not produce either one of those sad results. . . . Here, in fact, liberty, far from being oppressed by the revolution, is born out of the revolution itself; not the liberty in name only, that to some would consist in the name they give to a form of government, that is to say, in a purely negative concept whose results are uncertain: but in real liberty, which means that the citizen is assured, through just laws and stable institutions, against despotic orders by the ruling power, that the power itself is immune to the predominance of the oligarchic society and is not swayed

by the rash impulses of the uncultured and agitated mob: tyranny and enslavement of power which were, sometimes together, the two ways in which oppression was practiced in France at some moments of the revolution, the first under a mask of legal authority, the second under a mask of popular will" (from a facsimile reproduction published in *L'Unità d'Italia, Albo di Imagini 1855–1861*, RAI, Radiotelevisione Italiana).

2. "When the *Nautonier*, bringing Garibaldi to Rio de Janeiro, draws near the port, he sees a crowd with hands and handkerchiefs waving, amid shouts of 'There he is! There he is! There he is!' Descending, he finds himself in the arms of Luigi Rossetti, nephew of Gabriele, the poet, who has been there two years, after fleeing Genoa because of problems similar to Garibaldi's. And behind him, another familiar face! Was it true? Was he dreaming? The same Gianbattista Cuneo, the coreligionary that he had met in Taganrog, still in hiding, directing Rio's Mazzinian newspaper under another name—Farinata degli Uberti. . . . The two *carbonari* presented to the rest their companion, who had spoken with Mazzini and who had a death sentence on his head" (*Garibaldi*, by Indro Montanelli and Marco Nozza).

3. "I arrived at a cottage that I had seen from the boat, and there I had a very pleasant meeting with a very charming young woman. . . . She told me that the overseer or steward of the ranch was her husband. . . . When I told her that I wished to have a bull to provide us with meat on board, she assured me that her husband would be happy to oblige me and told me to wait for him. . . . He and I agreed to go hunt the bull the following day. . . . At dawn, I went where Maurizio was waiting for me, although I felt uneasy, quite inexperienced in this part of America, I knew that there were tigers, which were less complaisant than the horses or the bulls. Soon Maurizio appeared with a roped bull which he killed, beheaded and quartered in minutes: such is the dexterity of these men in these bloody practices" (Garibaldi, *Memorie*).

4. "Mastei—the future Pius IX—remembers with disdain in his diary the 'Israelite aspect' of Rivadavia, and the 'disgusting pompous rhetoric' with which he received them. As for the minister, he gave vent to his ill humor by sending the ecclesiastical government an indecorous note in which, basing his arguments on the fact that he did not recognize the public character of that 'individual,' he forbade him to exercise any religious function, whether in public or in private. To which the purveyor, Zabaleta, added the last straw by writing Monseigneur Muzi that he was amazed at his coming to America to disturb the citizens' peace, and that it was excessively bold of him to attempt an infringement on others' jurisdiction" (Pedro de Leturia, *Relaciones entre la Santa Sede e Hispanoamérica*).

CHAPTER 10

1. In the National Assembly of France, the delegate Adolfe Gueroult said: "The exactions, extortions, violences are real; they were very numerous; but seriously and sincerely, can a European power demand that in a country that is involved in a civil war, disrupted by anarchy, our nationals, who come there with perfect knowledge of the facts, knowing perfectly the state of disorder in which the country is now enveloped, enjoy the security of which not even the nationals themselves know of?" (Manuel Tello, *Voces Favorables a México en el Cuerpo Legislativo de Francia* (*1862–1867*).

2. Ernesto Picard said in his speech before the National Assembly of France: "The Jecker banking house was Swiss; its director was Swiss; he was born in Porentruy at a time when this city did not belong to France. Gentlemen, do any of you know in which moment this creditor, who was going to be protected, had come to be French? Do you know the date of his naturalization? The date of his naturalization is March 26, 1862. I refer to the *Bulletin des Lois* of August 31, 1862, which publishes a decree, dated the preceding March 26, giving the French nationality to him on whose behalf we claim today an enormous sum, whose claim has been one of the causes for the breaking in Mexico of the London Convention and the departure of the allies" (p. 77, vol. 1). Jules Favre says in his speech as member of the Assembly: "Jecker declared himself bankrupt in the month of May, 1860. I have here the letter of the meeting held by his creditors in the month of September, 1860. . . . In one of the letters published by the *Monitor*, dated August 31, 1862, the correspondent announces to Jecker, as a priceless conquest, the publication in the *Bulletin des Lois* of his letter of naturalization. This is a true fact and in my opinion it is unexplainable. How is it, that after our debates, when it had already been revealed that the Jecker credits concealed a real swindle, Jecker is taken in by the higher administration, which makes of him a French citizen!" (Manuel Tello, *Voces Favorables a México*).

3. The secretary of state, William H. Seward, in his answer to the communication sent jointly by the representatives of the queen of Spain, the emperor of the French, and the queen of England, says to them: "The United States is seriously anxious to preserve the security and welfare of the Republic of Mexico and has authorized its Ministers residing in that Republic to negotiate a Treaty with the Mexican republic, by means of which it shall be granted material aid and other advantages which may assist that Republic in meeting the demands and claims of the aforementioned Sovereigns and thus avoid a war that has already been decided by these Sovereigns against Mexico" (Benito Juárez, *Documentos, Discursos y Correspondencia*).

4. In his speech before the National Assembly, the representative Jules Favre said: "Having stated the principle of nonintervention, there was yet, from the point of

view of general policy, another reason which imposed imperiously upon us its respect. It was impossible that after having proclaimed among us, as the foundation for our government, national sovereignty and suffrage for the country, we should not respect it among the others. The emperor has been elected by the people; he reigns and takes pleasure in it, by the will of the people; and you would have desired that beyond our frontiers he use the force which has been entrusted to him by that will of the people to repress the neighboring nations, to repress their aspirations, tearing away with his hands the titles to such sovereignty, to deny his own legitimacy" (Manuel Tello, *Voces Favorables a México*).

5. In *The Crown of México*, Joan Haslip summarizes in a few words the well-known interview with Princess Agnes Salm Salm, when she tried to pay off Palacio, Colonel Villanueva's brother, for the flight of the prisoner: "The princess was set on defeating Palacio. She not only tried to bribe him with money, but she also made him enter her room, locked the door and began to undress. Terrified, the colonel, so that his honor should not be questioned, threatened to throw himself out of the window if he were not permitted to leave immediately."

CHAPTER 11

1. With regard to works that have American themes, Otto de Greiff has had the kindness to write for the author of this book the list that follows, grouping not just those in which all is centered on a character, subject, or event pertaining to the New World but those that have passing references as well, as in the case of operas based on Abbé Prevost's novel, *Manon Lescaut*, where the heroine ends her life in the vicinity of New Orleans, or the curious case of *Un Ballo in Maschera*, where the plot is transferred to Boston for reason of political censorship. . . . This is Otto de Greiff's list:

1733	Vivaldi—*Montezuma* (Venice)
1735	Rameau—*Les Indes Galantes* (Paris)
1755	Graun—*Montezuma* (Berlin)
1771	Mysliveczek—*Montezuma* (Florence)
1773	Paisello—*Montezuma* (Rome)
1775	Sacchini—*Montezuma* (London)
1782	Zingarelli—*Montezuma* (Naples)
1786	Dalayrac—*Azémia ou le Nouveau Robinson* (Paris)
1797	Berton—*Ponce de León* (Paris)
1798	Portugal—*Fernando nel Messico* (Venice)
1800	Fomin—*Amerikantsi* (St. Petersburg)

1802	Tritto—*Gli Americani* (Naples)
1809	Spontini—*Fernand Cortes ou la Conquête du Mexique* (Paris)
1825	Seyfried—*Montezuma* (Vienna)
1828	Morlacchi—*Colombo* (Genoa)
1831	Carnicer—*Colombo* (Madrid)
1834	Jensen—*Robinson* (Copenhagen)
1845	Verdi—*Alzira*
1851	F. David—*La Perle du Brésil* (Paris)
1856	Auber—*Manon Lescaut* (Paris)
1859	Verdi—*Un Ballo in Maschera* (Rome)
1862	Verdi—*La Forza del Destino* (St. Petersburg)
1867	Offenbach—*Robinson Crusoe* (Paris)
1868	Offenbach—*La Périchole* (Paris)
1870	Gomes—*Il Guarany* (Milan)
1875	Offenbach—*La Créole* (Paris)
1892	Franchetti—*Cristoforo Colombo* (Genoa)
1893	Puccini—*Manon Lescaut*
1904	Puccini—*Madama Butterfly* (Milan)
1910	Puccini—*La Fanciulla del West*
1930	Milhaud—*Christof Columbus* (Berlin)
1932	Milhaud—*Maximilien* (Paris)
1950	Milhaud—*Bolivar* (Paris)

2. As a very curious complement to the American subjects chosen by European authors in their literary works, it is important to mention the dialogues in a series written by Abbott Lorenzo Ignazio Thjulen with the general title of *Dialoghi nel Regno de Morti*, which was published in Bologna in 1817. In these dialogues, which take place in the other world, the author brings together Charles V, Moctezuma, Cardinal Jiménez, Columbus, and Cortés in order to hold a trial, with the confrontation of these characters, on the injustices that were committed during the discovery and the conquest of America. Each actor's argument is presented with great propriety and remarkable knowledge of history, in the form of a dramatic debate. In Thjulen's series, these dialogues are numbers 17, 18, 19, and 20.

CHAPTER 12

1. From the life of Sir Walter Raleigh by Martin A. S. Hume: "The colonists who abandoned Virginia returned to Plymouth in Drake's fleet at the end of June, 1586, and brought with them, perhaps for the first time in England, the habit of smoking tobacco, which Raleigh himself made fashionable in court. The custom

at first met with the greatest resistance, and an ordinance was dictated against it, rejecting it as a habit of savage peoples. According to Camden, it was feared that such a habit would open the way for England's degeneration into a barbarian life."

2. In Drake's travel accounts, one reads that when he arrived in California, which he named Nova Albion, the natives were extremely friendly and offered him gifts of tobacco and potatoes. Camden says that the natives, naked, merry, and happy, jumped and danced tirelessly, and tore skin off their faces with their nails as a sign of sacrifice and adoration, all the time asking Sir Francis to be their king. The women went down in procession to where he was, bringing baskets of "tobah" (tobacco), some roots called "petah" (potatoes), boiled fish and seeds. Those who have commented on Raleigh's voyage do not agree on whether the "petah" that he mentioned was or was not potatoes. Dr. Kroeler (quoted by Wagner) believes that they were, and Wagner is of the same opinion. In any case, the general opinion is that Drake brought potatoes to England.

3. Irving Anthony in his life and times of Raleigh tells how the vagaries of politics forced him to spend some time in Ireland, where he introduced potatoes. While living in the guardian's house at a Dominican monastery in Youghal Bay, he found a quiet spot, whose seclusion enabled him to see the world around him more clearly. He thought of Virginia, his ideal colony, and the potatoes and tobacco of America. "From the garden entrance one could see the rows planted with this tubercule which would someday save Ireland from destruction by famine, and whose cultivation would extend from there to the whole of Munster."

Bibliography

Adamczewski, Jan. *Nicolas Copernico y Su Epoca*. (Spanish edition) Warsaw, 1972.

Ailly, Pierre d'. *Ymago Mundi*. Paris, 1930.

Arinos de Mello Franco, Alfonso. *O Indio Brasileiro e a Revolução Francesa, As Origens Brasileiras de Theoría da Bondade Natural*. Rio de Janeiro, 1937.

Armani, Alberto. *Les Institutions Politiques et Sociales dans les Réductions du Paraguay*. Montreal, 1961.

Armitage, Angus. *Sun, Stand Thou Still*. New York, 1947.

Arrázola, Roberto. *Palenque, Primer Pueblo Libre de América*. Cartagena, 1970.

Bacon, Francis. *New Atlantis*. London, 1838.

Baillet, Adrien. *La Vie de M. Descartes*. Paris, 1691.

Bailly, Augusto. *Montaigne*. Paris, 1942.

Bandin, Louis. *Les Incas du Pérou*. Paris, 1942.

Bataillon, Marcel. *Études sur Bartolomé de Las Casas*. Paris, 1965.

Batlloti, Miguel, S. J. *El Abate Viscardo. Historia y Mito de la Intervención de los Jesuitas en la Independencia Hispanoamericana*. Caracas, 1953.

Benedict, Ruth. *Race and Racism*. London, 1943.

Borrego Pla, María del Carmen. *Palenques Negros en Cartagena de Indias a Fines del Siglo XVIII*. Seville, 1973.

Bourgeois du Chastanet. *Nouvelle Histoire de Concile de Constance*. Paris, 1718.

Bruzen de la Martinère, Antoine Augustin. *Le Grand Dictionnaire Géographique et Critique*. The Hague, 1726–39.

Buarque de Holanda, Sergio. *Visão do Paraiso. Os Motivos Edenicos no Descobrimento e Colonização do Brasil*. Rio de Janeiro, 1959.

Bullock, Alan. *Hitler, A Study in Tyranny*. London, 1952.

Cabarrús, Francisco. *Cartas del Conde Cabarrús al Sr. D. Gaspar de Jovellanos*. Madrid, 1820.

Campbell, W. E. *Erasmus, Tyndale and More*. Milwaukee, 1950.

Campillo, José de. *Nuevo Sistema de Gobierno Económico para América*. Madrid, 1789.

Cardenas Nanetti, Jorge. *Nueva Historia de los Estados Unidos*. New York, 1970.

Carpentier, Alejo. *Concierto Barroco*. Mexico, 1975.

Cavour, Count Camillo Benso di. *Discorsi Parlamentari*. 3 vols. Florence, 1932–35.

Charleroix, Pierre François Xavier de. *Histoire du Paraguay*. Paris, 1754.

Chevalier, Auguste and H. F. Emmanuel. *Le Tabac*. Paris, 1942.

Chinard, Gilbert. *L'Exotisme Américaine dans la Littérature Française au XVII siècle*. Paris, 1911.

———— *L'Amérique et le Rêve Exotique dans la Littérature Française au XVII et aux XVIII Siècle*. Paris, 1913.

———— *George Washington as the French Knew Him*. Princeton, 1940.

———— *La Déclaration des Droits de l'Homme et du Citoyen et ses Antécédents Américains*. Washington, 1945.

———— *L'Homme contre la Nature*. Paris, 1949.

Ciasca, Raffael. *L'arte dei Medici e Speziali nella Storia e nel Commercio Fiorentino*. Florence, 1928.

Cioranescu, Alexandre. *L'Avenir du Passé. Utopie et Littérature*. Paris, 1972.

Combris, André. *La Philosophie des Races du Comte et Saportée Actuelle*. Paris, 1937.

Condorcet, Jean-Antoine Nicolás de Cariat, Marquis de. *L'influence de la Révolution de l'América en Europe. Extraites de sa Correspondance et de Celle de Ses Amis*. Paris, 1824.

Conte Corti, Egon Caesar. *Maximilian und Charlotte von Mexiko*. Germany, 1924.

Conway, Moncurse D. *The Life of Thomas Paine*. New York, 1892.

Copernic, Nicolas. *Des Revolutions des Orbes Celestes*. Paris, 1934.

Cresson, André. *Montaigne, sa Vie, son Oeuvre*. Paris, 1952.

Croce, Benedetto. *Histoire de l'Europe du Dix-neuvième Siècle*. Paris, 1959.

D'Alembert, Jean, and Denis Diderot. *Encyclopédie ou Dictionnaire Raisonné des Sciences, des Arts et des Metiers*. Paris, 1751–72.

Defourneaux, Marcelin. *Pablo de Olavide ou l'afrancesado, 1725–1803*. Paris, 1959.

Denis, Ferdinando. *Une Fête Brésilienne*. Paris, 1850.

Descartes, René. *Oeuvres*. Paris, 1901.

Devèze, Michel. *L'Europe et le Monde à la Fin du XVIII Siècle*. Paris, 1970.

Domergue, Lucienne. *Jovellanos et la Société Économique des Amis du Pays de Madrid (1778–1795)*. Toulouse, 1971.

Dutertre, Gral. François. *Départ du Temple pour Cayenne des Déportés de 17 et 18 Fructidor, An V.* Paris.

Du Tertre, P. *Histoire des Antilles.* Paris, 1654.

Echeverría, Durand. *Mirage in the West. A History of the French Image of American Society, to 1815.* Princeton, 1956.

Fay, Bernard. *L'Esprit Révolutionnaire en France et aux États Unis à la fin du XVIII Siècle.* Paris, 1925.

Fernández de Navarrete, Martín. *Colección de los Viajes y Descubrimientos que Hicieron por Mar los Españoles.* 4 vols. Madrid, 1825–37.

Feuillée, Le P. Louis. *Journal des Observations Physiques, Mathématiques et Botaniques Faites par l'Ordre du Roi sur les Côtes Orientales de l'Amérique Méridionale et dans les Indes Occidentales depuis l'Année 1707 jusque en 1712.* Paris, 1714.

Flynn, John Stephen. *The Influence of Puritanism on the Political and Religious Thought of the English.* New York, 1920.

Francastel, Pierre. *Utopie et Institutions au XVIII Siècle. La Pragmatique des Lumières.* Paris, 1963.

Frazer, Sir James George. *The Golden Bough.* London, 1914.

Garibaldi, Giuseppe. *Memorie.* Verona, 1972.

Gerbi, Antoinello. *Disputa del Nuevo Mundo.* Mexico, 1960.

―――― *Presencia de América en el Pensamiento Europeo.* Bogotá, 1952.

Giraldo Jaramillo, Gabriel. *Estudios Históricos.* Bogotá, 1954.

Gómez Hoyos, Rafael. *La Revolución Granadina de 1810.* Bogotá, 1962.

Guy, Alain. "Vives Socialista y la Utopía de More." *Moreana*, November 1971.

Hagen, Victor W. von. *The Green World of Naturalists.* New York, 1948.

―――― *South America Called Them.* London, 1949.

Haller, William. *The Rise of Puritanism.* New York, 1938.

Hark, W. *America: Ideal and Reality; The United States of 1776 in Contemporary European Philosophy.* London, 1947.

Haslip, Joan. *The Crown of Mexico.* New York, 1971.

Hazard, Paul. *La Crise de la Conscience Européenne* (1680–1715). Paris, 1935.

―――― *La Pensée Européenne au XVIII Siècle: De Montesquieu à Lessing.* Paris, 1935.

Hertsler, Y. O. *The History of Utopian Thought.* New York, 1926.

Hodgson, M. *Hemispheric Interregional History as an Approach to World History.* Paris, 1954.

Huizinga, Johan. *Le Déclin du Moyen Age.* Paris, 1958.

Iglesias, José María. *Revistas Históricas sobre la Intervención Francesa en México.* Mexico, 1966.

Imaz, Eugenio. *Topía y Utopía.* Mexico, 1946.

Isole, Maria dell'. *Mazzini: Promoteur de la République Italienne et Pionnier de la Fédération Européenne.* Paris, 1955.

Jones, H. M. *America and the French Culture (1750–1848).* Chapel Hill, 1927.

Jovellanos, Gaspar Melchor de. *Obras Escogidas.* 3 vols. Madrid, 1945–46.

Juárez, Benito. *Documentos, Discursos y Correspondencia.* 15 vols. Mexico, 1971.

Kester, Hermann. *Copernic et son Temps.* Paris, 1951.

King, Bolton. *The Life of Mazzini.* London, 1914.

Kuhn, Thomas S. *The Copernican Revolution, Planetary Astronomy in the Development of Western Thought.* Cambridge, 1957.

Labra y Martínez, Rafael M. *Los Presidentes Americanos en las Cortes de Cádiz.* Cádiz, 1912.

Ladame, Paul A. *Le Rôle des Migrations dans le Monde Libre.* Geneva, 1958.

Laffont, Robert. *Histoire du Développement Cultural et Scientifique de l'Humanité.* Paris, 1970.

Lafitau, Joseph François. *Moeurs des Sauvages Amériquains Comparées aux Moeurs des Premiers Temps.* 2 vols. Paris, 1724.

Lahontan, Louis, Baron de. *Dialogues Curieux entre l'Auteur et un Sauvage de bon Sens qui a Voyagé.* Paris, 1931.

Langlois, Ch. V. *La Vie en France au Moyen Age.* Paris, 1926.

Las Casas, Bartolomé de. *Historia de las Indias.* 3 vols. Mexico, 1951.

——— *Apologetica Historia.* 2 vols. Madrid, 1958.

——— *Tratado de las Indias y el Doctor Sepulveda.* Caracas, 1962.

Laufer, Bertholdt. *The American Plant Migration.* Chicago, 1938.

Lavisse, Ernest, and Alfred Rambraud. *Histoire Générale. Renaissance et Réforme.* Paris, 1970.

Leonard, Irving A. *Books of the Brave.* Cambridge, 1949.

Lery, François. *Le Cacao.* Paris, 1954.

Lery, Jean de. *Histoire d'un Voyage Fait en la Terre du Brésil.* 2 vols. Paris, 1880.

Leturia, Pedro de. *Relaciones entre la Santa Sede e Hispanoamérica.* 3 vols. Caracas, 1959.

Llinares, Armand. *Raymond Lulle, Philosophe de l'Action.* Grenoble, 1963.

Locke, John. *Fundamental Constitutions of Carolina.* London, 1720.

Luciani de Pérez Díaz, Lucila. *Miranda, su Vida y su Obra.* Caracas, 1968.

Luckwill, Leonard C. *The Genus Hicopersicon.* Aberdeen, 1943.

Lugon, Clovis. *A Republica Comunista Cristia dos Guaranies, 1610–1768.* Rio de Janeiro, 1968.

Lull, Ramon. *Le Livre des Bêtes.* Barcelona, 1905.

Madrillon, Jh. M. *Récherches Philosophiques sur la Découverte de l'Amérique.* Amsterdam, 1784.

Magron, Joseph. *Des Orchides à la Pomme de Terre.* Lagny-sur-Marne, 1943.

Manceron, Claude. *Les Hommes de la Liberté. Les Vingt Ans du Roi (1774–1778).* Paris, 1974.

——— *Le Vent d'Amérique (1778–1782).* Paris, 1974.

Mazzini, Giuseppe. *Epistolario.* 2 vols. Imola, 1938.

——— *Scritti Editi ed Inediti.* Imola, 1950.

Meade, Joaquin and Centli Iziz. *El Maíz, Orígenes y Mitología*. Mexico, 1948.

Miranda, Francisco. *The Diary of Francisco de Miranda*. Edited by William Spence Robertson. New York, 1928.

Mondranelli, Indro and Marco Nozza. *Garibaldi*. Milan, 1971.

Montaigne, Michel Eyquem de. *Oeuvres Complètes*. 4 vols. Paris, 1924–29.

—— *Essais*. edited by M. J. Leclerc. 5 vols. Paris, 1826–29.

Montani, Francesco. *Lettera sopra il Tabaco*. Urbino, 1957.

Morelly. *Code de la nature ou Véritable Esprit de ces Lois*. Abbeville, 1950.

Mornet, Daniel. *Les Origines Intellectuelles de la Révolution Française (1715–1887)*. Paris, 1947.

More, Sir Thomas. *Utopia*. London, 1557.

Muratori, Ludovico Antonio. *Rélations des Missions du Paraguay*. Paris, 1754.

Mürner, Magnus. *The Guarani Missions and the Segregation Policy of the Spanish Crown*. Rome, 1961.

O'Gorman, Edmundo. *La Idea del Descubrimiento de América, Historia de Esa Interpretación y Crítica de sus Fundamentos*. Mexico, 1951.

Omodeo, Adolfo. *L'Età del Risorgimento Italiano*. Naples, 1952.

Orbigny, Alcides Dessalines d'. *El Hombre Americano*. Buenos Aires, 1944.

Paine, Thomas. *The Writings of Thomas Paine*. Collected and edited by Moncure D. Conway. New York, 1892.

Palmer, R. R. *The Age of the Democratic Revolution. A Political History of Europe and America (1760–1800)*. Princeton, 1959–64.

Papini, Giovanni. *Tutte le Opere*. Milan, 1958.

Parra Pérez, C. *Miranda et la Révolution Française*. Paris, 1925.

Pauw, Jan Cornelis. *Récherches Philosophiques sur les Anglo-Américaines*. Paris, 1772.

Pernoud, Régine. *L'Amérique du Sud au XVIII Siècle*. Nantes, 1942.

Perry, Ralph Barton. *Puritanism and Democracy*. New York, 1944.

Picón Salas, Mariano. *Miranda*. Caracas, 1966.

Pinelo, Antonio León. *El Paraíso en el Nuevo Mundo*. Lima, 1943.

Plattard, Jean. *Les Cannibales de Montaigne*. Paris, 1939.

Pontrianne. *Un Évêque Français de XIV Siècle, Pierre d'Ailly, Évêque de Cambrai et Cardinal*. Le Puy, 1896.

Porras Barranechea, Raúl. *Los Viajeros Italianos en el Perú*. Lima, 1957.

RAI (Radiotelevisione Italiana). *L'Unità d'Italià. Albo di Immagini, 1859–1861*, Torin, 1961.

Raynal, Abbé. *Histoire de la Colonisation et du Commerce des Européens dans les Deux Mondes*. 4 vols. Geneva, 1780.

Recueil de Diverses Pièces Concernant la Pensylvaine. The Hague, 1684.

Renouvin, Pierre. *Histoire des Relations Internationales*. Paris, 1955.

Robertson, W. S. *La Vida de Miranda*. Caracas, 1967.

Rodríguez de Alonso, Josefina. *Le Siècle des Lumières, Conté par Francisco de Miranda*. Paris, 1947.

Ruyer, Raymond. *L'Utopie et les Utopies*. Paris, 1950.

Rybka, Eugeniusz. *Four Hundred Years of the Copernican Heritage*. Krakow, 1964.

Ryden, Stig. *Pedro Loefling en Venezuela*. Madrid, 1957.

Salaman, Redcliffe. *History and Social Influence of the Potato*. Cambridge, 1949.

Sarmiento, Domingo Faustino. *Viajes*. Buenos Aires, 1968.

Sarrailh, Jean. *L'Espagne Éclairée de la Seconde Moitié du XVIII Siècle*. Paris, 1964.

Schmidt, Max Georg. *Historia del Comercio Mundial*. Barcelona, 1927.

Sociedad Bolivariana de Venezuela. *Escritos del Libertador*. Caracas, 1967.

Solís, Ramón. *El Cádiz de las Cortes*. Madrid, 1969.

Spellanzon, Cesare. *Storia del Risorgimento e della Unità d'Italia*. 4 vols. Milan, 1933–38.

Staden, Hans. *Warhaftige Historia*. London, 1874.

Tello, Manuel. *Voces Favorables a México en el Cuerpo Legislativo de Francia (1862–1867)*. 2 vols. Mexico, 1967.

Thevet, André. *La Cosmographie Universelle d'Andrée Thevet cosmographe du Roi*. Paris, 1575.

Tocqueville, Alexis de. *La Démocratie en Amérique*. Paris, 1838.

Valle Iberlucea, Enrique del. *Las Cortes de Cádiz, la Revolución de España y la Democracia de América*. Buenos Aires, 1912.

Vaultier, Roger. *Le tabac à l'armée*. Marseille, 1954.

Vespucci, Amerigo. *El Nuevo Mundo*. Buenos Aires, 1951.

Vidarrue, Manuel Lorenzo. *Proyecto de Código Eclesiástico*. Paris, 1830.

Vignard, H. *Améric Vespuce*. Paris, 1917.

Villey, P. *Les Sources et l'Évolution des Essais de Montaigne*. 2 vols. Paris, 1933.

Vitoria, Francisco de. *Relectio de Indii o Libertad de los Indios*. Madrid, 1967.

Voltaire. *L'Orphelin de la Chine*. Paris, 1755.

—— *Essai sur les Moeurs*. Paris, 1756.

—— *Oeuvres Complètes*. Paris, 1877–85.

Weill, Georges. *L'Europe du XIX Siècle et l'Idée de la Nationalité*. Paris, 1938.

Whyte, A. J. *The Political Life and Letters of Cavour (1848–1861)*. London, 1930.

Williams, Eric. *From Columbus to Castro: The History of the Caribbean (1492–1969)*. London, 1970.

Zavala, Silvio. *La Utopía de Tomás Moro en la Nueva España*. Mexico, 1937.

—— *América en el Espíritu Francés*. Mexico, 1949.

—— *Recuerdo de Vasco de Quiroga*. Mexico, 1965.

Zea, Leopoldo. *América en la Historia*. Mexico, 1957.